Old Fashioned Wooden Toys

Old Fashioned Wooden Toys

Ed & Stevie Baldwin

HEARST BOOKS
New York

Created by The Family Workshop, Inc.

Dedicated in loving memory to
Holly Eugene
&
Nina Lillian Frier

The authors wish to thank Joan Nagy and Dale Timpe for their support and cooperation in the production of this book. Special thanks to the following companies for providing materials and tools: Shopsmith, Inc., Frank Paxton Lumber Company, Black & Decker, Louisiana-Pacific, and Swingline.

Inquiries should be addressed to Hearst Books, an affiliate of
William Morrow and Company, Inc.,
105 Madison Avenue, New York, N.Y. 10016.

Library of Congress Cataloging in Publication Data

Baldwin, Ed.
  Old-fashioned wooden toys.

  "Created by The Family Workshop, Inc."
  1. Wooden toy making.   I. Baldwin, Stevie.   II. Title.
TT174.5.W6B34   1983   745.592   82-15772
ISBN 0-87851-306-X

Created by The Family Workshop, Inc.

Editorial Director: Janet Weberling
Art Director: D. Curtis Hale
Illustration & Production: Roberta Taff, Jacqueline Nelson,
Christopher Berg, Dale Crain, Deborah Howell
Project Designs: Ed Baldwin & D.J. Olin

Contents

Tips & Techniques

This section provides the overkill that beginners will need, plus information pertaining to terms, materials, and techniques, for woodworkers of all skill levels.

Since you chose this book over a romance novel or a dictionary of idiomatic Spanish, we are assuming that you have some woodworking knowledge. While we have avoided using jargon understandable only to master craftsmen, we have also tried to avoid overkill in the step-by-step instructions.

Terms

Temporary assembly — When performing a temporary assembly, use nails that are smaller in diameter than the nails or screws you will be using for the final assembly, and drive them in just far enough to hold the pieces in place. Do not use glue. When you have achieved a good fit, mark the positions of the pieces. Carefully disassemble the pieces one at a time, apply glue, refit, and replace the temporary holding nails. When all parts have been glued, remove the temporary nails one at a time, and drive the proper size nails or screws into the existing holes.

Finish the open (or end) grain — When working with plywood, it is safer and more attractive to fill in the raw edges (open or end grain) with wood filler, wherever the edges will show or possibly come in contact with a child.

Dado — A dado is a groove cut into the side of a board, so that another board may be fitted into it. One or both boards may have the groove. The term "dado" also refers to the joint thus formed, which is most commonly used to assemble 2 boards at right angles, as shown in **Figure A**.

Router bits — Whenever a router is called for, we have specified the bit style you'll need to use. Several commonly used router bits, and the design that each will create in the wood, are shown in **Figure B**.

Nominal wood sizes — Finished boards and lumber are named after their rough, pre-finished dimensions. The 2 x 4 that you purchase from a lumber dealer actually measures 1½ x 3½ inches (if dry), or 1 9/16 x 3 9/16 inches (if green). We have taken into account the fact that actual dimensions are different than nominal ones. Nominal metric sizes which conform closely to the actual dimensions of the finished wood are indicated in parentheses after the nominal imperial sizes in this book (see "Metrics" under "General tips and techniques" below).

Substitutions

Nailset — If you do not have a nailset, a large common nail will work just as well to recess finishing nails. If your hammering technique is not quite professional, a nailset will help you avoid unsightly hammer marks on exposed wood surfaces, but it will not save your thumbs and fingers.

Compass — If you don't have one, devise a homemade compass from a length of string and a pencil. Tie the string to the pencil and measure off, from the pencil to a point along the string, a distance equal to the radius of the circle you wish to draw. Pin the string to the wood stock at the designated point, and draw the circle.

Clamps — C-clamps and wood clamps are invaluable little critters which can be adjusted to hold assembled parts in place. Pipe clamps can be used on extremely wide or long assemblies. When using pipe or C-clamps, place blocks of scrap wood between the clamp ends and the wooden parts, to avoid scoring your work. If you don't wish to purchase clamps, just place a heavy weight (large dictionary or loud-mouthed assistant) on top of the assembly.

Wood filler — Mix carpenter's glue and sawdust (heavy on the sawdust) for a substitute wood filler. See the "General tips and techniques" section below for tips on using filler.

Lubricant — On assemblies where 1 wooden part must move against another wooden part, you'll get smoother action if you lubricate the contact points. Beeswax is a good wood lubricant, but you can substitute non-hardening paste wax, or hard soap.

Wood — If you cannot find a particular wood size called for, substitute with stock that is the same thickness, and at least as wide as that specified. Wood of a different thickness will almost always necessitate some alteration in the assembly of the project. Wooden dowel rod of a different diameter will require different drill bit sizes than those called for. If you must substitute materials for any of the large riding toys, be sure that you do not weaken the design structurally. It is always safer to use a thicker material than a thinner one. We have specified pine for most of the projects because it is soft, reasonably affordable, and easy to work with. If you are an experienced woodworker, use hardwood for longer lasting toys.

Washers — Metal washers are usually called for in this book, but you can substitute plastic or wooden washers. Cut plastic washers from bleach bottles or other plastic containers. Wooden washers can be made by drilling a small hole through the center length of a dowel rod, and cutting thin, washer slices from the drilled rod.

Designs — If you are prone to creative urges and wish to alter any of our designs, you have our blessings. However, we suggest that you work out the changes on paper (to scale) before you plunge into your wood shop and start flailing about with saws and nails. A little careful planning will save you from screaming frustration, and from return trips to the lumber store.

Kraft paper — The project plans in this book contain scale drawings, from which you will make full-size paper patterns (see "Enlarging scale drawings" under "General tips and techniques" below). We have specified kraft paper for this purpose, but flattened grocery bags or shelf paper will work just as well.

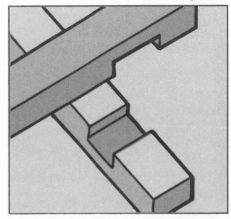

Figure A

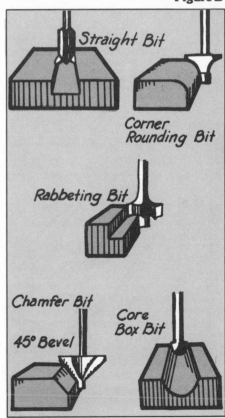

Figure B

Straight Bit

Corner Rounding Bit

Rabbeting Bit

Chamfer Bit

45° Bevel

Core Box Bit

General tips and techniques

Cutting identical pieces — When the instructions call for 2 or more identical pieces, use your full-size paper pattern to cut the first piece. Use the resulting wooden piece (preferably clamped to the cutting material) as a pattern to cut the subsequent pieces.

Enlarging scale drawings — Each scale drawing is shown on a background grid of squares. Each square on the grid equals 1 inch (25.4) on the full-size project. To enlarge, draw a grid of horizontal and vertical lines, spaced 1 inch (25.4) apart, on a piece of kraft paper. (A pantograph is an instrument that will speed this process. Consider using one if you plan to make very many of these projects.) Draw the same number of squares on the paper as shown on the scale drawing. Copy the drawing to the larger grid, one square at a time, as shown in **Figure C**.

Allowance for waste — If you arrange the patterns carefully, you should have no problem getting all of the pieces for each project out of the specified amounts of materials. However, it won't hurt to purchase a little extra, to allow for the width of saw cuts, imperfections in the wood, and unforeseeable mistakes (try to ignore the fact that we used that word). Just save any excess lumber for use in another project.

Measuring — Use a carpenter's square to check the alleged right angle at each corner of the stock before you start measuring and cutting. As the old saying goes, "Measure twice, cut once." When you are measuring between holes, or between a hole and some other designated point, measure from the center of the hole, not from the edge.

Wood filler — This is a very handy product for filling holes and covering imperfections. When filling a hole that is deeper than ¼ inch (6), apply the filler in shallow layers, allowing each layer to dry between applications. Wait until the top layer has dried completely before you sand the surface. If you plan to finish any project with wood stain instead of paint, be sure to select a wood filler that will accept the stain.

Metrics — For metric-speaking readers, the numbers which appear in parentheses after each imperial dimension or measurement are the metric equivalents **in millimeters**, unless otherwise specified. While converting specific measurements was no problem, we contracted a large and persistent headache trying to ferret out the nominal metric sizes of lumber, dowel rod, screws, drill bits, and other essential doodads. You'll know if we've erred along the way when you ask your hardware dealer for, let's say, a 6.35 mm. drill bit, and he bursts into uncontrollable laughter. Should this occur, we offer our apologies, and suggest that you purchase whatever is closest in size to the specified material or tool.

Figure C

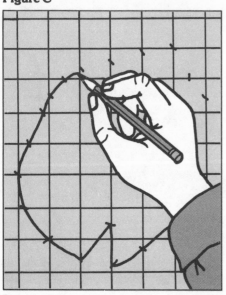

"With a hop, skip, and a jump"
Toys that move

Waddling Ducks

Mama duck and her 3 little ducklings are as easy to make as they are fun to watch. Because the axle holes in the wheels are drilled off-center, this family of quackers waddles back and forth with hilarious realism.

Metric equivalents in millimeters are indicated in parentheses.

Materials

6-inch (153) length of 2 x 8-inch (38 x 185) clear pine lumber.
16-inch (407) length of 1 x 8-inch (17 x 185) clear pine lumber.
21-inch (534) length of ¼ x 1¾-inch (6 x 45) wooden lattice.
40 square inches (260 sq. cm.) of ½-inch (13) thick pine lumber, at least 2 inches (51) wide.
3-foot (915) length of ¼-inch (6.35) diameter wooden dowel rod.
6-foot (1830) length of cotton cord, ¼ inch (6.35) or smaller in diameter.
Finishing nails: two 1 inch (25) long, two ¾ inch (20) long, and fourteen ½ inch (13) long.
Carpenter's wood glue, small quantity of wood filler, carbon paper, medium and fine sandpaper, and kraft paper.

Tools

Saber saw (or coping saw), hammer, wood rasp, nailset, electric or hand drill, and drill bits of the following diameters: ¼-inch (6.35) and ⅜-inch (10).
A circle-cutting drill attachment will help you cut the wheels.

Mama

Cutting the pieces   **1.** Full-size patterns for the pieces required to build Mama duck are given in **Figure A.** Make a kraft paper pattern for each piece.
2. Cut 1 Body from the pine 2 x 8 (38 x 185), and 2 Feet from the lattice. Cut 1 Base, 3¼ x 5 inches (83 x 127), and 2 Wings from the pine 1 x 8 (17 x 185). Cut 4 Wheels, each 2 inches (51) in diameter, and 2 Legs from the ½-inch (13) thick lumber. Sand each piece to eliminate sharp edges.

3. Cut 2 Axles, each 4¾ inches (121) long, from the wooden dowel rod.

4. Figure B shows placement of the axle holes in the Base and Wheels. Drill 2 axle holes through the Base where indicated, using the larger diameter bit. Drill an off-center axle hole through each Wheel, using the smaller bit.

Assembly **1.** An assembly diagram for Mama duck is given in **Figure C.** Begin by attaching the Feet to the Legs, using glue and ¾-inch (19) long nails driven through the bottoms of the Feet and up into the Legs.

2. Attach the Legs to the Body where indicated in **Figure C,** using glue and the 1-inch (25) long nails. Recess the nails, cover the holes with wood filler, and sand the resulting lumps smooth.

3. To give the Wings a more attractive shape, use the wood rasp to contour the edge all the way around 1 side of each Wing, as shown in **Figure D.** Sand the contoured Wings smooth, and glue the Wings to the Body where indicated in **Figure C.**

4. Attach Mama duck to her Base, centering the Feet between the front, back, and side edges, using glue and ½-inch (13) long nails. Recess the nails, fill the holes with wood filler, and sand the resulting lumps smooth.

5. Insert the Axles through the axle holes in the Base, leaving equal extensions on each side.

6. To achieve the optimum waddle, it is necessary to attach the Wheels correctly. If you will look at 1 Wheel you will see that, since the axle hole is drilled off-center, there is a larger portion of the Wheel on 1 side of the hole than on the other. Glue a Wheel to each axle end on the left side of the Base, so that the larger portion of each Wheel is at the top **(Figure E).** Glue the remaining 2 Wheels to the axle ends on the right side of the Base, so that the larger portion of each Wheel is at the bottom. (Be sure that the axles do not spin, changing the positions of the left-hand Wheels, when you turn the assembly around to attach the right-hand Wheels.) The outer sides of the Wheels should be flush with the axle ends, leaving a short gap between the Base and each Wheel.

Figure B

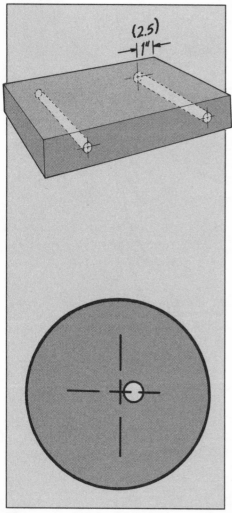

(2.5)

|←1"→|

Figure C

Figure D

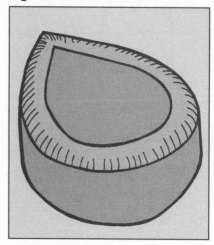

Figure E

Figure F

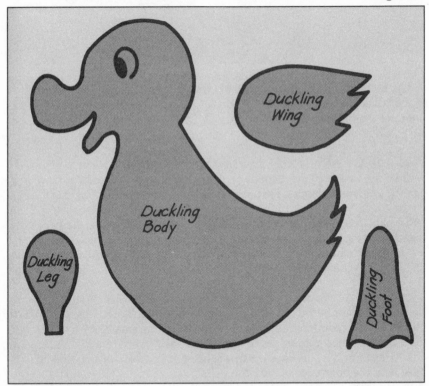

Ducklings
Cutting the pieces 1. Full-size patterns for the pieces required to build the ducklings are given in **Figure F**. Make a kraft paper pattern for each piece.
2. Cut 3 Bases, each 2 x 3 inches (50 x 75), and 3 Bodies from the pine 1 x 8 (17 x 185). Cut 6 each of the Feet, Wings, and Legs from the lattice. Cut 12 Wheels, each 1¼-inches (32) in diameter, from the ½-inch (13) thick lumber. Sand the pieces, eliminating all sharp edges.

Figure H

3. Cut 6 Axles, each 3½ inches (89) long, from the wooden dowel rod.

4. Drill 2 axle holes through each Base, using the larger diameter bit. Placement of the holes is shown in **Figure G**. Use the smaller diameter bit to drill an axle hole ⅜-inch (10) off center, through each Wheel.

Assembly   An assembly diagram for the Ducklings is given in **Figure H**. Follow the assembly instructions for Mama duck as you build the Ducklings, with a few minor changes. Do not attempt to use nails when attaching the Feet to the Legs, as the ends of the Legs are extremely small and may split if you drive nails into them. Use the remaining smallest nails to attach the Feet to the Bases, and the Wings to the Bodies. (There is no need to contour the Wings.) As you attach the Wheels, be sure to follow carefully the instructions given for the Mama's Wheels (see **Figure E**).

Finishing   **1.** You may wish to connect the duck family with lengths of cord so that they can be pulled along in a row. If so, you'll need to drill holes in the Bases to accommodate the cotton cord. Use the smaller bit to drill a hole near the front and rear edges of each Base, taking care to avoid drilling into the Axles. (For the Duckling which will be at the end of the line, drill only the hole near the front edge of the Base.) Cut three 12-inch (305) lengths of cord, and use them to tie the Bases together. Tie the remaining length of cord to the hole near the front edge of the Mama's Base, and use it to pull the entire crew along.

2. Paint or stain your Duck family, and add facial features with paint or felt tip markers when the base coat has dried completely.

Although these ducks waddle like champs, they're not strong in the vocal department. You may need to audition the neighborhood kids if you're not inclined to provide your own quackery.

Figure G

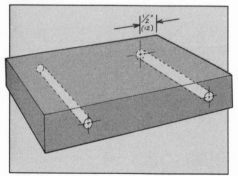

Bobbing Tortoise, Hopping Hare, & Speedy Fox

Materials
3-foot (915) length of 2 x 8-inch (38 x 184) pine.
4½-foot (1372) length of 1 x 8-inch (17 x 184) pine.
4-foot (1220) length of ¼-inch (6.35) diameter wooden dowel rod.
6-inch (152) length of ordinary string or twine.
3 yards (2743) of cotton cord, no larger than ¼ inch (6) in diameter.
3 small eyebolts, with ¼-inch (6) or larger diameter eyes.
Carpenter's wood glue, medium and fine sandpaper, kraft paper, carbon paper, and small quantities of non-toxic paint or stain in the colors of your choice (optional).

Tools
Saber or coping saw, wood rasp, and an electric or hand drill with ⅛-inch (3), ¼-inch (6.35), and ⅜-inch (9.5) diameter bits. A circle-cutting drill attachment and 2 C-clamps will be helpful, but are not required.

The Tortoise
Cutting the pieces 1. Enlarge the scale drawings given in **Figure A** to full-size patterns on kraft paper. Transfer the facial features and all placement markings to the paper patterns.
2. Cut the following pieces from the 2 x 8-inch (38 x 184) pine: 1 Center Shell, 1 Head, and 1 Tail. Use the side view patterns for the Head and Tail to cut the pieces, and the top view patterns for contouring.
3. Cut the following pieces from the 1 x 8-inch (17 x 184) pine: 2 Inner Shells, 2 Outer Shells, and 1 Head Support. In addition, cut 4 Wheels, each 1½ inches (38) in diameter.

According to Aesop (of fable fame), the tortoise won the race against the hare, while in an entirely different neck of the woods the fox was scorning the grapes he could not reach. ("Sour grapes!" he purportedly cried.) We've done a little fable-fuddling to bring you all three critters, respectively bobbing, hopping, and loping along in one gala race.

Metric equivalents in millimeters are indicated in parentheses.

Figure A

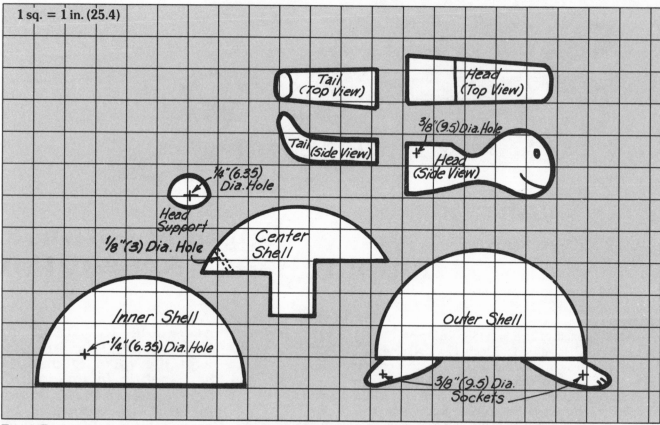

1 sq. = 1 in. (25.4)

Tail (Top View)

Head (Top View)

Tail (Side View)

3/8" (9.5) Dia. Hole

Head (Side View)

1/4" (6.35) Dia. Hole

Head Support

1/8" (3) Dia. Hole

Center Shell

Inner Shell

1/4" (6.35) Dia. Hole

Outer Shell

3/8" (9.5) Dia. Sockets

Figure B

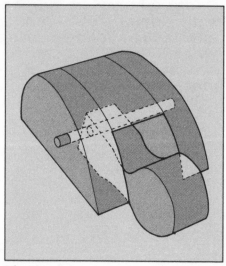

4. Sand all of the pieces. Transfer the placement markings to the wooden pieces using carbon paper and a pencil. (The facial features will be transferred later, after the critters have been painted or stained.)

5. Drill the holes which are indicated on the scale drawings by cross marks and dotted lines. Use the ⅜-inch (9.5) diameter bit to drill the hole through the neck portion of the Head. Use the ¼-inch (6.35) diameter bit to drill the hole through the Head Support and each Inner Shell and, in addition, a hole through the center of each Wheel.

Assembly 1. Spread glue on the outer edges of the Center Shell and sandwich it between the 2 Inner Shells, with the rounded edges flush. Apply C-clamps (or place the assembly under a weight) so that the bond will not be disturbed as you continue to work.

2. Cut a 3-inch (76) length of dowel rod to use as a pivot for the Head piece. Insert the dowel through the hole in 1 of the Inner Shells, and align the Head piece so that you can slide the dowel on through the hole in the Tortoise's neck and into the hole in the other Shell (**Figure B**). The ends of the dowel should not extend beyond the outer edges of the Shells.

Figure C

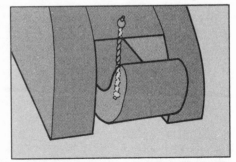

3. Figure C shows how the Tortoise's Tail is attached. Drill a ⅛-inch (3) diameter hole through the center of the Tail, from top to bottom. Use the same bit to drill a hole diagonally through the Center Shell, near the rear edge. Tie a large knot in 1 end of the short piece of string. Thread the unknotted end of the string through the hole in the Tail and then through the hole in the Center Shell. Adjust the string so that the Tail hangs about ¾ inch (19) below the Shell, and tie it off securely. Cut off the excess string.

4. Drill a ⅜-inch (9.5) deep axle socket on the inner edge of each of the Tortoise's feet. (The feet are those cute little protrusions at the lower edge of each Outer Shell.) Use the ⅜-inch (9.5) diameter bit to drill the sockets where indicated in **Figure D**. Cut 2 Axles, each 3 ¾ inches (95) long, from the wooden dowel rod.

5. Insert 1 of the Axles through the hole in the Head Support, leaving equal extensions on each side. Slip a Wheel over each end of the Axle, leaving slightly less than ⅜ inch (9.5) of space between the Head Support and each Wheel. Put the Front Axle aside while you assemble the Rear Axle.

6. Slip a Wheel over each end of the Rear Axle, leaving ½ inch (13) of space between the outer edge of the Wheel and the axle end.

7. Final assembly of the Tortoise is shown in **Figure E.** Spread glue on the flat sides of the Inner Shells and make a Tortoise sandwich, as shown in the illustration. First attach 1 Outer Shell, aligning the curved upper edge with the curved edge of the inner assembly. Insert (but do not glue) the Front and Rear Axles into the axle sockets in the attached Outer Shell. Add the remaining Outer Shell, inserting the free ends of the Axles into the sockets.

Figure D

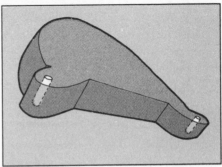

Figure E

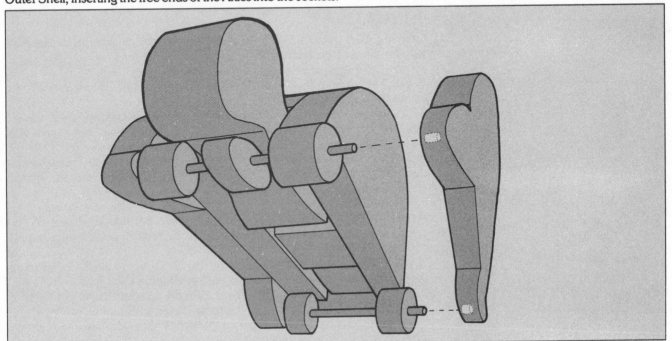

Figure F

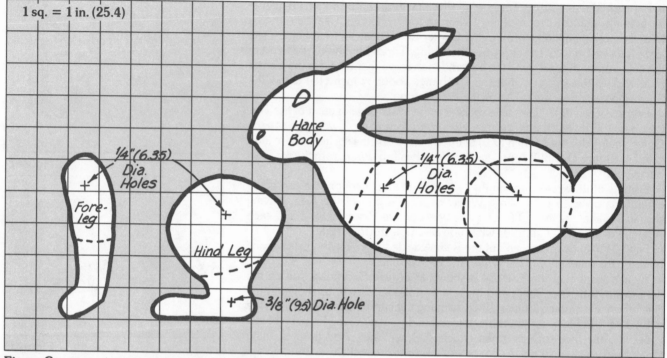

1 sq. = 1 in. (25.4)

¼" (6.35) Dia. Holes

Hare Body

¼" (6.35) Dia. Holes

Fore-leg

Hind Leg

3/8" (9.5) Dia. Hole

Figure G

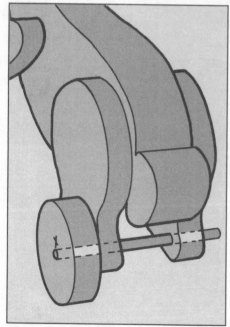

The Hare

Cutting the pieces   **1.** Enlarge the scale drawings given in **Figure F** to full-size patterns on kraft paper. Transfer the facial features and placement markings to the paper patterns.

2. Cut 1 Body from the 2 x 8-inch (38 x 184) pine. Cut 1 Front Wheel, 1½ inches (38) in diameter, from the same material.

3. Cut two 2½-inch (64) diameter Rear Wheels, 2 Forelegs, and 2 Hind Legs from the 1 x 8-inch (17 x 184) pine. Sand all of the pieces and transfer the placement markings.

4. Drill the holes where indicated on the scale drawings. Use the ⅜-inch (9.5) diameter bit to drill the lower hole through each Hind Leg, and the ¼-inch (6.35) diameter bit for the other holes.

Assembly   **1.** Cut two 3-inch (76) lengths from the wooden dowel rod. Insert these dowels through the holes in the Body, leaving equal extensions on each side.

2. Follow the placement lines as you glue the Hind Legs to the Body, inserting the dowel ends into the upper holes in the Legs (**Figure G**).

3. Cut a 4⅝-inch (117) long Rear Axle from the wooden dowel rod. Insert it through the lower holes in the Hind Legs as shown in **Figure G**, leaving equal extensions on each side. Drill a ¼-inch (6.35) diameter axle hole through each of the large Wheels, about ⅜-inch (10) off center.

Figure H

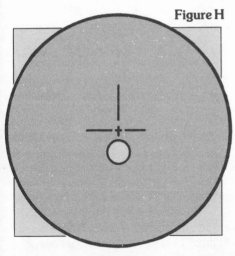

Figure I

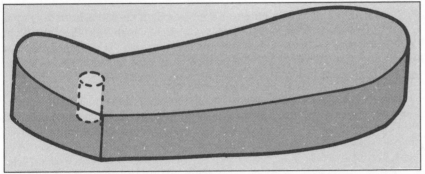

Figure J

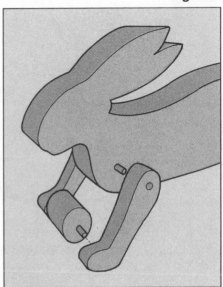

4. It is important to attach the Wheels correctly if you want your Hare to hop in true bunny fashion. Note that there is a larger portion of each Wheel on 1 side of the axle hole than on the other **(Figure H)**. Glue a Wheel over 1 end of the Rear Axle, flush with the Axle end **(Figure G)**. Rotate the Axle so that the larger portion of the Wheel is at the top. Hold the Axle firmly in position as you glue the remaining Wheel over the free end of the Axle, so that the larger portion of this Wheel is also at the top. (We repeat — it is crucial that the Wheels be attached so that the larger portion of each is pointing in the same direction. If they are not attached in this manner, your Hare will waddle instead of hop, and you'll get sniggers instead of cheers at the grand unveiling.)

5. To assemble the front section of the Hare, you'll need to drill a ⅜-inch (9.5) deep axle socket into the inner edge of each front foot. Use the ¼-inch (6.35) diameter bit, and place the sockets where indicated in **Figure I**. You'll also need to cut a 2¼-inch (57) length of dowel rod for the Front Axle, and drill a ⅜-inch (9.5) diameter hole through the center of the Front Wheel.

6. Assembly of the front section is shown in **Figure J**. Glue 1 Foreleg to the Hare's Body, following the placement lines. Glue 1 end of the Front Axle into the socket in the attached Foreleg, and slip the Wheel onto the Axle. Glue the remaining Foreleg to the Body, inserting the free end of the Axle into its socket.

The Fox

Cutting the pieces **1.** Enlarge the scale drawings given in **Figure K** to full size patterns on kraft paper.

2. Cut one 1½-inch (38) diameter Rear Wheel, and 1 Body from the 2 x 8-inch (38 x 184) pine.

3. Cut two 3-inch (76) diameter Front Wheels, 2 Forelegs, and 2 Hind Legs from the 1 x 8-inch (17 x 184) pine.

4. Cut the following pieces from the wooden dowel rod: 2 Body Dowels, each 3 inches (76) long; 1 Front Axle, 4½ inches (114) long; and 1 Rear Axle, 2¼ inches (57) long.

5. Sand all of the pieces and transfer the placement markings from the paper patterns. Drill the holes where indicated. Use the ⅜-inch (9.5) diameter bit to drill the lower holes in the Forelegs and a hole through the center of the Rear Wheel. Use the ¼-inch (6.35) diameter bit to drill the remaining holes and to drill an axle hole ½ inch (13) off center through each of the Front Wheels.

Figure K

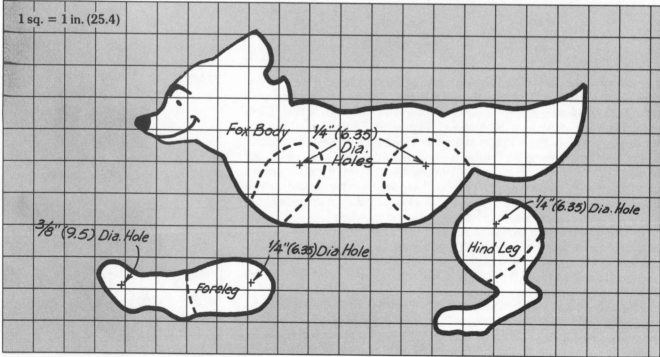

1 sq. = 1 in. (25.4)

Fox Body

¼" (6.35) Dia. Holes

¼" (6.35) Dia. Hole

⅜" (9.5) Dia. Hole

¼" (6.35) Dia. Hole

Foreleg

Hind Leg

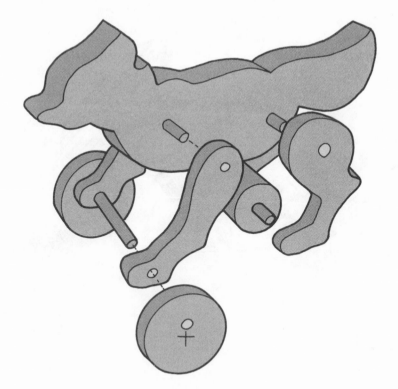

Figure L

Assembly

The Fox is assembled exactly like the Hare, except that the front and rear axle assemblies are reversed. As you can see in the illustration of the assembled Fox **(Figure L)**, the larger wheels with off-center axle holes are attached to the longer Front Axle. Follow the assembly instructions for the Hare as you build the Fox. When you get to step 5, refer to **Figure M,** which shows the placement of the axle sockets you'll need to drill into the inner edges of the Fox's hind feet.

Finishing

1. Carefully inspect all of your critters, and sand any remaining rough spots or sharp edges. Round off the curved edges of the Tortoise's Shell with a wood rasp, and finish with sandpaper. You may leave the natural wood finish, or use a non-toxic paint or stain to add color to the toys.

2. Use carbon paper to transfer the facial features from the paper patterns to both sides of each animal's head. If you use 2 sheets of carbon paper (non-carbon sides together) as you transfer the features to the first side of the head, the reverse outlines will automatically be transferred to the back of the paper pattern for use on the opposite side of the head. Use a heavy felt tip marker or paint to finish the facial features.

3. Install a small eyebolt on the front edge of each toy, and tie a 1-yard (914) length of cotton cord to each eyebolt.

Your work will be over when you find 3 little hands to hold the free ends of the cords — and the race will be on!

Figure M

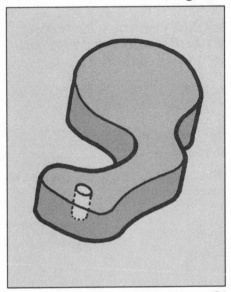

Spinning Tops

Toddlers took a liking to spinning tops centuries ago, and the love affair is still flourishing. These wooden tops are so easy to make, you may be tempted to build one for every little person you know.

Metric equivalents in millimeters are indicated in parentheses.

Materials

8-inch (203) length of 2 x 4-inch (38 x 89) clear white pine.
8-inch (203) length of 1 x 6-inch (17 x 140) clear white pine.
1-foot (305) length of ½-inch (13) diameter wooden dowel rod.
Two 30-inch (762) lengths of thin cotton string or twine.
A small quantity of non-toxic paint in 1 or more colors of your choice. If you prefer, use non-toxic wood stain, or simply rub vegetable oil into the wood.
Medium and fine sandpaper, kraft paper, and carpenter's wood glue.

Tools

Saber saw or coping saw, small paint brush (if you opt for a painted finish), wood rasp, and an electric or hand drill with ½-inch (13) and ⅛-inch (3) diameter bits.

Cutting the pieces   **1.** Scale drawings for 2 different Handles are given in **Figure A**. Either Handle design will work with either Top, so if you prefer, you can cut 2 Handles from the same pattern. Enlarge the drawings to full-size patterns on kraft paper.
2. Cut 2 Handles from the 2 x 4-inch (38 x 89) pine. The U-shaped notch in each Handle (indicated by dotted lines on the scale drawings) will be cut out after the Spindle sockets have been drilled. Refer to the top-view drawings given in **Figure B**, and use a wood rasp followed by sandpaper to contour the Handles, as shown.

Figure A

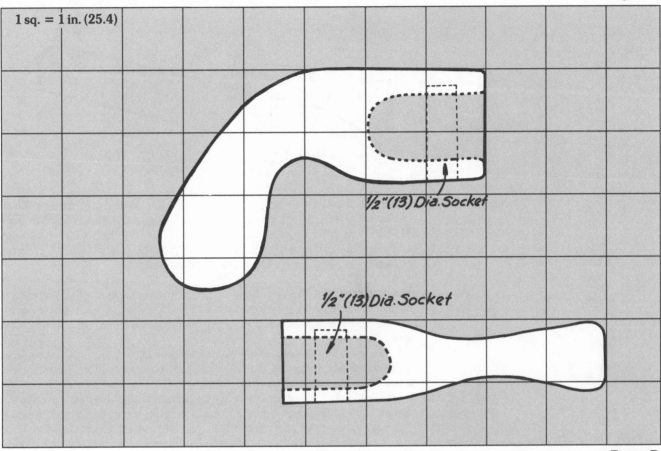

1 sq. = 1 in. (25.4)

½"(13) Dia. Socket

½"(13) Dia. Socket

Figure B

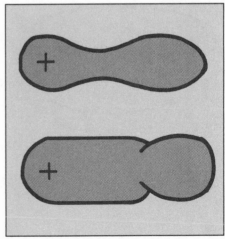

3. Drill a ½-inch (13) diameter socket into the spindle-support end of each Handle. Placement of the sockets is indicated by dotted lines in **Figure A**, and by cross marks in **Figure B**. To insure that you do not drill the sockets too long or short, measure the depth of each socket, and mark it on your drill bit.

4. Cut out the U-shaped notch in each Handle. Sand the Handles carefully, to eliminate sharp edges, and splinters. Use extra elbow grease to sand the sides of the sockets, so that the Spindles have plenty of spinning-space.

5. Cut the following circular pieces from the 1 x 6-inch (17 x 140) pine: 2 Disks, each 3 inches (76) in diameter; 2 Disks, each 2½ inches (64) in diameter; and 2 Disks, each 2 inches (51) in diameter. Drill a ½-inch (13) diameter hole through the center of each Disk. (Be sure to drill through the exact center, or your Tops will look tipsy, and spin that way too.) Take 3 Disks (1 of each size), and taper the circumference edges evenly, as shown in **Figure C**. Sand all of the Disks.

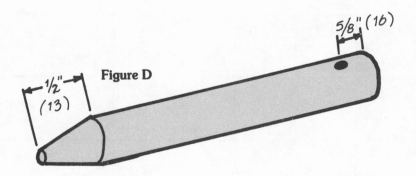

Figure D

½" (13)

5/8" (16)

6. Cut the dowel rod in half, to create two 6-inch (152) long Spindles. Taper a ½-inch (13) length at 1 end of each Spindle into a flat-tipped point (**Figure D**). The Tops will spin on these points, so be sure that they are precisely flat. Drill a ⅛-inch (3) diameter string hole through each Spindle, ⅝ inch (16) from the upper end, as shown in **Figure D**. Sand the Spindles.

Assembly   The trickiest assembly procedure (actually, it's the only assembly procedure, besides painting) is securing the Disks in place without smearing glue all over the Spindles. If you follow our suggested method, you shouldn't have any trouble.

1. Finish each of the pieces with paint, stain, or oil. Try not to get any finish inside the drilled holes, as that will slow the spinning motion. Allow several hours drying time.

2. Use the Disks with untapered edges as you assemble the first Top. Paint a ½-inch (13) wide band of glue around 1 Spindle, approximately 1½ inches (38) below the upper end. Slide the largest Disk over the Spindle, and down onto the band of glue, adjusting it so that it is level. Use a damp sponge to wipe away any glue that may have squished out around the hole.

3. Paint another band of glue around the Spindle, approximately ½ inch (13) below the attached Disk. Slide the medium-size Disk over the lower end of the Spindle, and up onto the band of glue. Level it, and wipe away the excess glue.

4. Attach the smallest Disk in the same manner, approximately ½ inch (13) below the medium-size Disk.

5. Assemble the second Top in the same manner, but attach the largest Disk approximately 2 inches (51) below the upper end of the Spindle, and allow only ¼ inch (6) of space between the Disks. Let the glue dry for several hours.

6. To play, turn the Tops upside down, and insert the Spindles into the Handles. Thread a length of string through the small hole in the Spindle, and hold it while you rotate the Top. When the entire string is wound around the Spindle, turn the Top and Handle right side up, and place the point of the Spindle on a flat, smooth surface. Pull the string in 1 quick, smooth motion to set the Top spinning. At the same time, lift the Handle straight up and off the Spindle.

Gather your favorite toddlers, and spin some magic for them with your Spinning Tops.

Figure C

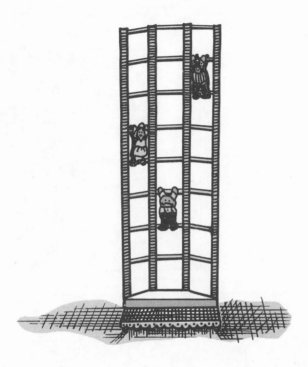

Tumbling Trio

This contraption is one of the most fascinating old fashioned toys around. Put the wooden acrobats on top of the ladders, and they'll somersault their way to the bottom, rung by rung.

Materials

Clear white pine: 21-inch (533) length of 2 x 4-inch (38 x 89); 52-inch (1321) length of 1 x 5-inch (17 x 114); 16-inch (406) length of 1 x 12-inch (17 x 286); 16-inch (406) length of 1 x 6-inch (17 x 140).

40-inch (1016) length of ¼ x 1¾-inch (6 x 45) pine lattice.

4 spherical wooden drawer pulls, each 1¼ inches (32) in diameter.

Handful of ½-inch (13) long finishing nails.

Small quantities of non-toxic paint in the colors of your choice.

Carpenter's wood glue, kraft paper, and carbon paper.

Tools

Table saw, band saw, hammer, carpenter's square, artist's fine paint brush, and an electric or hand drill with a ½-inch (13) diameter bit. You'll also need a tool called a mill bastard file. It is a long, flat file which (despite its disgraceful name) is the perfect tool for the small but important amount of filing work in this project.

Metric equivalents in millimeters are indicated in parentheses.

Cutting the pieces   The ladders are built from strips of wood that are ³⁄₁₆ inch (4.8) thick. We know that's a picky-sounding number, but the action of the toy depends on careful and precise measurements. (Just wait 'til you hear about the ⁷⁄₃₂-inch [5.6] wide slots!) Squareness is imperative here, so use your carpenter's square to true up the ends of all wood stock before cutting.

Figure A

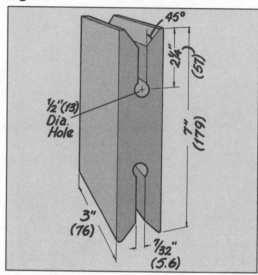

45°

2¼" (51)

½"(13)
Dia.
Hole

7" (179)

3" (76)

⁷⁄₃₂" (5.6)

Figure B

1 sq. = 1 in. (25.4)

1. To create stock of the correct thickness for the ladder parts, set your table saw guide to ³⁄₁₆ inch (4.8). Run the 1 x 5-inch (17 x 114) pine board through the saw lengthwise, to slice off a ³⁄₁₆ x ¾ x 52-inch (4.8 x 17 x 1397) strip. Repeat this procedure to cut 13 additional strips.

2. Cut a 45-inch (1143) length from each of 12 strips, for the Ladder Frames. The Rungs are cut from the remaining strips. They are the same thickness (³⁄₁₆ inch [4.8]) as the Frames, but are only ⁷⁄₁₆ inch (11) wide. Reset your table saw guide to ⁵⁄₁₆ inch (6), and run all of the remaining strips (2 long ones, and 12 short pieces) through the saw again, to reduce the width of each strip from ¾ inch (17) to ⁷⁄₁₆ inch (11). Cut 24 Rungs, each 6 inches (152) long, from the narrowed strips. Sand the ladder parts.

3. The Tumblers are fashioned from the length of 2 x 4-inch (38 x 89) pine. Run the wood through your table saw to reduce the width from 3½ inches (89) to 3 inches (76). Cut the block into three 3 x 7-inch (76 x 178) pieces.

4. The slots that allow the Tumblers to tumble are shown in **Figure A.** Drill a ½-inch (13) diameter hole 2¼ inches (57) from each end of 1 block, through the entire width. Cut a slot from each end of the block, up to the nearest hole. The slots should be exactly ⁷⁄₃₂ inch (5.6) wide, or as close to that as your humanness allows. Angle the sides of each slot at the open end, as shown. Repeat for the remaining 2 blocks. Sand the blocks, including the sides of the notches.

5. Front-view drawings of the Tumblers are given in **Figure B.** Make full-size patterns, and transfer the outlines and details to both sides of the wooden blocks. Use a band saw to cut around the outlines. Sand the newly-cut edges.

Assembly　　**1.** Paint the facial features and other details on both sides of each Tumbler. Avoid getting paint inside the notches, as that will hamper the swinging action.

2. Figure C shows how the ladders are assembled. Make 3 ladders, each consisting of 8 Rungs and 4 Frames. As you can see, the ends of each Rung are sandwiched between 2 Frames. Spacing is crucial, so be sure that there is exactly 5 inches (127) of space between Rungs. Assemble the ladders using glue and nails. Glue a small piece of leftover stripping as a spacer between the lower ends of the 2 Frames on each ladder side.

3. In order to achieve a good fit when you join the 3 ladders together, you will need to angle 1 long outer edge on 2 of the ladders. Cut the edges at the angles indicated in **Figure D,** and glue the ladders together in the configuration shown. Clamp or tape them together while the glue dries.

Figure D

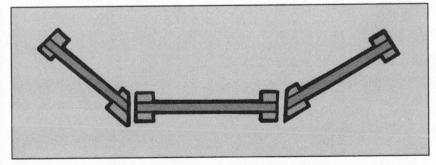

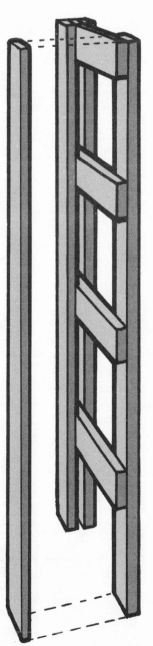

Figure C

4. The length of 1 x 12-inch (17 x 286) pine will serve as the Stage Floor. Scale drawings for the Stage Platform and Trim are given in **Figure E**. Make full-size, kraft paper patterns from the drawings.

5. Cut the Platform from the 1 x 6-inch (17 x 140) pine. To create the scalloped Trim, cut one 16½-inch (419) length and two 11¼-inch (286) lengths from the pine lattice. Transfer the scalloped Trim pattern to the lengths of lattice, and cut along the outlines.

6. Glue a wooden drawer pull underneath each corner of the Stage Floor. Glue the Stage Platform over the Floor, centered between the sides, with the long edge of the Platform 5 inches (127) from the front edge of the Floor. Glue the lower ends of the ladders over the Floor, flush with the rear edges of the Platform. Secure in place with nails driven through the Ladder Frames, into the Platform. Glue the Trim to the front and side edges of the Floor.

7. Paint the assembled stage in the colors of your choice. You may paint the Ladder Frames if you wish, but do not paint the Rungs, as that will cause the Tumblers to stick — and no one likes a sticky Tumbler. Allow the paint to dry.

8. Place the Tumblers, 1 at a time, on the top Rung of a ladder, and test the action. The Tumbler should swing smoothly from rung to rung, all the way down the ladder. If a Tumbler sticks, carefully file the sides of the offending notches. File a little at a time and retest often, because if you overkill with the file, the Tumbler will slide right off the ladder.

Set the stage and call the kids — they'll tumble to this entertainment right away, if not sooner.

Figure E

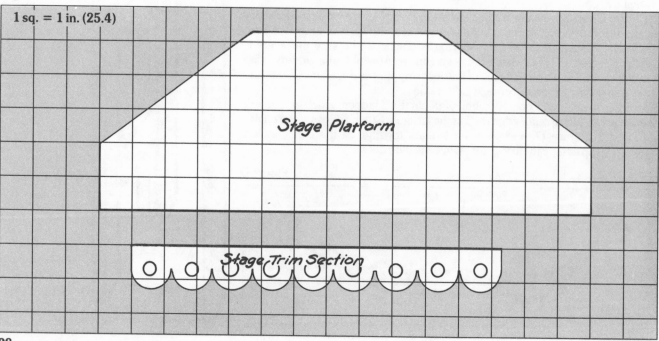

"All work and no play makes Jack a dull boy."
Toys that amuse

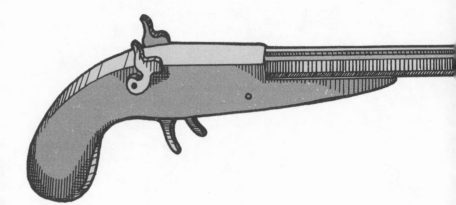

Rubber Band Shooting Iron

Made from a hardwood such as walnut, this working replica of a pre-Wild West pistol will be a handsome desk ornament for the sharpshooter in your family. You will need a reasonable amount of woodworking skill to complete the pistol, since hardwood is much more difficult to cut and drill than pine.

Metric equivalents in millimeters are indicated in parentheses.

Materials

1¼ square feet (1162 sq. cm.) of ¾-inch (19) thick hardwood lumber.

2½-inch (64) length of ⅛-inch (3) diameter wooden dowel rod.

2 brass escutcheon pins, each ½ inch (13) long. (These little critters are actually just glorified finishing nails, with slightly rounded heads and a fancy name.)

2 thin finishing nails, each 1¼ inches (32) long.

2 thin rubber bands, each 2½ to 3 inches (64 to 76) long. These will be used in the trigger tension mechanism.

Thin rubber bands, each approximately 3 inches (76) long, for ammunition. Caution: wide, short ammunition can be dangerous.

Medium and fine sandpaper, carpenter's wood glue, and kraft paper.

Tools

Hammer, wood rasp, band saw or jigsaw, and an electric or hand drill with ⅛-inch (3) and ⅜-inch (10) diameter bits. Since hardwood is normally available in ¾-inch (19) thickness, and the pieces for the gun require ¼-inch (6) thick wood, you'll need a table saw to split the wood. If you do not have access to this tool, you might convince your lumber dealer to split it for you. Do not have him split all of the stock, as the Horizontal Base, Barrel Support, and Barrels require the full thickness of the ¾-inch (19) stock.

Cutting the pieces **1.** Enlarge the scale drawings given in **Figure A** to full-size patterns on kraft paper.

2. If you plan to split the wood yourself (to create ¼-inch [6] thick stock) we suggest that you first cut the following rectangular blocks from the ¾-inch (19) thick hardwood, making each block slightly larger than the pattern piece: 2 Stocks, 1 Left Inner Handle, 1 Trigger, and 1 Inner Stock. (Although they may look identical at first glance, left- and right-side patterns are slightly different.) Use a table saw to split through the thicknesses of the rectangles, dividing them into thinner rectangles of the same width and length.

Figure A

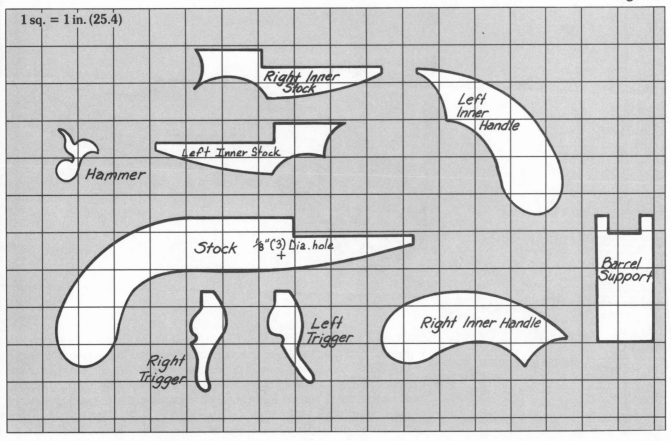

1 sq. = 1 in. (25.4)

Right Inner Stock

Left Inner Handle

Hammer

Left Inner Stock

Stock   ⅛"(3) Dia. hole

Barrel Support

Right Trigger

Left Trigger

Right Inner Handle

3. Cut the following pieces from the split rectangles: 3 Stocks, 2 Inner Handles (1 Right and 1 Left), 2 Inner Stocks (1 Right and 1 Left), and 2 Triggers (1 Right and 1 Left). Cut 2 Hammers from the remaining scraps of ¼-inch (6) thick wood. (The Barrel Support will be cut later.)

4. Each of the octagonal Barrels is formed from a 5¾-inch (146) length of ¾ x ¾-inch (19 x 19) hardwood. Simply trim each of the 4 corners at a 45 degree angle, along the entire length, so that the 8 resulting flat sides are of equal length (**Figure B**). Drill a ⅜-inch (10) diameter socket, approximately 1 inch (25) long, into 1 end of each Barrel.

Assembly   Think of your Shooting Iron as a 3-layer cake with frosting between the layers (but regardless of how hungry you feel, it will be tough chewing). The 3 identical Stocks serve as the 3 cake layers. The frosting between the layers consists of the Inner Handles (at the rear of the gun), and the Inner Stocks (at the front). The Triggers fit between the Inner Stocks and Handles in the frosting layers.

Figure B

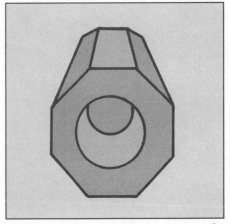

Figure D

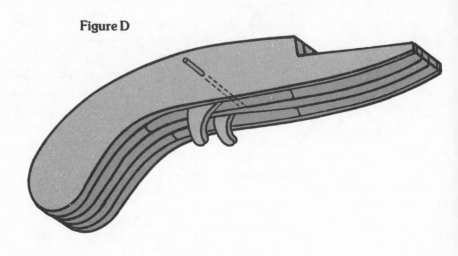

Figure C

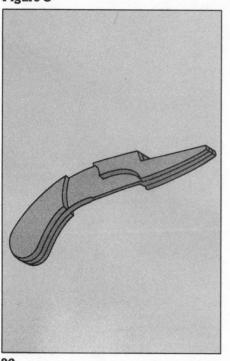

1. Choose 1 of the 3 identical Stocks to serve as the Center Stock. Refer to **Figure C**, and glue the Right and Left Inner Handles to the respective sides of the Center Stock, with curved edges even. (Right- and left-hand sides are determined as if you were holding the gun in a normal firing position, looking down the barrel.) Glue the Right and Left Inner Stocks to the respective sides of the Center Stock, with upper and lower edges flush. (Don't panic — that gap between the upper edges of the Inner Stocks and Inner Handles is supposed to be there.) Use a wood rasp followed by sandpaper to reduce the width of the Center Stock, along the lower edge between the Inner Stocks and Handles. This will give the Triggers room to move.

2. Glue the 2 remaining Stocks to the sides of the inner assembly, and allow the glue to dry for several hours. Use a wood rasp followed by sandpaper to trim the inside lower edge of each Outer Stock, between the Inner Stocks and Handles, to further widen the gap for the trigger mechanism.

3. The Triggers pivot on a length of dowel rod, as shown in **Figure D**. Cut a 1¼ inch (32) length of ⅛-inch (3) diameter dowel rod for the pivot. Slide the 2 Triggers into place, and drill a ⅛-inch (3) diameter hole through all 5 layers of the gun, to accommodate the pivot dowel. The hole should be placed approximately ½ inch (13) below the upper edge of the gun, on a line that will run through both Triggers (**Figure D**). Slide the pivot dowel through the hole. Glue only the very ends of the pivot dowel in place, flush with the outer sides of the Stocks.

4. Sand the partially assembled pistol. Use a wood rasp, if necessary, to round off the curved edges of the handle, and to taper the width of the Outer Stocks, as shown in **Figure E**.

5. Drill a ⅛-inch (3) diameter hole through the entire assembly where indicated on the scale drawing for the Stock. Cut a 1⅛-inch (29) length of ⅛-inch (3) diameter dowel rod, to be used as a support for the trigger spring mechanism. The spring mechanism is assembled as shown in **Figure E**. Insert the dowel through the hole in the left stock, until the end of the dowel is about half way across the left trigger gap. Take 1 rubber band, twist it and double it over so that it forms a double circle, and place the doubled rubber band over the dowel end. Continue to push the dowel through the Center Stock, and half way into the right trigger gap. Twist and double over the remaining rubber band, place it over the dowel, and finish by pushing the dowel end into the hole in the right Stock. If the dowel ends extend beyond the outer sides of the Stocks, trim them flush. (Do not glue them into the holes, as you will need to remove the dowel in order to replace the rubber bands periodically.) Stretch the doubled left-hand rubber band back over the Left Trigger, seating it in the small notch at the rear edge of the Trigger. Repeat for the right-hand rubber band and Trigger, to complete the spring mechanism.

6. Glue the Barrels and Hammers in place (**Figure F**), and secure each of the Hammers with a brass escutcheon pin driven through the Hammer and into the Stock.

7. To make the stand for your assembled pistol, cut 1 Horizontal Base, 3 x 12½ inches (76 x 318) from the hardwood lumber. In addition, cut 1 Barrel Support, using the pattern you made from the scale drawing in **Figure A** . Sand both of the pieces to eliminate sharp edges. Glue the Support to the Base, approximately 2¾ inches (70) from 1 end, as shown in **Figure G**, and drive 2 finishing nails through the underside of the Base, into the Support.

Loading and Firing   If you will look at the upper edge of your pistol, and pull back on the right-hand trigger, you will see a small gap open as the upper end of the trigger moves forward. Place 1 end of a rubber band into this gap, and release the trigger. Grab the opposite end of the rubber band and stretch it along the top of the gun, until you can pull it over the end of the right-hand barrel. Load the left-hand side in the same manner, take aim, and fire when ready, as they say.

The trigger tension can be adjusted by changing the length of the doubled-over rubber bands in the trigger spring mechanism. We strongly recommend that only enough tension be put on the triggers to enable a rubber band to be fired a short distance. As an added precaution, fire only the size rubber bands described in the "Materials" section above. A smaller rubber band will be stretched too tightly and, when fired, will have too great a force for safety's sake. This is not a child's toy.

A little target practice is in order, before you start bragging about what a Deadeye Dan you are. To get into the mood as you knock off unsuspecting tin cans and flies, rehearse some appropriate Old West phrases, like, "Reach fer the sky, ya' mizrable sidewinder, or I'll fill ya' full of elastic!"

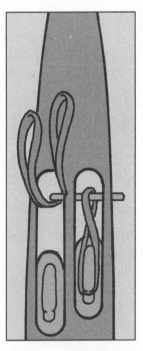

Figure E

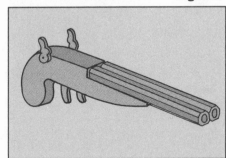

Figure F

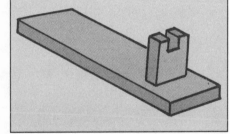

Figure G

Umbrella Lady Whirligig

Whirligigs made their appearance in America in the early 1800 s. The simplest ones were designed as "Sunday toys" for quiet play on the Sabbath.

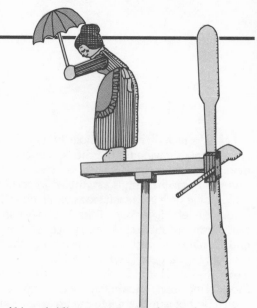

Metric equivalents in millimeters are indicated in parentheses.

Materials

16 x 26-inch (406 x 660) piece of ¼-inch (6) exterior grade plywood.
19-inch (483) length of 1 x 3-inch (17 x 64) pine.
7-inch (179) length of 2 x 8-inch (38 x 184) pine.
7-inch (179) length of ¼-inch (6.35) diameter wooden dowel rod.
14-inch (356) length of 1½-inch (38) diameter wooden closet rod.
5 metal washers, each ½ inch (13) in diameter, with a ¼-inch (6) diameter center hole.
17-inch (432) length of ⅛-inch (3) diameter metal wire, somewhat more bendable than coathanger wire.
2 flat head wood screws, each 1¼ inches (32) long.
Handful of ½-inch (13) long finishing nails; a 2½-inch (64) long common nail; a 1-inch (25) long common nail; and a ½-inch (13) long escutcheon pin. To guard against rust stains, the nails, screws, and other metal hardware for this project should be the galvanized variety.
Small quantities of non-toxic paint in the colors of your choice.
Carpenter's wood glue, kraft paper, carbon paper, and sandpaper.

Tools

Hammer, screwdriver, saber saw or table saw, band saw, artist's fine paint brush, small flat paint brush, and an electric or hand drill with bits of the following diameters: 1½-inch (38), ¼-inch (6.35), ⅛-inch (3), and a 1/16-inch (1.6) bit capable of drilling through the metal wire. If you do not have access to a table saw, you'll need a miter box and a router with a straight bit.

Cutting the pieces   **1.** Enlarge the scale drawings given in **Figure A** to full-size patterns on kraft paper. Cut 1 Upper Body, 2 Lower Bodies, 2 Arms, 2 Umbrellas, and 4 Paddles from plywood.
2. Cut the following additional pieces from plywood: 1 Spacer Block, ¾ x 1½ inches (19 x 38); 2 Base Covers, each 1⅛ x 7 inches (29 x 178); and 1 Shaft Cover, 2½ x 5⅝ inches (64 x 143).
3. Cut a 13½-inch (343) length from the pine 1 x 3 (17 x 64) for the Base. In addition, cut 1 Pivot Block and 1 Hub, each 2½ x 2½ inches (64 x 64), from the same material.

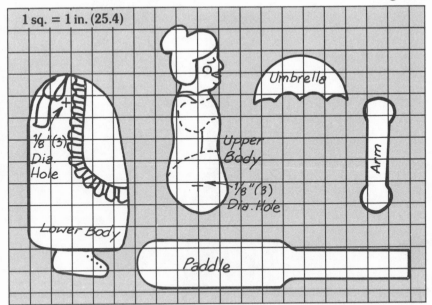

Figure A

1 sq. = 1 in. (25.4)

⅛ "(3) Dia. Hole

Lower Body

Umbrella

Upper Body

⅛ "(3) Dia. Hole

Arm

Paddle

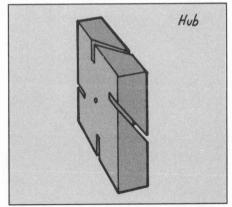

Figure B

Hub

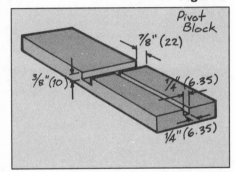

Figure C

Pivot Block

⅞" (22)

³⁄₈" (10)

¼" (6.35)

¼" (6.35)

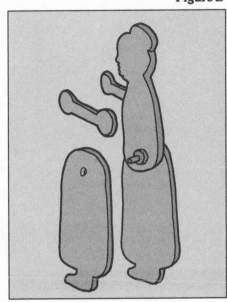

Figure D

4. Drill the holes indicated by cross marks on the scale drawings, using the specified drill bits. Drill a hole through the center of the Pivot Block, using a bit that is slightly larger than the shank diameter of the longest common nail.

5. Drill a ⅛-inch (3) diameter hole through the center of the Hub. The Paddles are set into notches cut into the edges of the Hub. Refer to **Figure B**, and cut a notch into each edge of the Hub, at a 45 degree angle. You can either set your table saw to cut the notches at the correct angle, or use a miter box to mark the angles.

6. Use a table saw or router to cut 2 rectangular grooves into the Base, as shown in **Figure C**.

7. Sand and label all of the pieces. Transfer the facial features, costume outlines, and placement lines to both sides of the Upper Body piece. Transfer the costume lines to opposite sides of the 2 Lower Body pieces.

Assembly   You'll cruise right through these assembly procedures if you will fribbitz the canoodle on the left-hand ordleter. No wait, that's a different project. (How embarrassing.)

1. Begin by assembling the umbrella-wielding lady. Glue and nail 1 Arm to each side of the Upper Body, along the placement lines. Sandwich the Upper Body between the 2 Lower Bodies, aligning the small holes, and placing a washer between each wooden piece (**Figure D**). Do not glue these pieces in place, as they should be free to move. Slip a washer over the end of the shorter common nail, and insert the nail through the aligned holes and washers. To secure the assembly, use a hammer to tap lightly on the point of the nail until if flattens and spreads slightly. (This is called "peening.")

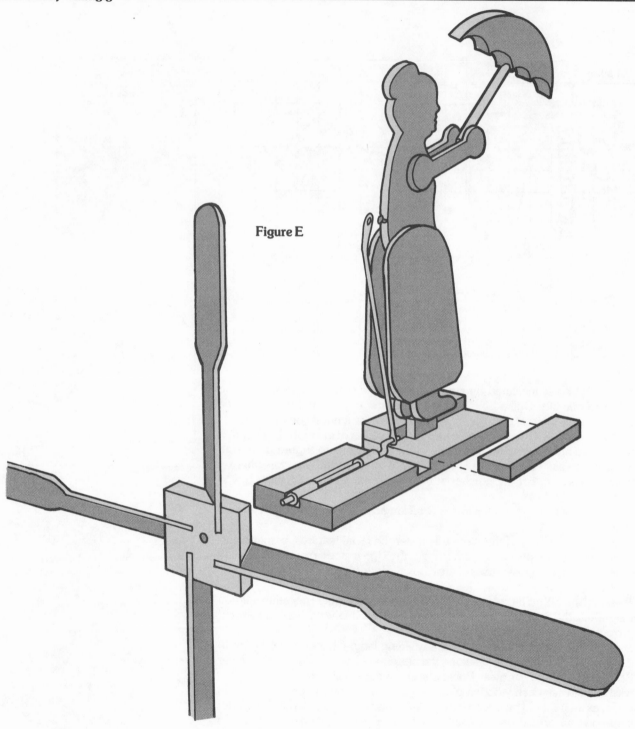

Figure E

2. Glue the 2 Umbrellas together, allow the glue to dry, and round off the curved upper edges. Drill a ¼-inch (6.35) diameter socket, ½ inch (13) deep, into the center of the scalloped lower edge. Cut a 4½-inch (114) length of ¼-inch (6.35) diameter dowel rod for the Umbrella Handle. Glue 1 end of the Handle into the socket in the Umbrella, and the other end between the hand portions of the lady's arms.

3. Paint the assembled lady in your choice of colors. Try to avoid getting any paint between the Upper and Lower Body pieces.

4. Before you start to assemble the support structure (including the mechanism which makes the lady rock back and forth), refer to the assembly diagram given in **Figure E**, so you'll have a good idea of where you're headed. Begin by cutting the wire into 2 pieces; one 8 inches (203) long (this will be the horizontal Shaft), and one 9 inches (229) long (the vertical Stem). Bend a ¾-inch (19) length at 1 end of the Shaft into the configuration shown in **Figure F**. Use your hammer to flatten a ⅜-inch (10) length at each end of the Stem, and drill a ¹⁄₁₆-inch (1.6) diameter hole through each flattened portion. Insert the bent end of the Shaft through the hole in 1 end of the Stem, and peen the end of the Shaft so that it can't slip out.

5. As you can see in **Figure E**, the Shaft runs through the narrow, lengthwise groove in the Base. To make Stabilizers for the Shaft, cut two 1-inch (25) lengths of ¼-inch (6.35) diameter dowel rod, and drill a ⅛-inch (3) diameter hole through the entire center length of each. Slip the Stabilizers onto the Shaft, and glue them into the groove at each end (**Figure G**).

6. Attach the Shaft Cover and Base Covers over the Base, as shown in **Figure H**. Glue the Spacer Block between the 2 Base Covers where indicated. Attach the wooden lady over the Base Covers, glueing and nailing her feet to the Spacer Block. Raise the Stem to a vertical position, bending it slightly so that you can drive the escutcheon pin through the hole in the Stem, into the rear edge of the Upper Body.

7. Glue a Paddle into each of the notches in the Hub. Slip a washer and the Hub over the end of the Shaft. Drive 2 small finishing nails into the hole, one on either side of the shaft (**Figure I**), so that the Shaft will rotate with the Hub.

8. To create the lower support assembly, first enlarge 1 end of the hole in the Pivot Block, to create a shallow socket that will accommodate the head of the long common nail. Insert the nail through the enlarged end of the hole, slip a washer over the end of the nail, and drive it into the center of 1 end of the closet rod. Drive the nail all the way into the rod, but leave a small amount of space, so that the Block can spin on the nail.

9. The Pivot Block is attached underneath the Base, at the balance point. To find the balance point, place the upper assembly on a table, perpendicular to an edge. Slide the assembly out over the edge, a little at a time, until it begins to tip. The point which lies along the table edge when the assembly begins to tip is the balance point. Glue the Pivot Block underneath the Base, centered under the balance point. Insert 2 wood screws through the Block and into the Base, being careful to avoid the shaft grooves.

10. Drill a 1½-inch (38) diameter socket into the center of 1 side of the 2 x 8 (38 x 184), and glue the lower end of the closet rod into the socket. Paint the assembled whirligig, carefully avoiding the working mechanisms.

If there are no prevailing breezes, break out the fan to demonstrate your bobbing, spinning whirligig.

Figure F

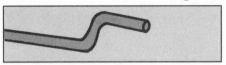

Figure G

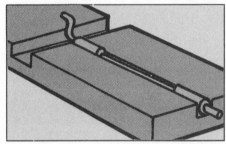

Figure H

Figure I

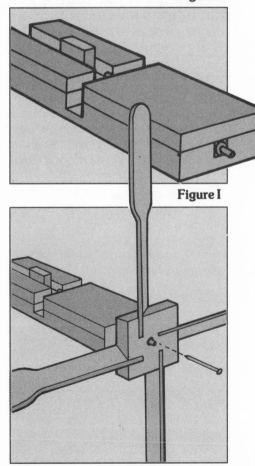

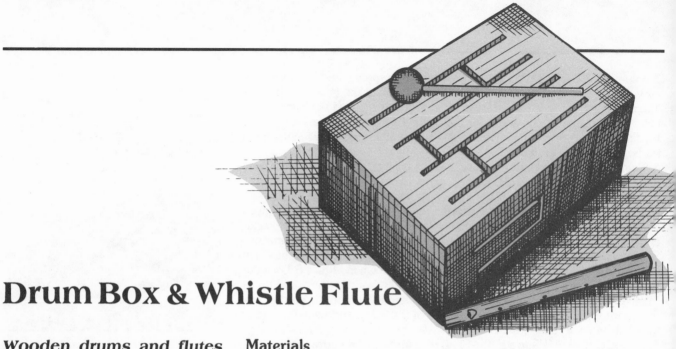

Drum Box & Whistle Flute

Wooden drums and flutes have been around since ancient times. This Drum Box will produce eight different, clear tones, and is a real favorite with both children and practicing musicians. Wooden flute designs have evolved over the centuries, but the simpler ones, like this model, are still popular with youngsters.

Metric equivalents in millimeters are indicated in parentheses.

Materials

For the Drum Box:

5-foot (1524) length of ½-inch (13) thick lumber, at least 7 inches (178) wide. The drum looks and sounds best when made from hardwood, but pine will work just fine.

15-inch (381) length of ¼-inch (6.35) diameter wooden dowel rod.

2 spherical wooden drawer pulls, each approximately 1 inch (25) in diameter. These will serve as the mallet heads, and will produce clear, sharp tones. For a softer sound, substitute hard rubber balls.

4 small rubber bumper pads, to cushion the bottom of the Drum.

Handful of 1-inch (25) long finishing nails.

For the Whistle Flute:

Wooden dowel rod: 10-inch (254) length of ¾-inch (19) diameter, 1¾-inch (45) length of ½-inch (13) diameter.

Carpenter's wood glue, sandpaper, non-toxic wood stain (optional), vegetable oil, and wood filler.

Tools

Saber saw, coping saw, or table saw; nailset; hammer; wood rasp; 2 or more clamps, each with a 7-inch (178) or larger mouth; vise or table clamp; and an electric or hand drill with ½-inch (13), ¼-inch (6.35), and ⅛-inch (3) diameter bits. The ½-inch (13) bit should be at least 5 inches (127) long.

Drum Box

Cutting the pieces   You could build the Drum Box by cutting a solid piece for each wall, and then go through drilling or routing gyrations to create the slots. Instead, you'll cut several rectangular pieces and small spacers for each of the slotted walls, and glue them together. Since you'll be cutting a mess of rectangles of varying sizes, we suggest that you label them as you cut.

1. Cut 2 Inner Walls, each 5½ x 7 inches (140 x 178); and 1 Floor, 7 x 11 inches (178 x 279).

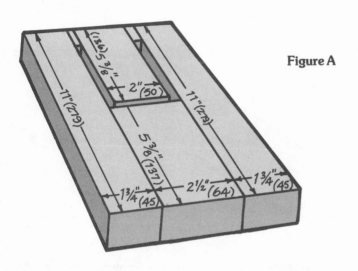

Figure A

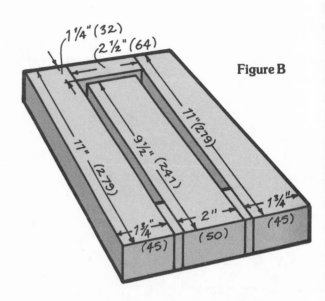

Figure B

Figure C

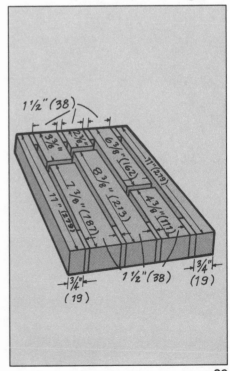

2. For 1 Outer Wall, cut 4 rectangular pieces to the dimensions given in the assembly diagram, **Figure A**. In addition, cut 2 Spacers, each ¼ x 1⅜ inches (6 x 35). Refer to **Figure B**, and cut 4 rectangular pieces for the other Outer Wall. Cut 2 additional Spacers for this wall.

3. For the Lid, cut 8 rectangular pieces to the dimensions given in **Figure C**, and 8 spacers. Sand all of the pieces lightly, to eliminate burrs.

Assembly   1. Begin with the pieces for the first Outer Wall. Glue them together along the edges as shown in **Figure A**, and clamp the assembly while it dries. Repeat this procedure to assemble the second Outer Wall (**Figure B**), and the Lid (**Figure C**).

2. To assemble the box, glue and nail the 2 Inner Walls over the short ends of the Floor. Attach the Lid over the Inner Walls. Add the Outer Walls over the open sides of the box. Recess the nails, and fill the holes with wood filler.

3. Use a wood rasp followed by sandpaper to round off the corners and long edges of the assembled Drum. Sand all remaining edges and surfaces. Glue a rubber bumper under each corner of the Floor. Finish with wood stain followed by vegetable oil, or simply use the oil. The Drum Box should be oiled regularly, to keep the wood from drying out.

4. To create a mallet, cut the dowel rod into 2 equal lengths. Drill a ¼-inch (6.35) diameter socket, approximately ½ inch (13) deep, into each wooden drawer pull or rubber ball. Glue the rods into the sockets. Sand, and finish the mallets as you did the Drum.

5. When playing the Drum Box, you will get the best tones by striking the slotted Walls and Lid at the closed ends of the slots.

Figure G

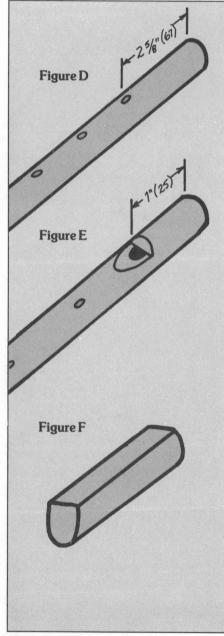

Figure D

← 2⅝" (67) →

Figure E

← 1" (25) →

Figure F

Whistle Flute

Cutting and assembly **1.** Drill out the entire center length of the larger dowel rod, using the ½-inch (13) diameter bit. Since this is a 10-inch (254) length, you'll need to clamp the rod in a vise and drill as straight as possible, first from 1 end, and then from the other.

2. To create the finger holes shown in **Figure D**, drill a ⅛-inch (3) diameter hole, 2⅝ inches (67) from 1 end of the rod. This will be the mouthpiece end. Drill 2 additional holes in a straight line with the first hole, spacing them 1⅞ inches (48) apart.

3. To create the angled tone opening shown in **Figure E**, make a straight cut, ³⁄₁₆ inch (5) deep, 1 inch (25) from the mouthpiece end of the Flute, in line with the finger holes. Make a second, angled cut up to the straight cut, starting approximately ½ inch (13) below it.

4. Cut a 1-inch (25) length from the smaller dowel rod for the mouthpiece Insert. Cut a slice approximately ¹⁄₁₆ inch (1.6) thick from the length of the Insert (**Figure F**). Glue the Insert into the mouthpiece end of the Flute, so that the sliced side is lined up with the tone and finger holes. (Be very careful that you do not clog the air passage, or you'll have very blue-faced flautists producing no sounds at all.) Glue the remaining, unsliced length of dowel rod into the opposite end of the Flute.

5. This step is optional. Make another angled cut, as shown in **Figure G**, to remove a section from the lower side of the mouthpiece. Angle the cut sharply, making it no longer than ⅞ inch (22).

6. Sand the Flute lightly, and finish with stain and/or oil. To play, cover the finger holes tightly and blow gently into the mouthpiece. Lift your fingers 1 at a time to produce different tones. Blow harder, and you'll get 3 additional tones in a higher register.

With ear plugs inserted firmly, teach your little toots to flute, and your aspiring drummers to percuss.

"School days, school days"
Toys that teach

Country Puzzle Picture

Young children will enjoy this old-time jigsaw puzzle, and learn something about barnyard animals at the same time. The twelve puzzle pieces, each with a dowel-rod handle, are easy to recognize and place.

Metric equivalents in millimeters are indicated in parentheses.

Materials

16½ x 36-inch (419 x 914) piece of ¼-inch (6) thick, interior grade plywood.
10½-inch (267) length of ¼-inch (6.35) diameter wooden dowel rod.
Small quantities of non-toxic paint in the colors of your choice.
Carpenter's wood glue, sandpaper, wood filler, kraft paper, and carbon paper.

Tools

Band saw or jigsaw, artist's fine paint brush, small flat paint brush, and an electric or hand drill with a ¼-inch (6.35) diameter bit. If you do not have access to a band saw or jigsaw, use a saber saw to cut puzzle pieces with simplified outlines (e.g., cut a simple square around the chicken). The puzzle will still work just fine, and the details will be provided by the painted design.

Cutting the pieces   **1.** Cut 2 square pieces from the plywood, each 16½ x 16½ inches (419 x 419). One of these pieces will be the Backboard.

2. Cut a 1-inch (25) wide Frame Strip from each side of the remaining plywood square (**Figure A**). The Frame Strips will be used later to form a frame (what else, pray tell?) around the puzzle. The smaller plywood square will serve as the Puzzle Board.

3. A scale drawing of the puzzle picture is given in **Figure B**. Make a full-size pattern, and transfer the darker cutting lines to the Puzzle Board.

4. Cut out each puzzle piece, starting at the lower edge of the Board. Make a short cut across the background portion of the Board where necessary, to get to the remaining pieces.

5. The Cow and Chicken present special problems since it will be impossible to cut the small corners without destroying the surrounding background area. For this reason, we suggest that you cut into the pieces where necessary, to achieve the proper cutout in the background, and cut a new Cow and Chicken from excess plywood. (You will, nonetheless, need to make 1 long saw cut across the Barn to get to the Chicken outline.)

6. Drill a hole through the center of each puzzle piece, to accommodate a dowel Handle. Sand the pieces and the Puzzle Board. Pay special attention to the cutout edges, so that the pieces will slide in and out easily. Sand the Frame Strips and Backboard, rounding off the outer corners.

7. Cut twelve ¾-inch (19) long Handles from the wooden dowel rod, and sand each of them.

Assembly   **1.** To repair the background saw cuts, fill them with wood filler. Allow the filler to dry, and sand smooth.

2. Glue the Frame Strips along the edges of the Backboard. Use wood filler to fill the open grain on each of the outer raw edges, allow it to dry, and sand the edges smooth.

3. Glue a dowel Handle into each puzzle piece.

4. It's now painting time at the farm. You can follow our color scheme (see the color photograph in the center section of the book), or stand by your artistic license and create your own color scheme. Paint each Handle to match the color immediately surrounding it. Try to avoid getting paint on the edges of the puzzle pieces or on the edges of the cutouts in the Puzzle Board.

5. Glue the Puzzle Board over the Backboard, inside the Frame. Allow the glue to dry, and put the puzzle pieces in place.

With just a short demonstration, your pint-size puzzlers will catch on post-haste — and probably just as quickly start clamoring for another new picture puzzle!

Figure A

Figure B

14½" (368)   1" (25)

Puzzle Board

16½" (419)

1 sq. = 1 in. (25.4)

Alphabet Train

If those zany educational television shows have taught us anything, it's that children learn faster when they're having fun. So sharpen your saw, dust off your dictionary, and make this entertaining learn-to-spell toy for the kids.

Metric equivalents in millimeters are indicated in parentheses.

Materials

The letters, Engine, Caboose, and the bases on which they stand are cut from a length of 2 x 8-inch (38 x 184) pine. The length you'll need will depend on how many letters you want to produce. (You may wish to cut out only the letters in your child's name. If you want to go all out for a more educational toy, cut 1 or more of each letter in the alphabet.) To determine the specific length of pine you'll need, allow approximately a 4-inch (102) length for each letter you plan to cut. (This will also accommodate the base of the letter.) Add an additional 14 inches (356) for the Engine and Caboose, and you have the total length of the pine board you'll need to purchase.

The axles are cut from ¼-inch (6.35) diameter wooden dowel rod. Allow 9 inches (229) of dowel for each letter and for the Caboose, plus 13 ½ inches (343) for the Engine.

Standard metal cup hooks will be used to connect the bases so that the train can be pulled along as a unit. You'll need 2 hooks for each letter, plus 1 each for the Engine and Caboose.

Wheels. You can purchase pre-made wheels or cut them yourself. You'll need 4 wheels for each letter and for the Caboose, and 6 wheels for the Engine. Each wheel should be 2 inches (51) in diameter and approximately ¾ inch (19) thick, with a ¼-inch (6.35) diameter center hole.

Non-toxic paint or stain (optional), in bright colors of your choice.

Nails or screws. Purchase two 2-inch (51) long nails or flat head wood screws for each letter you intend to make, plus 2 each for the Engine and Caboose.

Small quantities of wood filler and epoxy cement.

Carpenter's wood glue, medium and fine sandpaper, and kraft paper.

Tools

Hammer, carpenter's rule, saber saw or coping saw, screwdriver (if you intend to use wood screws), and an electric or hand drill with a ⅜-inch (10) diameter bit. In addition, you'll need a ¼-inch (6.35) diameter bit if you plan to cut your own wheels. If you intend to use wood screws, you'll also need a bit slightly smaller than the diameter of the screw shanks, and a bit slightly larger than the diameter of the screw heads. You can use a router with a small core box bit to add dimensional designs to the letters, but it is not necessary (and certainly not easy).

Cutting the pieces   **1.** A scale drawing for each letter of the alphabet is given in **Figure A**. For each letter you wish to cut, enlarge the scale drawing to a full-size pattern on kraft paper.

2. Cut the letters from the pine board. In addition, cut a 2½ x 4-inch (64 x 102) base for each letter. (Please note that while most of the letters will fit on a 4-inch [102] long base, you may wish to alter the length for unusually wide or narrow letters, like "W" and "I." But do not make any of the bases shorter than 3¼ inches [83], or the wheels will not fit.)

Figure A

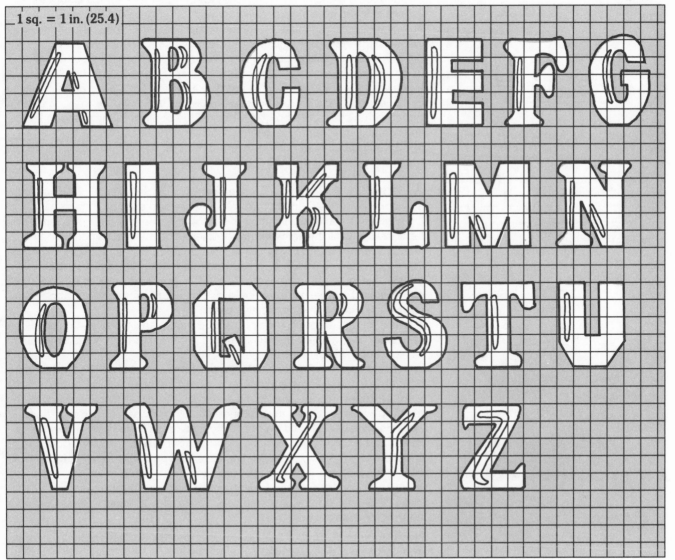

1 sq. = 1 in. (25.4)

3. Scale drawings for the Engine and Caboose are given in **Figure B**. Enlarge the drawings to full-size patterns on kraft paper.

4. Cut 1 Engine and 1 Caboose from the pine board. In addition, cut a base to accommodate the length of each.

5. Drill 2 axle holes through each base, using the ⅜-inch (10) diameter bit, where indicated in **Figure C**. If you cut any short bases for the narrow letters, allow at least 2¼ inches (58) between the holes. Drill an extra axle hole through the Engine base, 2¼ inches (58) from 1 of the existing holes.

6. Cut three 4½-inch (115) long axles for the Engine, 2 for the Caboose, and 2 for each letter, from the wooden dowel rod.

7. If you did not purchase pre-made wheels, cut and drill them at this time, following the dimensions given in the "Materials" section above.

8. (This is an extremely optional step because it is for looks only, and is difficult to do well unless you are a whiz with a router. To option out, skip to step 9.) If you will look at **Figure A** once again, you will notice shaded areas on some of the letters. These are "dimensional designs" which can be created using a router with a small core box bit. Transfer the outlines to the wooden letters, and carefully run your router between the lines on each design.

9. Carefully sand all of the pieces you have cut, to eliminate splinters, rough spots, and all sharp edges and corners.

Assembly **1.** Center the Engine over its base. Secure it in place with glue and 2 nails or screws driven through the base and into the Engine. (Pre-drill the screw holes to avoid splitting the wood.) Recess the nails or countersink the screws, and fill the holes with wood filler. (You might consider this needless work, since the fasteners won't show. But children, as you probably know, will invariably examine, rub, lick, pinch, and otherwise probe every surface of the objects that make up their world — so this is a safety precaution, to avoid scratches and scrapes.) Follow the same procedure to attach the Caboose and each of the letters to their respective bases.

2. Insert an axle through each of the axle holes, leaving equal extensions on each side. Glue a wheel over each axle end, so that the end of the axle is flush with the outer side of the wheel.

3. Install a cup hook at the center of the front and rear edges of each letter base. Apply epoxy cement to the hook shanks before you insert them, so that it will be impossible for little people to remove them. The open section of the rear hook on each base should point directly downward, and that of the front hook on each base should point directly right or left (**Figure D**). This way, any letter may be connected to any other letter. Insert a hook (pointing downward) into the rear edge only of the Engine base, and another (pointing right or left) into the front edge only of the Caboose base.

4. Paint or stain the letters, Engine, and Caboose. If you prefer the natural wood finish, we suggest that you rub the wood with vegetable oil to keep it from drying out.

Hook up your Alphabet Express, roll it into the littlest engineer's room, and sit for a s-p-e-l-l. (Arrrgh!)

Figure B

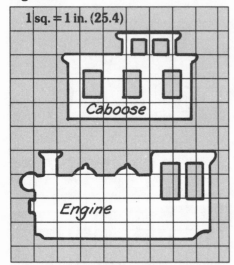

Figure C

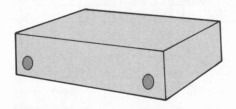

Figure D

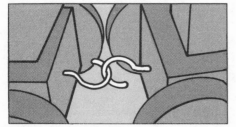

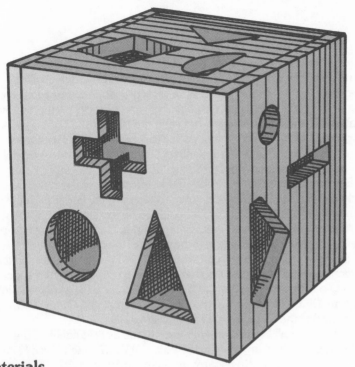

Size & Shape Box

This simple project is a definite contender for the world title in the "Easiest-to-Build, Most Entertaining Toys for Toddlers" category. Can you think of a better way to teach the kids that age-old lesson about round pegs and square holes?

Materials

2-foot (610) length of 2 x 8-inch (38 x 184) pine.
51-inch (1295) length of 1 x 12-inch (17 x 286) pine.
9½ x 10½-inch (241 x 267) piece of ¼-inch (6) thick plywood.
Non-toxic paint in several bright colors.
Handful of 1¼-inch (32) long finishing nails.
Carpenter's wood glue, medium and fine sandpaper, kraft paper, and a small quantity of wood filler.

Tools

Saber saw or coping saw, small paint brush, carpenter's rule, hammer, nailset, electric or hand drill with a ½-inch (13) diameter bit, and a router with a ¼-inch (6) straight bit. If you do not have access to a router, a small wood chisel will do the job.

Cutting the pieces
1. Scale drawings for the shaped Blocks are given in **Figure A**. Enlarge the drawings to full-size patterns on kraft paper.
2. Cut 1 of each Block pattern from the 2 x 8-inch (38 x 184) pine. Cut the following additional Blocks from the same material: 1 circle with a 1½-inch (38) diameter; 1 circle with a 2¾-inch (70) diameter; 1 rectangle, 1½ x 3½ inches (38 x 89); and 1 square 3½ x 3½ inches (89 x 89). Carefully sand each of the Blocks to eliminate splinters and sharp edges.
3. Cut the following pieces for the box from the pine board: 2 Outer Walls, each 10½ x 10½ inches (267 x 267); 2 Inner Walls, each 9 x 9¼ inches (229 x 235); and 1 Roof, 9 x 10½ inches (229 x 267). The 9½ x 10½-inch (241 x 267) piece of plywood will serve as the Floor.

Metric equivalents in millimeters are indicated in parentheses.

4. To create the cutouts in the Walls and Roof of the box, first separate the Blocks into 5 piles (3 Blocks per pile). It makes no difference which Blocks you group together, but try to mix the sizes in each pile, so that you avoid having 3 very large Blocks in any 1 pile. Arrange 1 group of Blocks on the box Roof, leaving at least 1 inch (25) of space between the Blocks and the edges of the Roof (**Figure B**). Draw the outline of each Block on the Roof. Repeat this procedure 4 more times, using the 4 remaining piles of Blocks and the 4 box Walls.

5. Drill 3 holes through the Roof and each of the Walls, placing 1 hole inside of each Block outline. Insert your saw blade through 1 of the holes, and cut out the shape. We suggest that you cut the shape slightly larger than the outline, so that your little ones will not be frustrated by too close a fit. Repeat this procedure to cut out each of the remaining shapes. Sand all of the box parts carefully, paying particular attention to the edges of the cutouts.

6. The box Floor will be slid into grooves cut into the Outer Walls, so that it can be opened and closed. Use a router or chisel to cut a straight, ¼-inch (6) wide groove on the inner side of 1 Outer Wall, ¼ inch (6) above the lower edge (**Figure C**). Cut an identical groove in the remaining Outer Wall. Sand the grooves so that the Floor will slide along them easily.

7. We attached a small Lip underneath each of the 2 short edges of the Floor to provide a handhold when opening the box. Cut 2 Lips, each ¼ x 8¾ inches (6 x 222), from the leftover pine boards, and sand them carefully.

Figure A

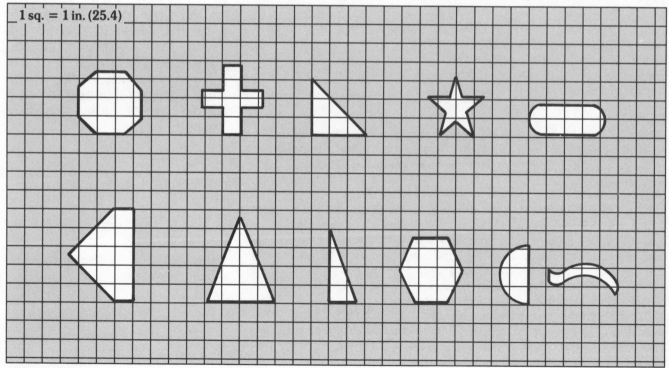

1 sq. = 1 in. (25.4)

Figure B

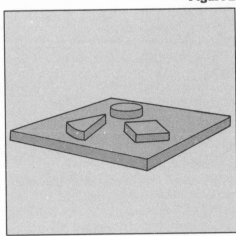

Figure C

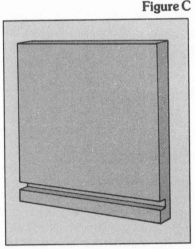

Figure D

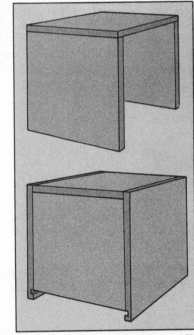

Assembly   All there is left to do is put the box together and paint every-thing. While you assemble the box, why not let the kids have at it with the Blocks and paint? (Why not, indeed! We have 5 kids of our own, so we're all too familiar with why not. But we regularly fling all caution to the winds any-way, cover every exposed surface with plastic, and shout encouragement to the budding artists from a safe distance.)

1. Glue and nail the Roof over the edges of the 2 Inner Walls, as shown in **Figure D**. Attach the 2 Outer Walls over the raw edges of the Roof and Inner Walls. (The grooved portions of the Outer Walls should extend below the Inner Walls, so that the Floor can be inserted between the grooves.)

2. Spread glue on 1 long side of 1 of the Lips. Center, and attach the Lip under-neath 1 short edge of the Floor, as shown in **Figure E**. Attach the remaining Lip underneath the opposite short edge of the Floor.

3. Slide the Floor into the assembled box, and test it to make sure that it will move back and forth in the grooves without undue effort. If it is too difficult to move, sand the lower edges of the grooves slightly. The Floor should move easily, but not so easily that it will slide open by itself when the box is turned.

4. Sand any remaining splinters or sharp edges on the box, and give it to the pint-size painters. If you've decided against apprentice painters, you'll have to paint the box and all of the Blocks yourself.

After you present the Size & Shape Box to the toddlers (and patiently show them how it works), there are bound to be lengthy silences in the playroom. While this is usually cause for alarm, fear not! In this case, it's purely a sign of intense concentration.

Figure E

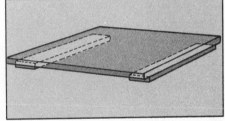

Tell-Time Clock

This large, easy to read, clown-faced clock will help the kiddos learn about hours and minutes in practically no time at all! Unlike the plastic models available in most toy outlets, your Tell-Time Clock will last for generations. It's also a very simple project to build.

Metric equivalents in millimeters are indicated in parentheses.

Materials

10 x 20-inch (254 x 508) piece of ¼-inch (6) thick interior grade plywood.
38-inch (965) length of 1 x 4-inch (17 x 89) clear white pine.
3-foot (914) length of ¼ x 1¾-inch (6 x 45) pine lattice.
⅜-inch (10) length of 1-inch (25) diameter wooden dowel rod.
1 small gauge, round head wood screw, 1½ inches (38) long.
2 metal washers, each approximately ¾ inch (19) in diameter, with a center hole slightly larger than the diameter of the wood screw shank.
8 thin finishing nails, each 1¼ inches (32) long; and 16 thin finishing nails, each ¾ inch (19) long.
Non-toxic paint in 3 or 4 bright colors of your choice.
Carpenter's wood glue, medium and fine sandpaper, kraft paper, and a small quantity of wood filler.

Tools

Hammer; nailset; saber saw or coping saw; small paint brush; screw driver; and an electric or hand drill with 2 bits, 1 slightly smaller and 1 slightly larger than the diameter of the wood screw shank.

Cutting the pieces 1. Cut the piece of plywood in half widthwise to create 2 pieces, each 10 x 10 inches (254 x 254). These will be the Face and Rear Wall of the Clock.

2. Cut the following pieces from the clear white pine: 2 Inner Frames, each 8½ inches (216) long; and 2 Outer Frames, each 10 inches (254) long.

3. Make kraft paper patterns from the full-size drawings given in **Figure A**, and cut the following pieces from the pine lattice: 2 Eyes, 1 Mouth, 1 Big Hand, 1 Little Hand, 5 of the Numeral 1, 2 of the Numeral 2, and 1 each of the Numerals 3 through 0. Sand all of these pieces.

4. Drill a hole through the center of the round portion of each Hand, using the bit which is slightly larger than the diameter of the wood screw shank. Drill a hole through the center of the short length of dowel rod, from 1 flat side to the other, using the bit that is slightly smaller than the diameter of the wood screw shank. Use the same bit to drill a hole through the exact center of 1 plywood Wall. (This will be the Face.)

Assembly   We suggest that you paint all of the small pieces before assembling the Clock, so you won't have to go through the tedious ordeal of masking, or worse yet, cleaning up paint spots from adjoining surfaces, repainting, re-cleaning the new spots, re-repainting, and ad nauseum, as the ancient Romans used to say.

Figure A

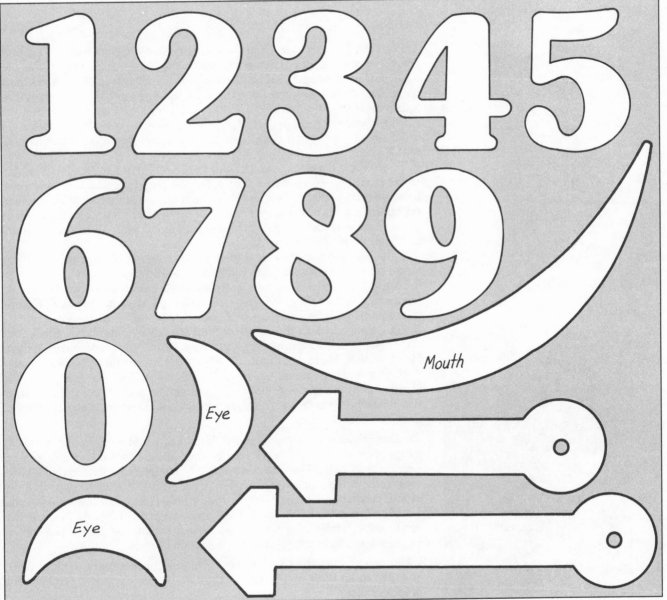

1. Paint the Eyes and Mouth in 1 color, and all of the Numerals in a second color. The short length of dowel rod will be the Nose, which will serve as the base to which the Hands will be attached. Paint the Nose and Hands in a third color. The clock case (consisting of Walls and Frames) will be painted in a fourth color after it is assembled. (These are our suggestions but you may, of course, choose to paint your clock differently. Keep in mind that a small child will need all the help he or she can get, to sort out the separate elements of the Clock.)

2. To assemble the clock case, first glue the Outer Frames flush over the edges of the Inner Frames to form a square. Secure each joint with 2 of the longer finishing nails. Glue the Face and Rear Wall over the raw edges of the Frames, on opposite sides of the square, and use the shorter nails to secure them in place. Recess all nails, and fill the holes with wood filler. Allow several hours for the glue and wood filler to dry.

3. Carefully sand the clock case, to eliminate splinters, sharp edges, and any lumps created by the wood filler. Paint the case, and allow it to dry.

4. Lay the Numerals on the Face, and play with the arrangement until you have the spacing correct. Glue the Numerals in place, 1 at a time, so you don't lose your carefully spaced arrangement. Glue the Eyes and Mouth in place.

5. Glue the Nose over the center of the Face, aligning the holes. Stack (but do not glue) the following pieces on top of the Nose, in this order: washer, Little Hand, washer, Big Hand (**Figure B**). Align the stack and insert the wood screw through the aligned holes, tightening it until the head sits flat against the Big Hand. Adjust the screw so that the Hands can be turned, but will hold their positions when you let go. The screw tension should be checked periodically, once the Clock is in use.

Caution: Even some very young children are surprisingly handy at taking things apart, especially if they have observed an adult at work. With access to a screwdriver or the like, and given enough unsupervised time, a clever child could remove the screw from this clock. If you suspect that such ingenuity lurks in your children, substitute a wooden peg for the screw. This will involve some modifications in the hole sizes for the Hands, washers, and Nose. Measure the peg length carefully, to achieve proper tension on the Hands. The peg should be glued securely into the Nose. (No, not the child's nose.)

When you present the Clock to your fledgling timekeepers, set it at 5:00, and give them their first lesson — time for tea (or the liquid refreshment of your choice).

Figure B

"Sailing, sailing, over the bounding main"
Toys to sail imaginary seas

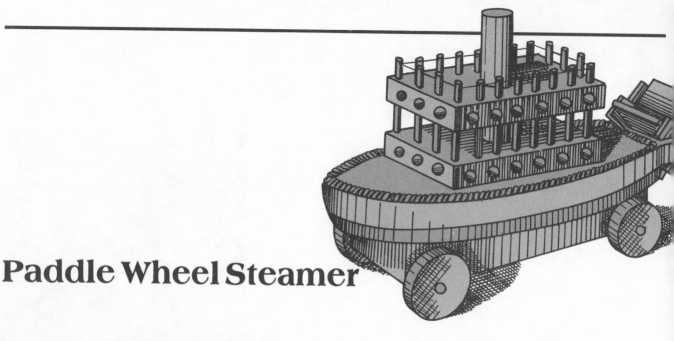

Paddle Wheel Steamer

In 1787, John Fitch successfully launched the first workable steamboat in the United States. Twenty-five years later, Nicholas J. Roosevelt (a great-granduncle of President Theodore Roosevelt) launched the paddle wheel steamer New Orleans, which completed the first steam powered trip down the Mississippi River. By 1846, nearly 1,200 steamboats ran up and down the Mississippi on regular schedules.

Metric equivalents in millimeters are indicated in parentheses.

Materials

10-inch (254) length of 2 x 4-inch (38 x 89) pine.
40-inch (1016) length of 1 x 8-inch (17 x 184) clear white pine.
11-inch (279) length of ¼ x 1¾-inch (6 x 45) wooden lattice.
Wooden dowel rod: 4 feet (1219) of ¼-inch (6.35) diameter; 5 inches (127) of ½-inch (13) diameter; 4½ inches (114) of 1-inch (25) diameter.
32-inch (813) length of hemp rope, approximately ¼-inch (6) in diameter.
21-inch (533) length of string or twine, no larger than ⅛ inch (3) in diameter.
1-yard (914) length of cotton cord, no larger than ¼ inch (6) in diameter.
1 metal screw eye, approximately 1 inch (25) long, with a ¼-inch (6) or larger diameter eye.
16 thin finishing nails, ½ to ¾ inch (13 to 19) long.
Carpenter's wood glue, a small quantity of epoxy cement, medium and fine sandpaper, kraft paper, and small quantities of non-toxic paint or wood stain in the colors of your choice.

Tools

Hammer, saber saw or coping saw, carpenter's rule, small paint brush, and an electric or hand drill with bits of the following diameters: ⅛-inch (3), ¼-inch (6.35), ⅜-inch (10), ½-inch (13), ¾-inch (19), and 1-inch (25).

Cutting the pieces   **1.** Enlarge the scale drawings given in **Figure A** to full-size patterns on kraft paper.
2. Cut the following pieces from the 1 x 8-inch (17 x 184) pine: 4 Wheels, each 2 inches (51) in diameter; 2 Decks, each 4 x 6 inches (102 x 152); 1 Upper Hull; and 1 Lower Hull.
3. Use the ¼-inch (6.35) diameter bit to drill a hole through each of the rear extensions of the Upper Hull, where indicated by dotted lines on the scale drawing. Drill two ½-inch (13) diameter holes through the Lower Hull where indicated. Angle the edges of the Lower Hull as shown.

Figure A

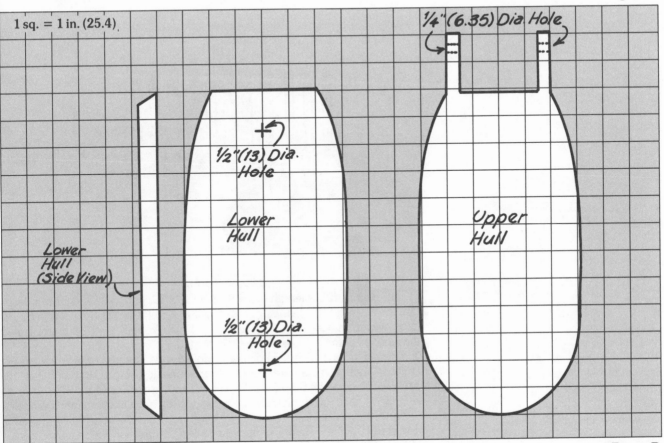

1 sq. = 1 in. (25.4)

¼" (6.35) Dia. Hole

½" (13) Dia. Hole

Lower Hull

½" (13) Dia. Hole

Lower Hull (Side View)

Upper Hull

Figure B

4. You will need to drill a whole mess, as they say (we hope it's not), of perfectly aligned holes through the 2 identical Decks, to accommodate the Rails. Stack the Decks, 1 on top of the other, and drive 2 temporary holding nails near the center point. Begin by drilling a ¼-inch (6.35) diameter hole near each corner (drill all holes completely through both Decks). Drill 6 holes in a straight line near each long edge, evenly spaced between the corner holes. Drill 2 holes in a straight line near each short edge, evenly spaced between the corner holes. Remove the temporary nails, and drill a 1-inch (25) diameter hole through the exact center of both Decks.

5. Now you get to drill another mess, this time of sockets, into the edges of the 2 Decks. These sockets are decorative only, so exact alignment is not crucial. But since the sockets will be drilled horizontally into the edges of the Decks, you'll need to take care to avoid drilling into any of the vertical holes that you just drilled. Use the ⅜-inch (10) diameter bit to drill the shallow sockets as shown in **Figure B**, placing 7 sockets in a straight line along each long edge, and 3 along each short edge.

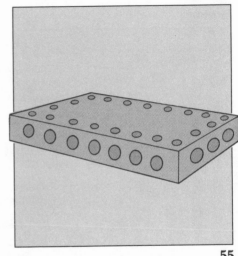

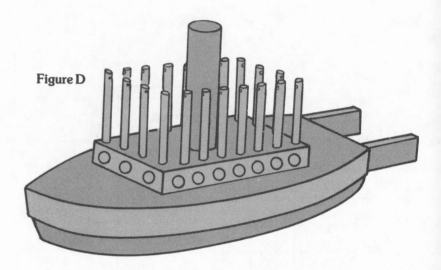

Figure D

6. The 10-inch (254) length of 2 x 4-inch (38 x 89) pine will serve as the Base. Use the ⅜-inch (10) diameter bit to drill 2 axle holes through the width of the Base where indicated in **Figure C**. Drill two ½-inch (13) diameter holes through the depth of the base where indicated.

7. The length of 1-inch (25) diameter dowel rod will serve as a Smokestack. Drill a ¾-inch (19) diameter socket, approximately ¾ inch (19) deep, into the center of 1 end of the Smokestack. (This will be the upper end.)

8. Drill a ¼-inch (6.35) diameter hole through the exact center of each Wheel.

9. Cut 20 Rails, each 3 inches (76) long, from the ¼-inch (6.35) diameter dowel rod. Drill a ⅛-inch (3) diameter hole through each Rail, approximately ¼ inch (6) from 1 end.

10. Cut 4 Paddles, each 1½ x 2½ inches (38 x 64) from the pine lattice. Cut 4 Paddle Supports, each ¾ x 2½ inches (19 x 64), from the same material.

11. Sand all of the pieces to eliminate splinters, rough spots, and sharp edges.

Assembly **1.** Glue the Upper Hull over the Lower Hull, and glue 1 of the Decks (this will be the Lower Deck) to the Upper Hull, as shown in **Figure D**. Insert the Smokestack into the center hole. Glue the Rails in place, aligning the small holes in the upper ends of the Rails so that a length of string can be passed straight through them.

2. Spread a thin belt of glue around each of the Rails, approximately 1 inch (25) below the upper edge. Slide the Upper Deck down over the Rails and Smokestack until there is about 1 inch (25) of space between the Upper and Lower Decks. (If you use a hammer for this procedure, place blocks of scrap wood over the Deck, to avoid hammer marks.) Perform this step as quickly as possible, so that the glue does not grab the Upper Deck in an uneven position. Use a wet sponge to wipe away any excess glue that may have squished out of the holes.

Figure C

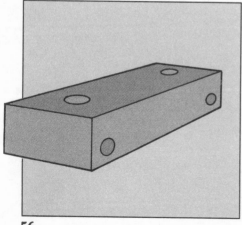

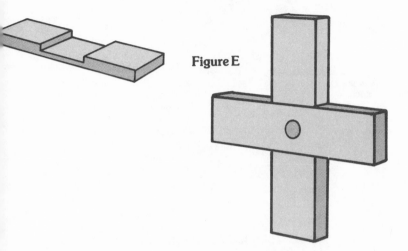

Figure E

3. To assemble the Paddle Supports, refer to **Figure E** and cut a ¾-inch (19) dado, ⅛ inch (3) deep, across each Support where indicated. Glue 2 of the Supports together, matching dadoes, to form a cross. Drill a ⅜-inch (10) diameter hole through the center of the crossed support assembly, as shown. Repeat the gluing and drilling procedure, using the 2 remaining Supports.

4. Glue and nail the 4 Paddles between the 2 paddle support assemblies as shown in **Figure F**. Be sure to leave enough space at the center of the assembly for the axle rod.

5. Cut a 4-inch (102) length of ¼-inch (6.35) diameter dowel rod for the Paddle Axle. Place the paddle assembly between the rear extensions of the Upper Hull, and insert the axle through the aligned holes. Glue the axle ends into the holes in the Hull extensions.

6. Paint or stain the Steamer. When the paint has dried, glue the length of hemp rope over the edge of the Upper Hull, and thread the length of string or twine through the aligned holes in the Rails.

7. To assemble the base, cut two 5-inch (127) long axles from the ¼-inch (6.35) diameter dowel rod, and insert the axles through the axle holes, leaving equal extensions on each side. Glue a Wheel over each axle end. Cut two 5-inch (127) lengths of ½-inch (13) diameter dowel rod, and glue these rods into the remaining holes in the Base, with lower edges flush.

8. Paint or stain the assembled base. When it is dry, place the Steamer on the base, sliding it down over the upright dowels.

9. Apply epoxy cement to the shank of the screw eye, and install it at the front of the base. Tie the 1-yard (914) length of cotton cord to the screw eye, and hand the cord to the proud new owner.

When you present the Paddle Wheel Steamer to the kids, caution them that they may only pretend to plunge the Paddler into a puddle or pond. This model's for landlubbers only!

Figure F

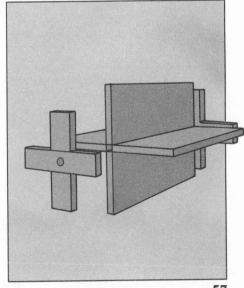

Sailing Sloop

This graceful sailboat will be a real joy to bathtub skippers of all ages. It has a working tiller, a removable cabin roof, and swinging booms. The trailer can be hitched up to a wooden car or truck, for transport to the local yacht basin.

Metric equivalents in millimeters are indicated in parentheses.

Materials
43-inch (1092) length of 1 x 6-inch (17 x 140) clear white pine.

18-inch (457) length of ¼ x 1¾-inch (6 x 45) pine lattice.

Wooden dowel rod: 22-inch (559) length of ½-inch (13) diameter; 22-inch (559) length of ¼-inch (6.35) diameter; 4-inch (102) length of ⅛-inch (3) diameter; and a ⅛-inch (3) length of ¾-inch (19) diameter.

4 wooden plugs, each ⅜ inch (10) in diameter.

4 wooden wheels, each 2 inches (51) in diameter and ½ inch (13) thick, with a 5⁄16-inch (8) diameter center hole. You can purchase pre-made wheels, or cut them yourself.

2 brass cup hooks, each approximately 1¾ inches (45) long, with a shank diameter no larger than ⅛ inch (3).

3 tiny metal screw eyes, each approximately ⅝ inch (16) long.

1 extremely small, nautically experienced, talking parrot (optional) to provide colorful (and possibly embarrassing) atmosphere.

A small quantity of marine grade wood sealer or spar varnish.

Paint or wood stain in the colors of your choice (optional).

¼ yard (229) of unbleached muslin.

Medium and fine sandpaper, kraft paper, carpenter's wood glue, a small quantity of epoxy cement, and white sewing thread.

Tools
Carpenter's rule; saber saw or coping saw; table clamp or vise; sewing machine or needle; medium-size paint brush; artist's fine-tipped paint brush (optional); and an electric or hand drill with bits of the following diameters: ⅛-inch (3), ¼-inch (6.35), ⅜-inch (10), and ½-inch (13). You'll also need a 5⁄16-inch (8) diameter bit if you plan to cut your own wheels.

You'll need to do some contouring to achieve the proper hull shape. A belt sander is the best power tool for this job, but it can also be accomplished with a wood rasp followed by sandpaper.

To cut the notch which serves as a seat for the keel, you will need either a circular saw or a wood chisel.

Figure A

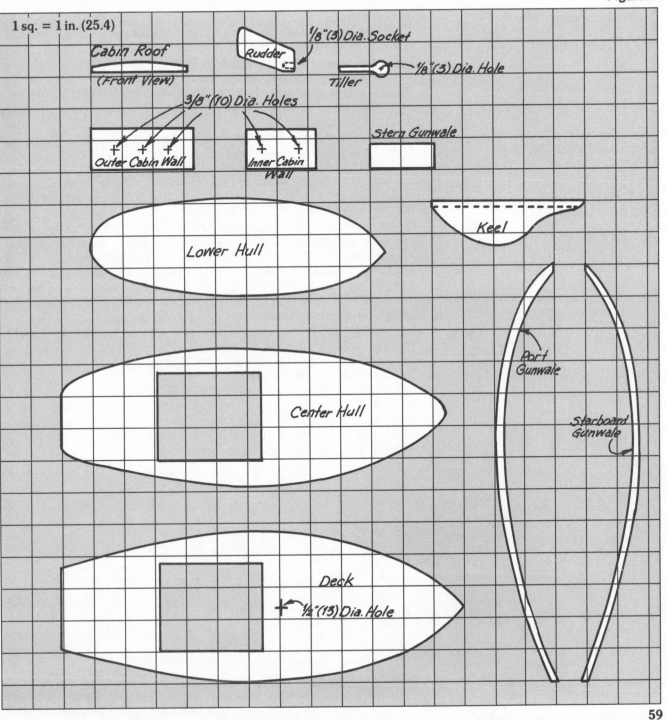

1 sq. = 1 in. (25.4)

Cabin Roof (Front View)

Rudder — 1/8"(3) Dia. Socket

Tiller — 1/8"(3) Dia. Hole

3/8"(10) Dia. Holes

Outer Cabin Wall

Inner Cabin Wall

Stern Gunwale

Lower Hull

Keel

Center Hull

Port Gunwale

Starboard Gunwale

Deck

1/2"(13) Dia. Hole

The Sloop
Cutting the pieces   In case you are a landlubber, we ought to explain a few nautical terms used here. "Port" and "starboard" refer to the left- and right-hand sides of a boat, respectively (if you're standing in the boat, facing front). "Bow" and "stern" refer to the front and back ends, respectively. A "gunwale" is the portion of a boat's side wall which extends up above the deck. The word is sometimes spelled "gunnel," and is always pronounced that way, to rhyme with "tunnel."

1. Refer to **Figure A**, and enlarge the scale drawings given to full-size patterns on kraft paper.

2. Cut 1 Deck, 1 Center Hull, 1 Lower Hull, 1 Port Gunwale, and 1 Starboard Gunwale from the 1 x 6-inch (17 x 140) pine. Cut the rectangular openings in the Deck and Center Hull, and drill a ½-inch (13) diameter hole through the Deck where indicated.

3. Cut 2 Outer Cabin Walls, 2 Inner Cabin Walls, 1 Rudder, 1 Tiller, 1 Stern Gunwale, and 1 Keel from the pine lattice. In addition, cut 1 Cabin Roof, 3 x 3⅝ inches (76 x 92), from the same material. Drill holes through the Tiller and Cabin Walls where indicated. Drill a shallow, ⅛-inch (3) diameter socket into the upper edge of the Rudder, as indicated by dotted lines on the scale drawing. Use a wood rasp followed by sandpaper to contour the Cabin Roof as shown in the front view drawing. Sand all of the pieces.

4. Cut a 14-inch (356) length of ½-inch (13) diameter wooden dowel rod for the Mast. Sand the Mast, gently tapering it so that the upper end measures approximately ¼-inch (6) in diameter. Try to taper it evenly, beginning about 8 inches (203) below the upper end.

5. A "boom" is a horizontal pole (or spar) along which the lower edge of a sail is attached. A sailboat may have 1 or more booms, connected to the upright mast so that they can swing from side to side, to catch the prevailing winds. Cut a 5½-inch (140) long Boom and an 8½-inch (216) long Boom from the ¼-inch (6.35) diameter dowel rod.

Figure B

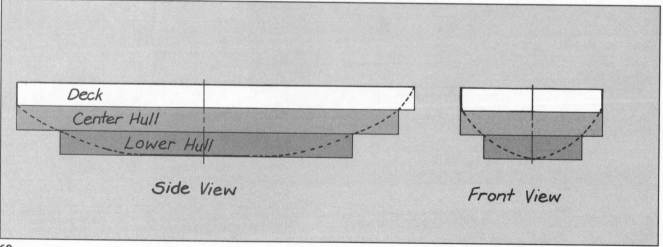

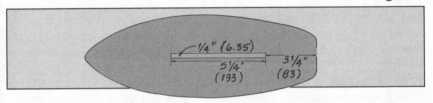

Figure C

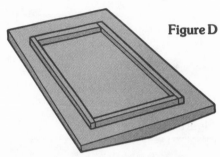

Figure D

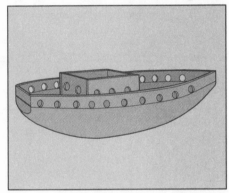

Figure E

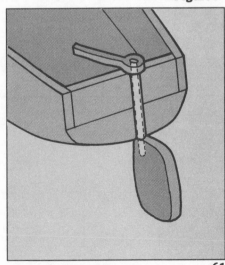

Figure F

Assembly

The trickiest part of this project is contouring the Hull. We've arranged it so you can get that over with right away, and breeze through the remainder of the assembly procedures.

1. Glue the Deck, Center Hull, and Lower Hull together, carefully positioning them as shown in the side view drawing, **Figure B.** Place the assembly in a vise or table clamp, and allow the glue to dry for several hours.

2. Use a belt sander or a wood rasp followed by sandpaper to contour the assembled hull. Begin by shaping the fore and aft (front and back) portions, following the dotted contour outlines shown in the side view drawing. Shape the sides, following the contour outlines shown in the front view drawings.

3. Cut a shallow notch along the center line on the underside of the assembled hull, to accommodate the Keel. Placement and dimensions of the notch are given in **Figure C.**

4. To assemble the Cabin, glue the 2 Inner Walls between the 2 Outer Walls. Glue the assembled cabin walls over the hatch opening in the Deck. You will need to cut 4 short lengths of ⅛ x ⅛-inch (3 x 3) wood stripping from the pine lattice, to serve as a frame on the underside of the Cabin Roof. (The frame will keep the Roof from sliding off.) Cut two 2¾-inch (70) lengths, and two 2-inch (51) lengths. Glue them in a rectangular pattern to the underside of the Cabin Roof, as shown in **Figure D.**

5. Glue the Port and Starboard Gunwales over the edges of the Deck, and add the Stern Gunwale (**Figure E**). Drill ten ⅜-inch (10) diameter holes through each of the side Gunwales where indicated, after the glue has dried.

6. Install a screw eye at the upper end of the Mast. Coat the shank with epoxy cement before you install the screw eye, so that it can not be removed by little fingers. Glue the lower end of the Mast into the hole in the Deck. To create a wooden ring, drill a ½-inch (13) diameter hole through the center of the ¾-inch (19) diameter dowel rod. Slip the ring over the Mast, and slide it down until it is approximately ½ inch (13) above the level of the cabin walls.

7. Cut a 1⅝-inch (41) length of ¼-inch (6.35) diameter dowel rod for the Rudder Shaft Housing. Clamp the Shaft Housing in a vise, and drill a ⅛-inch (3) diameter hole straight through the length, along the center line. Cut a 2⅛-inch (54) length of ⅛-inch (3) diameter dowel rod for the Rudder Shaft. To assemble the steering mechanism (**Figure F**), glue 1 end of the Rudder Shaft into the hole in the Tiller, so that the end of the Shaft is flush with the upper edge of the Tiller. Slip the Housing over the Shaft, and glue the exposed lower end of the Shaft into the socket in the upper edge of the Rudder. Glue the assembled steering mechanism to the stern of the Sloop, as shown in **Figure F.**

8. On each Boom, install a screw eye at 1 end, and a cup hook at the opposite end. (Coat the shanks with epoxy cement before you insert them.) Bend the hooks until they are almost closed. Slide the hook of the longer Boom down over the Mast, and add the shorter Boom. Glue the Keel in place underneath the hull.

9. Allow the glue to dry before adding paint or stain. Use a felt tip marker to letter the Sloop's name on 1 side, near the bow. The yacht will require careful sealing, and a test for proper balance, if you plan to put her to sea. Balance can be achieved by gluing lead fishing weights to the deck.

10. Cut 2 triangular muslin Sails and hem the edges so that the lower hems will accommodate the Booms. Install the Sails, using thread to attach the upper corners to the screw eye atop the Mast.

Figure G

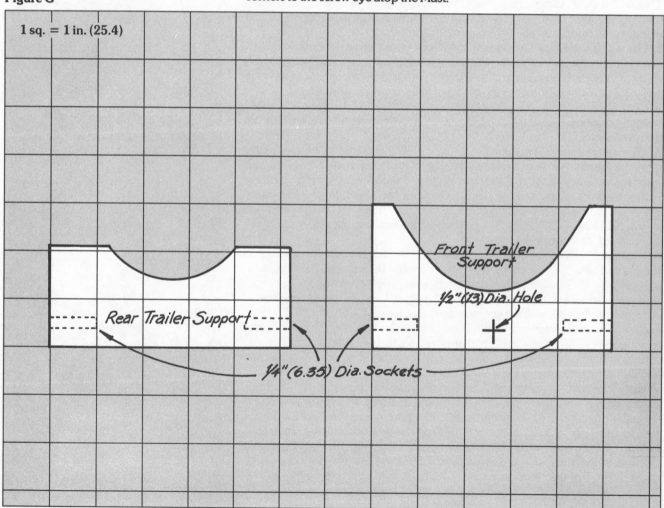

1 sq. = 1 in. (25.4)

Rear Trailer Support

Front Trailer Support

½" (13) Dia. Hole

¼" (6.35) Dia. Sockets

Trailer
Cutting the pieces   **1.** Enlarge the scale drawings given in **Figure G** to full-size patterns on kraft paper.

2. Cut 1 each of the Front and Rear Supports from the pine board. Drill 2 axle peg sockets into each Support. Placement of the sockets is indicated by dotted lines on the scale drawings. Drill a ½-inch (13) diameter hole through the Front Support where indicated. Cut 2 Lower Supports, each ¾ x 5¾ inches (19 x 146), from the pine board.

3. To make the tongue sections, cut one 5-inch (127) length and one 3¾-inch (95) length from the ½-inch (13) diameter dowel rod. The tongues will be connected with a pivoting "mortise and tenon" joint. To make the mortise, cut a notch into 1 end of the longer tongue, as shown in **Figure H.**

4. .Round off 1 end of the shorter tongue. Trim a small section on each side of the rounded end (**Figure I**), to create the tenon. Fit the tenon into the mortice, and drill a ⅛-inch (3) diameter hole through the joint (**Figure J**). Remove the shorter tongue, and enlarge the hole in the tenon slightly.

Assembly   **1.** Realign the 2 tongue sections, and insert a ½-inch (13) length of ⅛-inch (3) diameter dowel rod through the hole in the joint. Glue the ends of the rod into the holes in the notch.

2. Drill a ⅛-inch (3) diameter hole near the free end of the shorter tongue (**Figure J**). Cut a 1¼-inch (32) length of ⅛-inch (3) diameter dowel rod, and glue it into the hole, leaving equal extensions on each side.

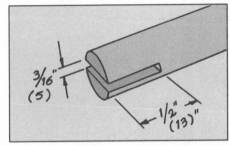

Figure H

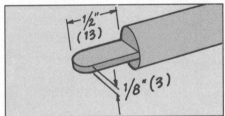

Figure I

Figure J

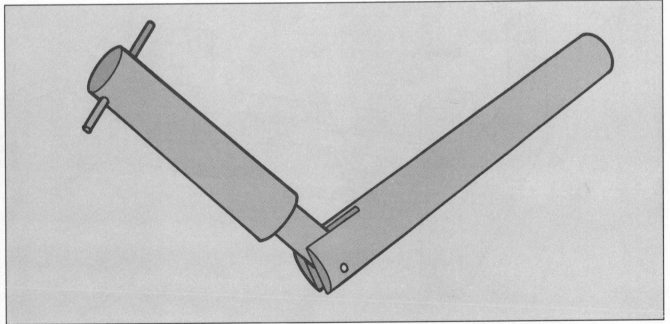

3. To assemble the trailer body (**Figure K**), glue the 2 Lower Supports between the Front and Rear Supports, with lower edges flush. Leave approximately ⅜ inch of space between the Lower Supports, to accommodate the keel when the Sloop is in place.

4. To make the axle pegs, cut four 1¾-inch (45) lengths from the ¼-inch (6.35) diameter dowel rod. Drill a shallow ¼-inch (6.35) diameter socket into the flat end of each of the wooden plugs, and glue a plug over 1 end of each of the pegs.

5. If you did not purchase pre-made wheels, cut them from the pine board, following the dimensions given in the "Materials" section above. Slip a wheel over each of the assembled axle pegs, and glue the pegs into the sockets in the Front and Rear Trailer Supports. Glue the tongue assembly into the hole in the Front Support.

6. Paint or stain the assembled Trailer.

You ought to learn these few additional nautical terms, to pass along to the pint-size person who will be the skipper of the Sloop. "Weigh" means hoist, as in "Weigh anchor!" When something is "aweigh," it is just clear of the ground, as in "Anchors aweigh!" (from the tune of the same name, or vice-versa). "Avast!" means cease or stop, as in "Avast heaving on the poop deck!" (Quit tossing your cookies all over the cabin roof!) or "Avast, me heartie!" (Stop right where you are, sailor!)

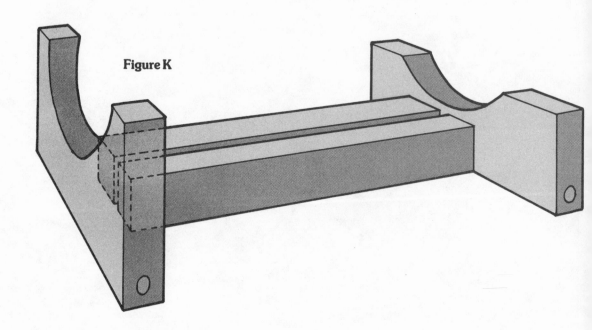

Figure K

Noah's Ark

Materials

3-foot (915) length of 2 x 6-inch (38 x 140) pine.

3-foot (915) length of 1 x 8-inch (17 x 184) pine.

12 x 18-inch (305 x 457) piece of ½-inch (13) thick interior plywood.

16 x 18-inch (407 x 457) piece of ¼-inch (6) thick interior plywood.

20-inch (508) length of ⅜-inch (9.5) diameter wooden dowel rod.

Handful each of ¾-inch (19) long and 1¼-inch (32) long finishing nails.

Carpenter's wood glue, carbon paper, kraft paper, medium and fine sandpaper, and a small quantity of wood filler.

Paint. You'll need several different colors of non-toxic paint, but only a small quantity of each. We used red, blue, yellow, brown, green, orange, gray, tan, black, and white. You might prefer to use a medium point black felt tip marker for the detail work on the animals. You can get by with the primary colors (red, blue, and yellow) plus black and white if you wish to mix your own secondary colors. Mixing colors is not at all difficult. (That's what they all say, right?) Any 2 primary colors mixed together will yield a secondary color. The basic formulas are: blue plus yellow equals green; red plus yellow equals orange; red plus blue equals purple. To mix a secondary color, start with a small amount of the darker primary color, and add small quantities of the lighter primary color until you have achieved a "hue" you like. You can lighten the "shade" of any primary or secondary color by adding white. All 3 primary colors mixed together will yield brown, and white added to brown will yield tan. To get gray, start with white, and add black.

Tools

Hammer, nailset, saber saw or coping saw, small and medium size paint brushes, and an electric or hand drill with ⅜-inch (9.5) and ½-inch (13) diameter bits.

Our rendition of Noah's famous Ark, complete with 7 pairs of animals, will provide hours of creative entertainment for your children. It will also make a charming display in a child's bedroom or in the family den. This model is slightly different than the original, which our Biblical authority informs us was made of gopher wood, and measured 30 cubits x 50 cubits x 300 cubits.

Metric equivalents in millimeters are indicated in parentheses.

Figure A

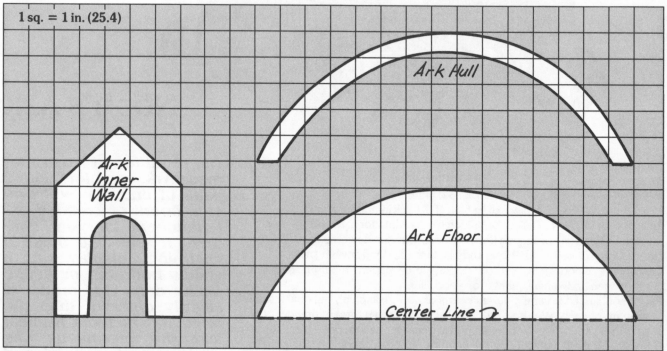

1 sq. = 1 in. (25.4)

Ark Hull

Ark Inner Wall

Ark Floor

Center Line

Figure B

The Ark

Cutting the pieces 1. Scale drawings for the Inner Wall, Hull, and Floor are given in **Figure A**. Enlarge the drawings to full size patterns on kraft paper.

2. Cut the following pieces from the ¼-inch (6) thick plywood: 2 Outer Walls, each 5 x 7 inches (127 x 178); 1 Roof, 5 x 9 inches (127 x 229); 1 additional Roof, 4¾ x 9 inches (121 x 229); and 2 Inner Walls.

3. Cut 4 Axle Blocks, each 2 x 2 inches (51 x 51); and 2 Hulls from the 2 x 6-inch (38 x 140) pine. Cut 1 Floor from the ½-inch (13) thick plywood.

4. Cut 2 Axles, each 10 inches (254) long, from the wooden dowel rod. The four 2-inch (51) diameter wheels can be cut from the ½-inch (13) thick plywood or from the 1 x 8-inch (17 x 184) pine. Sand all of the pieces. (Keep in mind that sanding is a somewhat tedious process. You might consider luring a few small fry or a particularly vocal back-seat woodworker into your shop for the sanding procedures.)

Assembly   **1.** An assembly diagram for the house portion of the Ark is given in **Figure B.** Glue the Outer Walls over the edges of the Inner Walls, and secure the joints with the shorter finishing nails. Recess the nails and fill the holes with wood filler. Bevel the upper edges of each outer wall to match the roof-slope angle of the inner walls.

2. Glue the shorter Roof section over the raw edges of the Walls on 1 side of the Ark, and add the longer Roof section to the opposite side. The longer Roof section will cover the upper raw edge of the shorter section, as shown in **Figure B.** Secure the Roof sections with the shorter finishing nails, recess the nails, and fill the holes with wood filler.

3. Refer to **Figure C** as you assemble the lower portion (Floor and Hull) of the Ark. Fit the 2 Hull sections together in the proper configuration, trimming the ends if necessary to achieve a good fit. Glue the sections together, and attach the assembled Hull to the Floor. Drive a few of the longer finishing nails through the Floor and into the Hull.

4. Paint the upper and lower assemblies before you join them together. We used red for the Roof, Floor, and Hull, and blue for the Walls. You can follow our inspired color scheme, or come up with some garish color combination of your own. We don't mind.

5. Full-size patterns for the painted wall designs are given in **Figure D.** Trace the designs onto paper. When the base coat of paint has dried, use carbon paper and a pencil to transfer the designs to the Walls.

6. Paint the designs in your choice of colors. We used yellow for the "Noah's Place" signs, brown for the cow and monkey, yellow for the banana, and white or yellow for the window background. Use black paint or a marker to fill in the lettering on the signs and other details.

Figure C

Figure D

Figure E

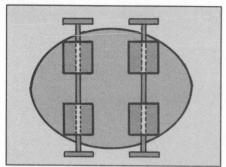

Figure F

1 sq. = 1 in. (25.4)

7. The axle assembly is shown in **Figure E.** Drill a ½-inch (13) diameter hole through the center of each Axle Block. Insert 1 Axle through 2 of the Blocks, and attach the Blocks to the Floor where indicated. Use glue and 2 of the longer finishing nails for each Block. Repeat this procedure for the remaining Axle and Blocks, attaching them where indicated.

8. Drill a ⅜-inch (9.5) diameter hole through the center of each Wheel. Adjust the Axles so that the ends extend equally on each side of the Floor, and glue a Wheel to each Axle end.

9. Glue the house assembly to the Floor, and secure it in place with a few of the longer finishing nails driven through the Floor and into the Walls.

The Animals
Cutting the pieces **1.** Drawings for the 7 different animals are given in **Figure F.** Make a full-size paper pattern for each animal. Transfer the facial features and other details to the patterns.

2. Since, as we all know, the animals joined Noah on the Ark in pairs, you'll need to cut 2 of each animal from the 1 x 8-inch (17 x 184) pine. Sand all of the animals.

Painting **1.** Paint the animals in your choice of colors.

2. Transfer the facial features and other details from the paper patterns to both sides of each animal, using carbon paper and a pencil. If you will use 2 sheets of carbon paper (non-carbon sides together) as you transfer the lines to the first side of each animal, the reverse outlines will automatically be transferred to the opposite side of the paper pattern. Use these reverse outlines for the second side of each animal.

3. Fill in the facial features and other details with black paint or marker.

Now you're prepared to set up your own Ark-ade! (Please pardon us — we just couldn't resist.)

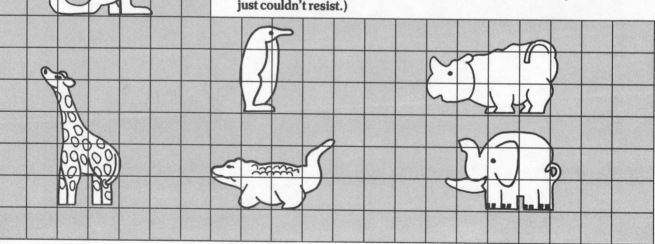

Ferryboat & Cars

This quaint replica of an old-time ferryboat includes a full cargo of automobiles. Although it is not exactly seaworthy, the Ferry will cruise quite smoothly on dry land, since we've added wheels underneath the keel.

Metric equivalents in millimeters are indicated in parentheses.

Materials

For the Ferryboat:

Exterior plywood: 12 x 23-inch (305 x 584) piece of ¼-inch (6), 28 x 38-inch (711 x 965) piece of ¾-inch (19).

Pine lumber: 11-inch (279) length of 2 x 3-inch (38 x 64), 3-foot (914) length of 2 x 6-inch (38 x 140).

Wooden dowel rod: 6-inch (152) length of ¼-inch (6.35) diameter, 7 feet (2134) of ½-inch (13) diameter, 3-inch (76) length of 1-inch (25) diameter.

Purchase a pre-made Smokestack or make one from a 5½-inch (140) length of 1½-inch (38) diameter dowel.

Six ½-inch (13) thick wooden wheels, each 1½ inches (38) in diameter, with a ¼-inch (6.35) diameter axle hole.

Six ¼-inch (6.35) diameter wheel pegs. These serve as short axles for the wheels. You can cut and assemble your own wheel pegs from a 1-foot (305) length of ¼-inch (6.35) diameter dowel rod and 6 wooden plugs, each ⅜ inch (10) in diameter. Directions for making the wheel pegs are given below.

8-foot (2438) length of cotton string, ⅛ inch (3) in diameter.

For the cars:

Pine lumber: 4-foot (1219) length of 1 x 4-inch (17 x 89), 26-inch (660) length of 1 x 6-inch (17 x 140), 2-foot (610) length of 2 x 4-inch (38 x 89), 13-inch (330) length of 2 x 6-inch (38 x 140).

6¼-inch (159) length of ¼ x 1¾-inch (6 x 45) pine lattice.

Wooden dowel rod: 2-foot (610) length of ½-inch (13) diameter, 9-inch (229) length of ¼-inch (6.35) diameter.

8 wooden wheels, each 2½ inches (64) in diameter with a ½-inch (13) diameter axle hole; 4 wooden wheels, each 2 inches (51) in diameter, with a ½-inch (13) diameter axle hole. All wheels should be ½ inch (13) thick.

12 metal washers, each 1½ inches (38) in diameter or larger, with a center hole at least ⅝ inch (16) in diameter.

Carpenter's wood glue, handful of 1-inch (25) long finishing nails, sandpaper, kraft paper, and non-toxic paint in your choice of colors.

Figure A

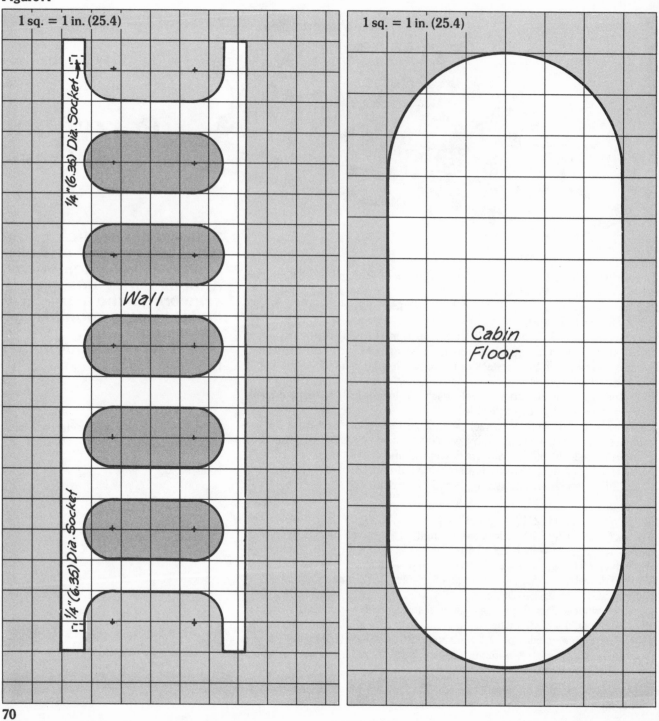

Figure A

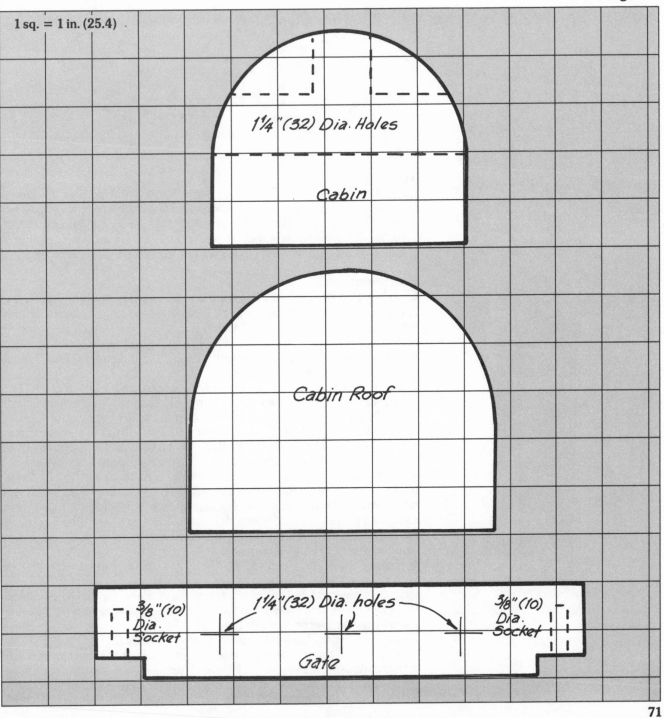

1 sq. = 1 in. (25.4)

1¼" (32) Dia. Holes

Cabin

Cabin Roof

3/8" (10) Dia. Socket

1¼" (32) Dia. holes

3/8" (10) Dia. Socket

Gate

Figure B

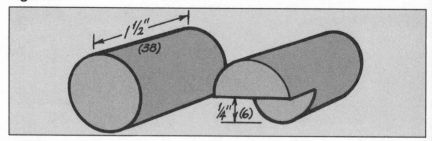

Tools

Saber saw, hammer, carpenter's square, scissors, paint brushes, C-clamps, wood rasp, plane, electric or hand drill, and drill bits of the following diameters: 1¼-inch (32), ⅝-inch (16), ½-inch (13), ⅜-inch (10), and ¼-inch (6.35). A sanding attachment for your electric drill (or an electric sander or lathe) will save elbow grease, but is not required to complete the project.

Ferryboat

Cutting the pieces **1.** Enlarge the scale drawings given in **Figure A** to full-size patterns on kraft paper. Cut 2 Walls, 2 Gates, and 1 Cabin Floor from the ¾-inch (19) plywood. Cut 2 Cabin Roofs from the ¼-inch (6) plywood, and 2 Cabins from the pine 2 x 6 (38 x 140). Cut out the oval-shaped openings in each of the Walls, and drill the three 1¼-inch (32) diameter holes through each Gate as indicated in **Figure A.**

2. Cut 1 Upper Deck, 11 x 22 inches (279 x 559), and 1 Lower Deck, 11 x 28 inches (279 x 711), from the ¾-inch (19) plywood. The corners of both decks should be rounded off with a wood rasp and sanded smooth.

3. Cut a 2½-inch (64) length of the pine 2 x 6 (38 x 140) for the Center Cabin, and a 24-inch (610) length for the Keel. Trim and sand the ends of the Keel to match the rounded ends of the Cabins. Cut the Keel in half lengthwise.

4. Cut 4 Gate Pegs, each 1½ inches (38) long, from the ¼-inch (6.35) diameter dowel rod. Cut 30 Rails, each 2½ inches (64) long, from the ½-inch (13) diameter dowel rod, and 2 Running Lights, each 1½ inches (38) long, from the 1-inch (25) diameter dowel rod. If you did not purchase Wheel pegs, cut six 2-inch (51) lengths of ¼-inch (6.35) diameter dowel rod, and glue a wooden plug onto 1 end of each peg.

5. Drill a ¾-inch (19) deep socket, 1¼ inches (32) in diameter, into the top of the Center Cabin. This will serve as a socket for the Smokestack. Drill a ¼-inch (6.35) diameter hole through each of the 30 Rails, approximately ½ inch (13) from 1 end. Drill the holes in the Walls, Gates, and Cabins which are indicated by dotted lines on the scale drawings.

6. Notch each of the Running Lights as shown in **Figure B.**

7. If you did not purchase a pre-made Smokestack, shape the 1½-inch (38) diameter dowel rod as shown in **Figure C**, using a wood rasp and sandpaper (or an electric sander or lathe if you have one). The lower end of the finished Smokestack should measure 1¼ inches (32) in diameter.

Figure C

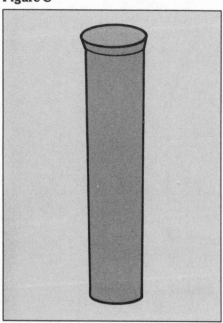

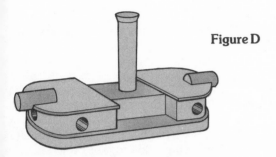

Figure D

Assembly
Top Cabin and center sections
1. Refer to **Figure D** for placement as you assemble and glue the pieces of the top cabin section. Attach the Center Cabin, and the 2 Cabins to the Cabin Floor. Add the Smokestack, Cabin Roofs, and Running Lights.

2. Center the assembled top cabin section over the Upper Deck and attach it with glue and nails.

3. The 30 Rails are placed around the edge of the Upper Deck as shown in **Figure E**. Mark the position of each Rail, beginning with the 4 corner positions and allowing equal distances between each Rail. Use the ¼-inch (6.35) diameter bit to drill a shallow socket into the deck at each mark. Glue the Rails into the sockets. The small holes in the tops of the Rails should be aligned so you can run the nylon cord through them in a straight line.

Figure E

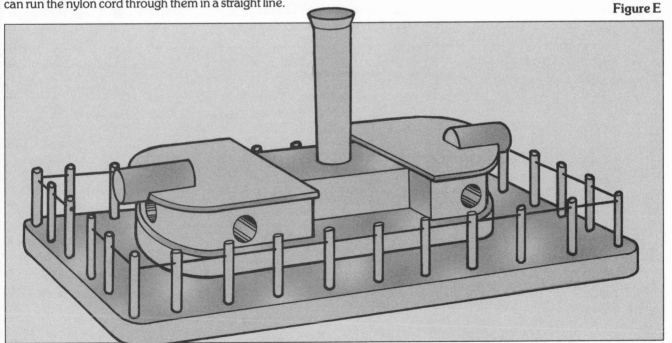

4. Glue a Gate Peg into the shallow socket at each end of the 2 Walls. Refer to **Figure F**, and use glue and nails to attach the Walls to the Upper and Lower Decks, centering the Walls between the ends of both decks. Slip the Gates onto the Gate Pegs.

Keel Section and ramp **1.** Refer to **Figure G**, and drill 3 wheel peg sockets, each ¾-inch (19) deep, and ¼ inch (6.35) in diameter, on the inside edge of each Keel half.
2. Insert a Wheel Peg through 1 of the wheels. Apply glue to the smaller end of the peg and insert it into 1 of the sockets on the inside edge of 1 Keel section. Repeat this procedure for the remaining 5 wheels.
3. Attach the 2 Keel halves to the bottom of the Lower Deck, close to the outer edges, as shown in **Figure H.**
4. Use the 11-inch (279) length of pine 2 x 3 (38 x 64) for the Ramp Support. Plane and sand 1 long edge of the Ramp Support at an angle to accommodate the Ramp, as shown in **Figure I**. Use the remaining piece of ¼-inch (6) plywood, trimmed to 11 x 16 inches (279 x 406), for the Ramp.
5. Position the Ramp and Ramp Support as shown in **Figure I**. You may wish to nail and/or glue the Ramp to the Ramp Support, but is not necessary. The 2 pieces will be more easily stored if left unjoined.

Making the cars Remove your ship builder's hat, and get ready for the automotive assembly line. There are 3 cars on board the Ferryboat: an antique-style Sport Coupe, a compact Pinto, and a futuresque X-17. Each car has the same basic, simple construction; an inner body piece sandwiched between 2 identical outer fenders.

Figure F

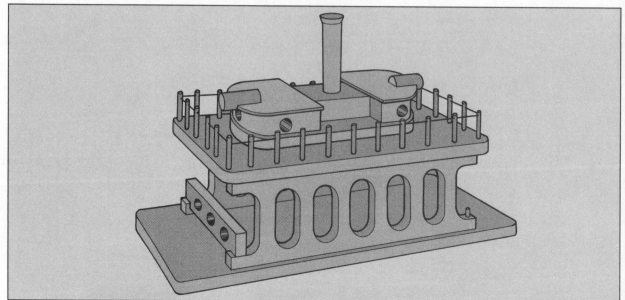

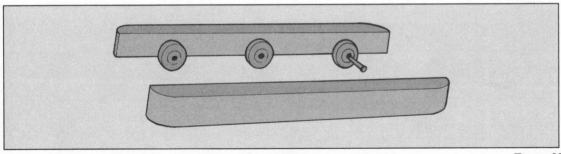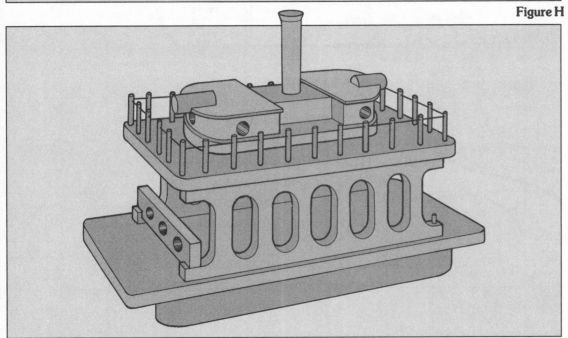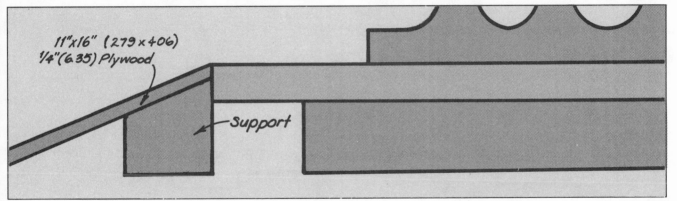

Ferryboat & Cars

Figure G

Figure H

Figure I

11"x16" (279 x 406)
1/4"(6.35) Plywood

Support

75

Figure J

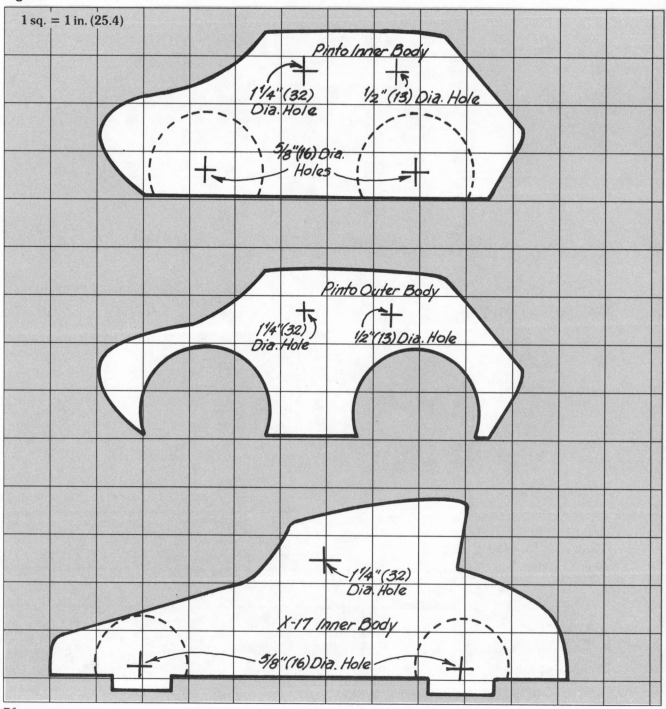

1 sq. = 1 in. (25.4)

Pinto Inner Body

1¼"(32) Dia. Hole

½"(13) Dia. Hole

⅝"(16) Dia. Holes

Pinto Outer Body

1¼"(32) Dia. Hole

½"(13) Dia. Hole

1¼"(32) Dia. Hole

X-17 Inner Body

⅝"(16) Dia. Hole

Figure J

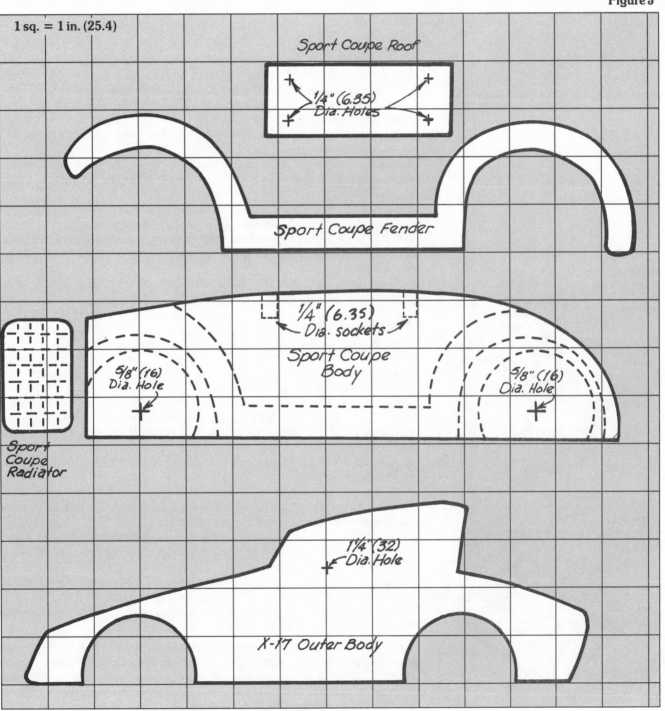

1 sq. = 1 in. (25.4)

Sport Coupe Roof

1/4" (6.35) Dia. Holes

Sport Coupe Fender

1/4" (6.35) Dia. sockets

Sport Coupe Body

5/8" (16) Dia. Hole

5/8" (16) Dia. Hole

Sport Coupe Radiator

1 1/4" (32) Dia. Hole

X-17 Outer Body

Cutting the pieces **1.** Enlarge the scale drawings given in **Figure J** to full-size patterns on kraft paper. Cut the following pieces for the X-17: 1 Inner Body from the pine 2 x 6 (38 x 140), and 2 Outer Bodies from the pine 1 x 6 (17 x 140). For the Sport Coupe, cut 1 Body from the pine 2 x 4 (38 x 89), 2 Fenders from the pine 1 x 4 (17 x 89), 1 Roof and 1 Radiator from the pine lattice. For the Pinto, cut 1 Inner Body from the pine 2 x 4 (38 x 89), and 2 Outer Bodies from the pine 1 x 4 (17 x 89).

2. Use the ¼-inch (6.35) diameter bit to drill 4 Roof Support holes into the upper edge of the Sport Coupe Body, where indicated by dotted lines on the scale drawing.

3. Transfer the placement lines for fenders and windows shown on the scale drawings. Drill the axle holes using a ⅝-inch (16) diameter bit.

4. Cut 6 Axles, each 4 inches (102) long, from the ½-inch (13) diameter dowel rod. Cut 4 Roof Supports, each 2¼ inches (57) long, from the ¼-inch (6.35) diameter dowel.

5. Thoroughly sand all of the pieces, eliminating sharp edges but leaving the window and fender placement lines intact.

Assembly All of the cars are simple to assemble. The Sport Coupe is a little different than the other 2 cars, so start with the Pinto or X-17.

1. Spread a thin coat of glue on the inner sides of the 2 Outer Body pieces. Sandwich the pieces on either side of the Inner Body, with roof edges flush. Clamp the assembly for several hours.

2. Drill the 1¼-inch (32) diameter front window through all thicknesses of wood. On the Pinto only, drill a ½-inch (13) diameter rear window.

3. Insert an Axle through each axle hole, leaving equal extensions on each side. Slip a washer onto each end, and attach the wheels to the Axles with spots of glue. Use 2-inch (51) diameter wheels for the X-17 and 2½-inch (64) diameter wheels for the Pinto.

Sport Coupe Assembly **1.** Glue the 2 Fenders to the Body and install the Axles and wheels as you did for the other 2 cars.

2. Glue a Roof Support dowel into each of the 4 roof support holes. Use a rasp and sandpaper to taper the Roof toward the front (**Figure K**). Glue it to the Roof Supports as shown.

3. Cut 2 short lengths from the leftover ½-inch (13) diameter dowel rod for Headlights. Glue 1 Headlight to the top of each front fender.

4. Cut a cross-hatch pattern of shallow grooves on 1 side of the Radiator, as shown in **Figure L**. Glue the Radiator between the fenders.

The Ferryboat and cars may be left with a natural wood finish, or you may wish to paint or stain them, using non-toxic materials. We don't recommend a float-test, but if you suspect your resident Ferryboat Captain will attempt a bathside launching ceremony, give the boat a couple of coats of high-quality polyurethane wood sealer.

Figure K

Figure L

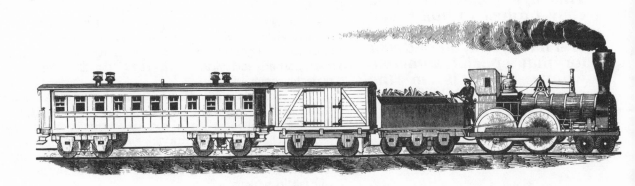

A long pull,
and a strong pull,
and a pull all together!
--Charles Dickens

"Yo, heave-ho!"
Toys to push and pull

Biplane Flying Machine

This flying machine is an easy project to build, and will make a great child's toy or a handsome bit of decor for that special someone whose head is in the clouds. It is modeled after a World War I biplane.

Metric equivalents in millimeters are indicated in parentheses.

Materials

15-inch (381) length of 2 x 4-inch (38 x 89) pine.

230 square inches (1484 sq. cm.) of ½-inch (13) thick pine.

10-inch (254) length of ¼-inch (6.35) diameter wooden dowel rod.

20-inch (508) length of ½-inch (13) diameter wooden dowel rod.

3 metal washers, each ⅝ to ¾ inch (16 to 19) in diameter, with a ⅜-inch (9.5) diameter center hole.

Pilot. You can make a pilot for the Biplane from a spherical wooden drawer pull or finial, 1 inch (25) in diameter, and a 1½-inch (38) length of ½-inch (13) diameter wooden dowel rod. (If you prefer to purchase a pre-made pilot, most hobby shops carry a variety of little dowel people.)

A piece of felt fabric, 1½ x 7½ inches (38 x 191), will make a spiffy pilot's scarf, and you can draw facial features and an aviator's cap onto the wooden head with felt tip markers.

Carpenter's wood glue, medium and fine sandpaper, handful of 1-inch (25) long finishing nails, carbon paper, and kraft paper. You can decorate the Biplane, using non-toxic paints in colors of your choice, or apply wood stain and sealer to enhance the natural wood grain.

Tools

Saber saw or coping saw, hammer, wood rasp, and an electric or hand drill with drill bits of the following diameters: ¼-inch (6.35), ⅜-inch (9.5), and ½-inch (13). Sanding and circle-cutting attachments for your drill will be helpful, but are not required.

Cutting the pieces

1. Enlarge the scale drawings given in **Figure A** to full-size patterns on kraft paper.

2. Cut 1 Wheel Support, 1 Nose Cone, and 1 Body from the 2 x 4-inch (38 x 89) lumber. Cut the following parts from the ½-inch (13) thick lumber: 1 Vertical Tail, 1 Horizontal Tail, 1 Propeller, 1 Upper Wing, 1 Lower Wing, and two 2¼-inch (57) diameter Wheels.

3. Cut the following parts from the smaller diameter dowel rod: 1 Axle, 3¼ inches (83) long; 1 Skid, 3 inches (76) long; and 1 Propeller Shaft, 3 inches (76) long. Cut 4 Wing Supports, each 4½ inches (114) long, and 3 Plugs, each ⅜ inch (10) long, from the larger diameter dowel rod.

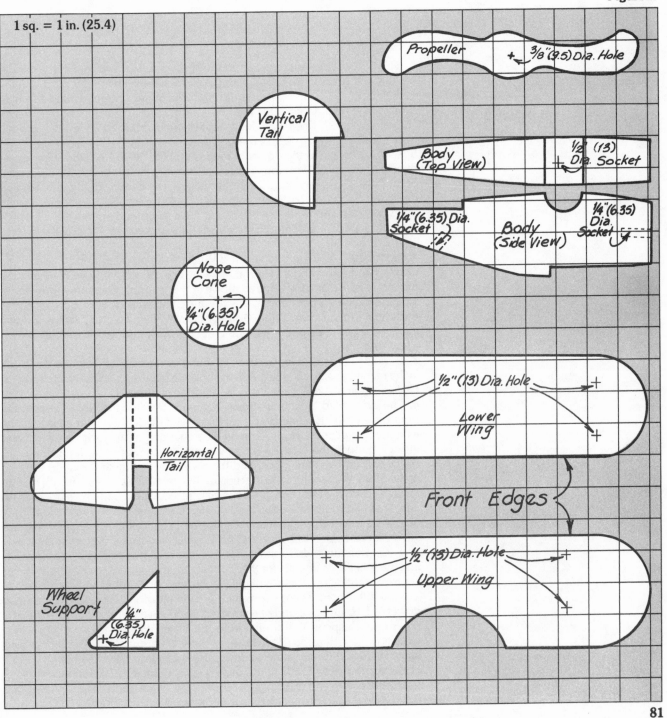

1 sq. = 1 in. (25.4)

Propeller   + 3/8"(9.5) Dia. Hole

Vertical Tail

Body (Top View)   1/2 (13) Dia. Socket

1/4"(6.35) Dia. Socket   Body (Side View)   1/4"(6.35) Dia. Socket

Nose Cone   1/4"(6.35) Dia. Hole

Horizontal Tail

1/2"(13) Dia. Hole   Lower Wing

Front Edges

1/2"(13) Dia. Hole   Upper Wing

Wheel Support   1/4"(6.35) Dia. Hole

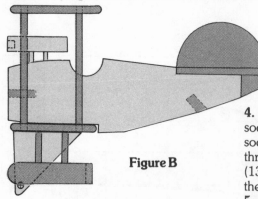

Figure B

4. The dotted lines and crosses on the scale drawings indicate placement of sockets and holes to be drilled. Use the ¼-inch (6.35) diameter bit to drill the sockets into the Body, the hole through the Wheel Support, and the hole through the Nose Cone. Drill the holes through each Wing using the ½-inch (13) diameter bit. Use the ⅜-inch (9.5) diameter bit to drill the hole through the Propeller and an axle hole through the center of each Wheel.

5. As you can see in the drawing, the front of the Nose Cone has been completely rounded off. Use the wood rasp to create the proper shape on 1 edge of the Nose Cone, and finish with sandpaper. The corners of the semi-circular dip in the Body (the cockpit) should also be rounded off. Get after these with the wood rasp and sandpaper until you have smoothed out the lines. Use the rasp and sandpaper to smooth the sharp edges and surfaces of all of the pieces.

Assembly   **1.** Glue and nail the Wheel Support to the underside of the Lower Wing, centering it between the wing tips. Attach the Lower Wing to the underside of the Biplane Body as shown in the assembly diagram, **Figure B.**

2. Spread glue on both ends of each Wing Support and insert 1 Support into each hole in the Lower Wing. Add the Upper Wing, carefully sliding it down over the upper ends of the Supports. Let the body and wing assembly dry for a few hours.

3. Glue the tail assembly together, inserting the Horizontal Tail into the notch in the rear edge of the Vertical Tail, as shown in **Figure C.** Attach the tail assembly to the rear of the Biplane Body as indicated in **Figure D.**

4. The assembled biplane is shown in **Figure D**. Glue the Nose Cone to the front edge of the Biplane Body, carefully aligning the hole in the Nose Cone with the socket in the Body. Spread glue on 1 end of the Propeller Shaft and insert it through the Nose Cone, pushing it into the socket as far as it will go. Slip a washer over the Shaft, add the Propeller, and glue a Plug to the end of the Shaft. We recommend that you drill a very shallow ¼-inch (6.35) diameter socket into the Plug and glue the Shaft into the socket. (It's an extra precaution, should an unmanned test flight occur someday when you're not looking.)

5. Insert the Axle through the hole in the Wheel Support, leaving equal extensions on each side. Add washers and Wheels, and glue a plug over each axle end. (Or preferably, drill a shallow socket into each plug and glue the axle ends into the sockets, as you did for the Propeller Shaft.)

Optional additions to the biplane are the wooden bombs and machine guns. To make the bombs, cut two 3-inch (76) lengths of 1-inch (25.4) diameter dowel rod. Round one end of each length, and cut a v-shaped groove into the other end. Suspend the bombs from the lower Wings with two 2-inch (51) lengths of ¼-inch (6.35) dowel rod, as shown in **Figure B**. The machine guns are constructed in the same manner, using 1½-inch (38) lengths of ¾-inch (19) diameter dowel rod for the guns. Drill a ¼-inch (6.35) diameter hole in the center of one end of each gun. Mount them at the front of the Biplane Body using short lengths of ⅛-inch (3.18) diameter dowel rods (**Figure B**).

6. Cut 1 end of the Skid dowel at an angle and glue the uncut end into the socket in the Biplane Body. The exact angle is not important, as long as the angled end will sit fairly level on the ground **(Figure D)**.

7. Paint or stain the assembled Biplane.

Adding the pilot

1. Drill a shallow socket, ½ inch (13) in diameter, into the spherical drawer pull or finial. Glue a 1½-inch (38) length of ½-inch (13) diameter dowel rod into the socket. Use felt tip markers to draw the pilot's facial features and an aviator's cap.

2. The shape of the pilot's scarf is shown in **Figure E**. Cut the piece of felt fabric into the correct shape, and slit the ends to create the fringe. Wrap the scarf around the pilot's neck.

3. Drill a shallow ½-inch diameter socket into the cockpit and insert the pilot in the socket. (If you purchased a pre-made pilot of a different size, use a corresponding size bit to drill the hole in the cockpit.)

Here's an interesting bit of trivia to pass along to admirers of your Biplane Flying Machine. In 1914, an American flyer named Tony Jannus began the world's first scheduled airline with a "fleet" consisting of 1 biplane very much like the model you have constructed. He carried passengers and freight across Tampa Bay, between St. Petersburg and Tampa, Florida. There was room on each flight for only 1 passenger, who paid a fare of $5.00 for the 22 mile journey. Unfortunately, Mr. Jannus became mired in financial difficulties, and the world's first scheduled airline folded after only a few months.

Figure C

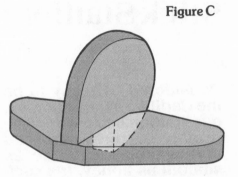

Figure D

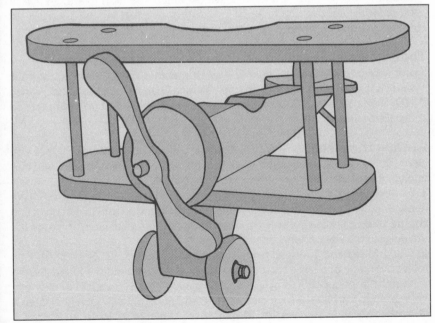

Figure E

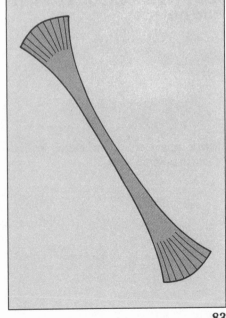

Stick Stallion

Considered by many to be the Cadillac of stick horses, our Stallion has a wheel assembly at the lower end that makes for a ride as smooth as honey. It's such an easy, inexpensive project to make, you might want to produce an entire herd of Stick Stallions for the neighborhood cowgirls and boys.

Metric equivalents in millimeters are indicated in parentheses.

Materials

15-inch (381) length of 2 x 12-inch (38 x 286) pine.

3-inch (76) length of 1 x 3-inch (17 x 64) pine.

40-inch (1016) length of ¾-inch (19) diameter wooden dowel rod.

1½-inch (38) length of ⅜-inch (10) diameter wooden dowel rod.

63-inch (1600) length of round braided polyester cord, crewel yarn, or rug yarn, approximately ¼-inch (6) in diameter, for the Stallion's mane and forelock. We used white braided cord, but you can use any of the suggested materials in the color of your choice.

A small quantity of non-toxic wood stain in the color of your choice. You'll also need a small quantity of non-toxic white paint if you wish to add an eye or other facial features.

Medium and fine sandpaper, carpenter's wood glue, and kraft paper.

Tools

Saber saw or coping saw, keyhole saw (sometimes called a miniature hack saw), and an electric or hand drill with ⅜-inch (10), ½-inch (13), and ¾-inch (19) diameter bits. You'll also need a small paint brush if you plan to add facial features.

Cutting the pieces   This project is primarily a cutting exercise. Once you have cut the pieces, the assembly will be a piece of cake. (Non-edible, and certainly not very tasty, but a piece of cake nevertheless.)

1. Scale drawings for the Head and Wheel Support are given in **Figure A.** (We know that the ears don't look exactly right in the drawing, but just trust us and cut the piece as drawn. You'll be shaping the 2 offset ears later.) Enlarge the drawings to full-size patterns on kraft paper.

2. Cut 1 Head and 1 Wheel Support from the pine 2 x 12 (38 x 286). (We took advantage of a large knot in the wood, and positioned the Head pattern so that the knot appears to be the Stallion's eye.) Drill a ¾-inch (19) diameter hole through the Head where indicated. In addition, drill a ¾-inch (19) diameter socket, about 1½ inches (38) deep, into the center of the lower neck edge.

Figure A

Figure B

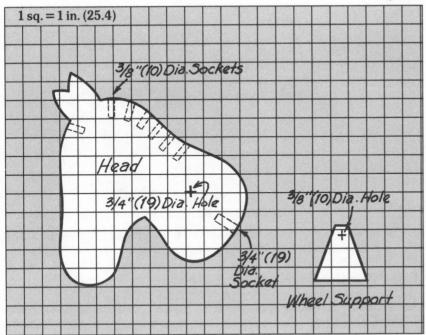

1 sq. = 1 in. (25.4)

3/8"(10) Dia. Sockets

Head

3/4"(19) Dia. Hole

3/8"(10) Dia. Hole

3/4"(19) Dia. Socket

Wheel Support

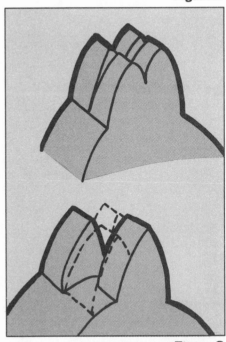

Figure C

3. Drill a series of 3/8-inch (10) diameter sockets, each approximately 5/8-inch (16) deep, along the center line of the upper edge of the Head. (Pieces of cord or yarn will be glued into these sockets later on, to create the mane and forelock.) Place 1 socket just in front of the ears, and 6 sockets in a straight row down the back of the neck, starting just behind the ears and leaving about 1 inch (25) between sockets.

4. Front and side view drawings of the contoured ears are given in **Figure B.** Cut a narrow V-shaped groove into the center width of the ear section to separate the right and left sides. Make paper patterns from the side view drawings for the right and left ears, and transfer the outlines to each side of the wooden Head. Use the keyhole saw to cut along the outline of each ear. (It will take a little longer to cut the ears with a hand saw than with a power saw, but you'll be less likely to make a regrettable, irreversible error.)

5. Sand the Head thoroughly, rounding off the edges.

6. Drill a 3/8-inch (10) diameter hole through the Wheel Support where indicated on the scale drawing. Cut a notch, 1 inch (25) wide and about 2 inches (50) deep, into the lower end of the Wheel Support, as shown in **Figure C.** The easiest way to accomplish this is to make a series of closely spaced cuts of the proper depth into the piece, thus shaving away the wood until you have a notch of the proper width.

7. Drill a 3/4-inch (19) diameter socket, approximately 1 inch (25) deep, into the center of the upper edge of the Wheel Support. Sand the Support, including the sides of the notch. There is no need to round off the edges, but sand them so that they are no longer sharp.

Figure E

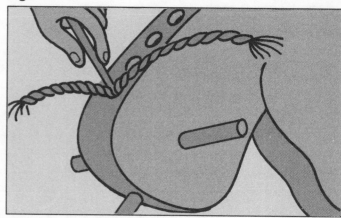

8. Cut a 2½-inch (64) diameter wheel from the 1 x 3-inch(17 x 64) pine. Drill a ½-inch (13) diameter hole through the exact center.
9. Cut a 7-inch (178) length of the larger wooden dowel rod for the Handle. The remaining length will be the Stallion's Body.

Assembly   **1.** Use the short length of ⅜-inch (10) diameter dowel rod as an axle for the wheel **(Figure D).** Insert the axle through 1 of the holes in the Wheel Support, on through the center hole in the wheel, and into the hole at the opposite side of the notch. Glue the axle ends in place. If they extend beyond the outer sides of the Wheel Support, trim them flush.
2. Glue 1 end of the Body dowel into the socket in the upper edge of the Wheel Support, and glue the opposite end into the socket in the lower edge of the Head. Insert the Handle dowel through the hole in the neck, leaving equal extensions on each side, and glue it in place.
3. Stain the assembled Stallion. When the stain is dry, you can add a painted eye or any other facial features you like. If you plan to paint features, we suggest that you draw them on the paper Head pattern to see how your designs will look before you apply any paint to the wooden Head. (We're not deriding your abilities as an artist — it's just that we've succumbed to the creative urge once too many times when it didn't come out exactly as we'd envisioned. The resulting mess, and the time spent trying to remove all traces of catastrophe, are not worth it.)
4. Cut the braided cord or yarn into 7 equal lengths, each approximately 9 inches (229) long. Fold 1 of the lengths in half, and coat the folded center point with a liberal amount of glue. Use a toothpick, unbent paper clip, ice pick, or other slim object to stuff the glued center portion down into 1 of the small sockets along the upper edge of the Head **(Figure E).** Tie the 2 exposed ends in a knot, just over the socket. Repeat this process for each of the remaining lengths of cord. After you have allowed the glue to dry for a few hours, untwist the exposed lengths of cord to form the mane and forelock.

Just for old time's sake, pardner, take the Stallion out for a spin before you hand him over to the kids.

Figure D

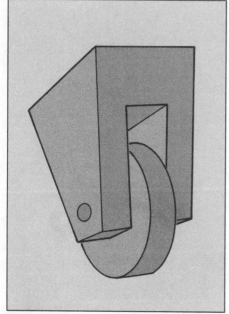

Old-Time Iron Horse

Materials

7 square feet (6503 sq. cm.) of ½-inch (13) thick clear white pine. Pine of this thickness is manufactured in different widths, so the length of the piece you'll need will depend upon how wide it is. A width as narrow as 5 inches (127) will accommodate the pieces you'll need to cut.

12-inch (305) length of 2 x 6-inch (38 x 140) clear white pine.

7-inch (178) length of 1 x 4-inch (17 x 89) clear white pine.

2-foot (610) length of ¼-inch (6.35) diameter wooden dowel rod.

40-inch (1016) length of ⅛-inch (3) diameter wooden dowel rod.

16 feet (4877) of small wood stripping, approximately ⅛ x ⅛-inch (3 x 3). Since most lumber yards do not carry stripping this small, you can purchase ¼ x ⅜-inch (6 x 10) lattice and cut it in half lengthwise.

5-foot (1524) length of ¼ x ¼-inch (6 x 6) wood stripping.

40-inch (1016) length of ¾-inch (20) wide cove molding (optional).

36 wooden wheels. You can purchase wheels or cut them yourself. You'll need 32 wheels, each approximately ½ inch (13) thick and 1½ inches (38) in diameter, and 4 wheels, each approximately ¾ inch (20) thick and 2¼ inches (57) in diameter. The center holes should be ⅜ inch (10) in diameter. If you plan to cut the wheels yourself, purchase extra ½-inch (13) thick lumber for the smaller wheels and a 4-inch (102) length of standard 1 x 10-inch (17 x 235) white pine for the larger wheels.

8-inch (203) length of 1-inch (25) diameter wooden dowel rod.

3-inch (76) length of 2-inch (51) diameter wooden rod for the Smokestack. You may wish to purchase a smokestack if you do not have an electric sander (or lathe) with which to shape the dowel. Many wood shops and hobby stores stock them.

8½-inch (216) length of 4 x 4-inch (89 x 89) white pine for the Engine Boiler. As you can see in **Figure G**, the block of wood has been turned on a lathe to create the decorative cylindrical shape of the Boiler. If you don't have access to a lathe, we suggest that you purchase a length of decorative porch post, which is available at most home improvement centers. They usually stock several different styles, so choose the style that most resembles the Engine Boiler shown here. It should be approximately 3½ inches (89) in diameter and 8½ inches (216) long.

Our wooden train pull toy is modeled after a 19th century steam locomotive and cars. Although the early trains were picturesque, and a definite improvement over stage coach travel, they were somewhat lacking in passenger comforts. While the fireman stoked the boiler, black smoke laden with soot, ash, and live sparks flew out of the smokestack and into the open windows of the passenger car.

Metric equivalents in millimeters are indicated in parentheses.

Wooden axle pegs. These can be purchased ready-made or you can make ordinary axles with plug ends. If you buy pegs, you'll need 2 different sizes: 40 pegs, each approximately 1¼ inches (32) long, with a ¼-inch (6.35) diameter shank and a ⅜-inch (10) diameter cap; and 4 pegs, each approximately 2 inches (51) long, with a ¼-inch (6.35) diameter shank and a ½-inch (13) diameter cap. (If you purchase ready-made wheels, be sure that the shank diameter of the axle pegs is slightly smaller than the diameter of the center holes in the wheels.) To make your own axles, purchase an extra 6 feet (1829) of ¼-inch (6.35) diameter wooden dowel rod and the following wooden plugs: 4 plugs each ½ inch (13) in diameter and 40 plugs each ⅜ inch (10) in diameter.

Whistle and Chimney pegs. The pegs on top of the Engine and Caboose are very much like axle pegs. The plugs, however, are shaped differently than the axle peg plugs. Purchase 2 pre-made pegs, each approximately 1½ inches (38) long or make them from a 2½ inch (64) length of ¼-inch (6.35) diameter dowel rod and 2 contoured plugs, each about ¾ inch (19) at the widest point.

Handful of very thin finishing nails, ¾ to 1 inch (20 to 25) long; carpenter's wood glue; medium and fine sandpaper; and kraft paper for enlarging the scale drawings.

Tools

Circular saw, saber saw (or hand coping saw), wood rasp, hammer, and an electric drill with 1-inch (25), and ⅛-inch (3) diameter bits. In addition, if you plan to make the axles, wheels, and smokestack, you'll need drill bits of the following diameters: ¼-inch (6.35), ⅜-inch (10), and ¾-inch (20). If you purchase the parts, you'll need a bit of the same diameter as the axle peg shanks, a bit slightly larger than the diameter of the peg shanks, and a bit of the same diameter as the lower end of the smokestack.

Optional tools include a lathe (to turn the Smokestack and Boiler), a circle-cutting attachment for your electric drill (to make the wheels), and an electric sander or sanding attachment for your drill (the smart or lazy man's sanding method, however you choose to look at it).

It probably won't take you as long to make this entire train as it did to get through the list of materials and tools. We've divided the project into 5 units, 1 for each car. You'll be getting underway with the easiest car. Unless otherwise specified, use glue and nails for all assembly steps.

To cut down on excess verbiage when specifying drill bit sizes, we will call for the ¼-inch (6.35) diameter bit when you are to drill a hole to match the diameter of the axle peg shanks. If you purchased axle pegs which have a different diameter, use a matching-sized bit. Similarly, when we specify the ⅜-inch (10) diameter bit, use the bit that is slightly larger than the shank diameter of the purchased axle pegs. Isn't that simple?

Coal Car

Cutting the pieces   **1.** Scale drawings for some of the Coal Car pieces are given in **Figure A**. (Additional parts, not shown in **Figure A,** require only simple cuts and will be explained in the cutting or assembly directions.) Enlarge the drawings to full-size patterns on kraft paper. (Save the paper patterns for all of the cars after you use them, as some will be called for again when you are cutting the pieces for the other cars. Label the patterns for easy reference.)

2. Cut the following pieces from ½-inch (13) thick lumber: 2 Sides, 1 Bed, 1 Connector, and 2 additional pieces for the Roof and Back, each 3½ x 3½ inches (89 x 89). Cut 1 Wheel Support from the pine 2 x 6 (38 x 140).

3. Drill 2 axle holes, each ¼ inch (6.35) in diameter, through the Wheel Support where indicated on the scale drawing. Drill a ⅜-inch (10) diameter hole through the tongue portion of the Bed and the Connector. Placement is shown in the scale drawings. Sand all of the pieces.

4. (If you purchased pre-made axle pegs, this step is unnecessary, and you may skip to "Assembly" below. But, for those of you who did not, we've included instructions to make the axles for each car.) Cut 2 Axles, each 3¼ inches (83) long, from the ¼-inch (6.35) diameter dowel rod.

Figure A

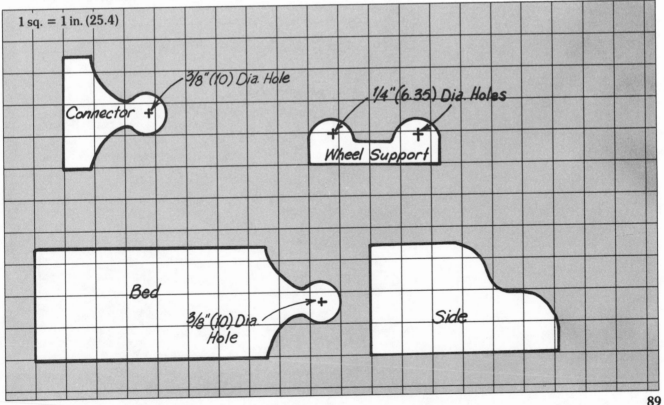

1 sq. = 1 in. (25.4)

Connector — ⅜" (10) Dia. Hole

Wheel Support — ¼" (6.35) Dia. Holes

Bed — ⅜" (10) Dia. Hole

Side

Assembly

1. An assembly diagram for the Coal Car is given in **Figure B.** Center and attach the Wheel Support to the underside of the Bed. Attach the Sides and Back to the top of the Bed, trimming the upper edges, if necessary, so that they are even.

2. Cut a 3½-inch (89) length of cove molding (optional), and attach it along the center line of the Roof as shown. Cut two 3½-inch (89) lengths of stripping, and attach them along the edges of the Roof. Place the Roof over the top edges of the Sides and Back, allowing it to extend about ½ inch (13) beyond the Back. Attach the Connector to the underside of the Bed.

3. Insert the Axles through the axle holes, leaving equal extensions on each side, and slip a Wheel over each Axle end. Glue a wooden plug over each axle end. (Use the smaller wheels and plugs unless otherwise indicated. If you purchased pre-made axle pegs, use them instead of the Axles.)

Passenger Car

Cutting the pieces

1. Scale drawings for the Passenger Car are given in **Figure C.** Enlarge the drawings to full-size patterns on kraft paper.

2. Cut the following pieces from the ½-inch (13) thick lumber: 2 Sides; 2 End Walls; 1 Bed; 1 Connector, using the Coal Car Connector pattern; and 1 Roof, 3½ x 12 inches (89 x 305). Cut 3 window openings through each of the Sides.

Figure B

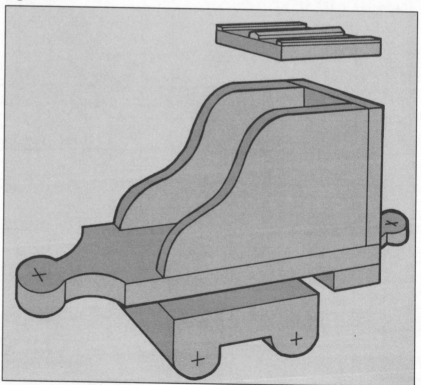

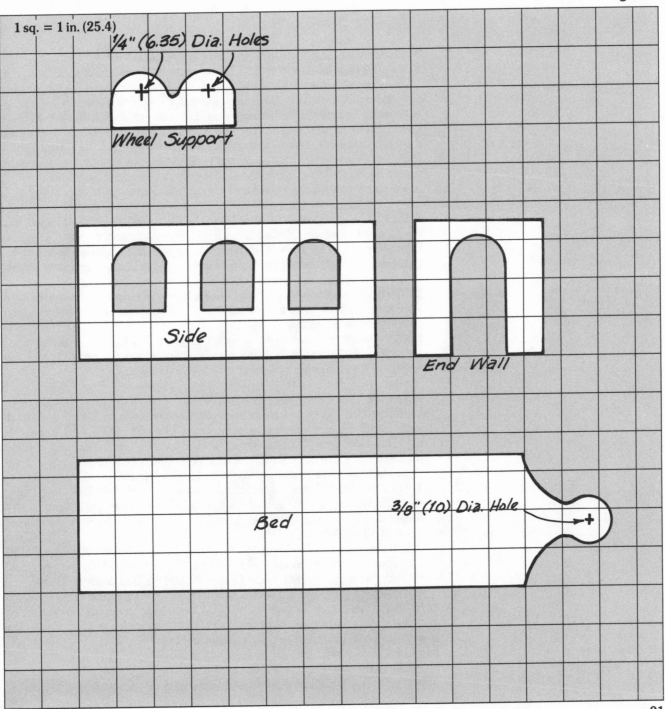

Figure C

1 sq. = 1 in. (25.4)

¼" (6.35) Dia. Holes

Wheel Support

Side

End Wall

Bed

3/8" (10) Dia. Hole

3. Cut 2 Wheel Supports from the pine 2 x 6 (38 x 140). Cut 4 Axles, each 3¼ inches (83) long, and 8 Gate Posts, each 1¼ inches (32) long, from the ¼-inch (6.35) diameter dowel rod. Cut 2 Gate Crossbars, each 3¼ inches (83) long, from the ⅛-inch (3) diameter dowel rod. Sand all of the pieces.

4. Drill two ¼-inch (6.35) diameter axle holes through each of the Wheel Supports where indicated on the scale drawing. Drill a ⅜-inch (10) diameter hole through the tongue portion of the Bed and Connector, as shown. Drill 4 shallow Gate Post sockets, ¼-inch (6.35) in diameter, in a straight line near each end of the Bed. Try to space them as evenly as possible. Use the ⅛-inch (3) diameter bit to drill a hole near 1 end of each Gate Post.

Assembly   **1.** Attach the 2 Sides to the Bed, centering them as shown in the assembly diagram **(Figure D).** Add the End Walls and the Roof. Glue the Gate Posts into their sockets, aligning the holes in the upper ends. Insert the Crossbars through the aligned holes. Turn the assembly upside down, and attach the Connector and Wheel Supports.

2. Insert an Axle through each of the axle holes, leaving equal extensions on each side. Install 8 wheels (1 on each end of each Axle), and glue a wooden plug to each axle end.

3. Cut a length of cove molding (optional), and 2 lengths of stripping, each 12 inches (305) long. Attach the cove molding along the center line of the Roof, and the stripping along the Roof edges, as shown.

Box Car
Cutting the pieces   **1.** Cut the following pieces from ½-inch (13) thick lumber: 8 Walls, each 3½ x 3½ inches (89 x 89); 1 Roof, 3½ x 12 inches (89 x 305); 1 Bed, using the Passenger Car Bed pattern; and 1 Connector, using the Coal Car Connector pattern. Cut 2 Wheel Supports from the pine 2 x 6 (38 x 140), using the Passenger Car Wheel Support pattern.

2. The Door Track Strips are cut from ¼ x ¼-inch (6 x 6) stripping. Cut 4 strips, each 2¾ inches (70) long, and 4 strips, each 9½ inches (242) long. Cut 4 Axles, each 3¼ inches (83) long, from the ¼-inch (6.35) diameter dowel rod. Sand all of the pieces.

3. Use the ¼-inch (6.35) diameter bit to drill 2 axle holes in each Wheel Support where indicated on the scale drawing. Drill a ⅜-inch (10) diameter hole through the tongue portion of the Connector and the Bed, as shown.

4. Two of the Walls will be used as sliding doors on the Box Car. Drill a ¼-inch (6.35) diameter hole through each of the Doors, to accommodate a dowel-peg "handle." Exact placement of the holes is not important, as long as they are at least ⅝ inch (16) from 1 edge, as shown in **Figure E.**

Assembly   **1.** Refer to **Figure E** and attach Door Track Strips to the top of the Bed where indicated. Attach additional strips underneath the Roof, using the same measurement guides.

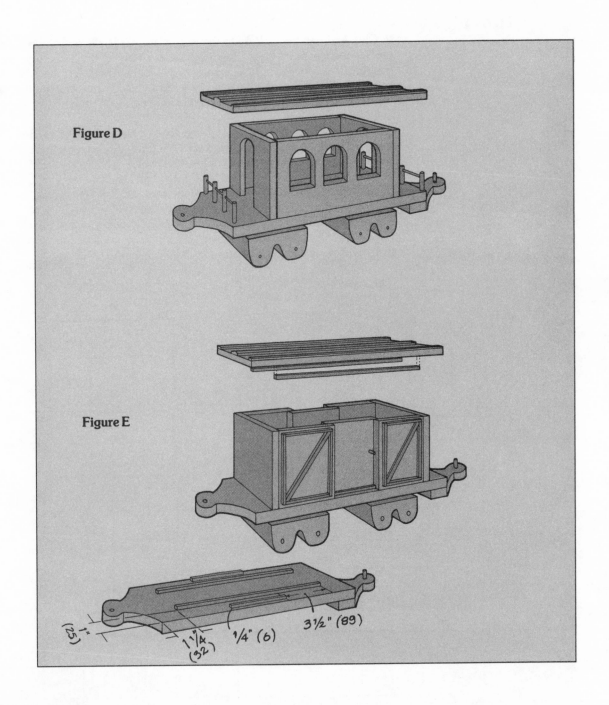

Figure D

Figure E

1" (25)

1 1/4" (32)

1/4" (6)

3 1/2" (89)

2. Glue and nail the 6 Walls to the Bed, placing 2 Walls on each side, and 1 each at the front and back. Butt the ends as shown in the assembly diagram. Put the Doors in place, with lower edges inserted between the Door Track Strips on each side of the Bed. Add the Roof, making sure that the tops of the Doors fit between the Door Track strips on each side of the Roof. Glue and nail the Roof in place.

3. Add the Wheel Supports and Connector to the underside of the Bed. Placement is shown in **Figure E.** Insert an Axle through each axle hole, and add the wheels and plugs as you did for the other cars.

4. Cut two 1¼-inch (32) lengths of the ¼-inch (6.35) diameter dowel rod. Glue a ⅜-inch (10) diameter plug onto 1 end of each. Glue these pegs into the holes in the Box Car Doors, as shown in **Figure E.**

5. Cut a 12-inch (305) length of cove molding (optional), and attach it along the center line of the Roof. Cut two 12-inch (305) lengths of stripping, and attach them along the edges of the Roof.

Figure F

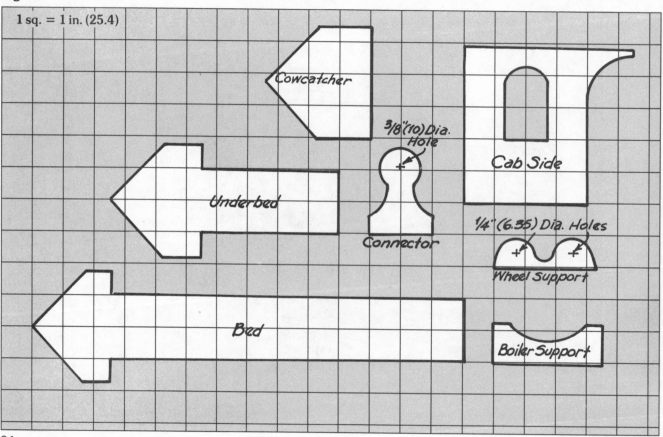

1 sq. = 1 in. (25.4)

Cowcatcher

⅜"(10) Dia. Hole

Underbed

Connector

Cab Side

¼" (6.35) Dia. Holes

Wheel Support

Bed

Boiler Support

6. Cut the following pieces of stripping for the Box Car wall trim: eight 3½-inch (89) lengths, eight 3¼-inch (83) lengths, and four 4⅝-inch (118) lengths. Glue a 3½-inch (89) length along the upper and lower edges of each wall, as shown in **Figure E.** Glue a 3¼-inch (83) length along both sides of each wall, between the upper and lower strips. Add a 4⅝-inch (118) length diagonally across each square of strips, trimming the ends to fit into the corners as shown. We discovered that a sharp pocket knife is easier to use for this trimming process than a saw or sandpaper.

Engine
Cutting the pieces   **1.** Scale drawings for some of the Engine parts are given in **Figure F.** Enlarge the drawings to full-size patterns on kraft paper.
2. Cut the following pieces from the ½-inch (13) thick lumber: 2 Cab Sides; 1 Connector; 1 Bed; 1 Underbed; 1 Cab Front, 3½ x 5 inches (89 x 127); 1 Cab Roof, 3½ x 6 inches (89 x 152); and 1 Cab Floor, 2½ x 4 inches (64 x 102). Cut window openings through each Cab Side.
3. Cut 1 Cowcatcher and 2 Boiler Supports from the pine 1 x 4 (17 x 89). Cut 2 Wheel Supports from the pine 2 x 6 (38 x 140), using the Engine Wheel Support pattern **(Figure F)** for the Front Wheel Support, and the Coal Car Wheel Support pattern for the Rear Wheel Support. Sand all of the pieces.
4. Cut 2 Pistons, each 3 inches (76) long, from the 1-inch (25) diameter dowel rod. Cut 2 Axles, each 3¼ inches (83) long, and 2 Axles, each 4 inches (102) long, from the ¼-inch (6.35) diameter dowel rod.
5. Drill 2 holes, each ¼ inch (6.35) in diameter, through each Wheel Support where indicated on the scale drawings. Drill a ⅜-inch (10) diameter hole through the Connector where indicated.
6. Shape the Boiler from the pine 4 x 4 (89 x 89). If you purchased a length of porch post to serve as the Boiler, the front will be cut flat, instead of tapered like the Boiler shown in **Figure G.** Use a wood rasp and sandpaper to round off the front circumference-edge of the Boiler. Drill a shallow 1-inch (25) diameter socket into the center front. Cut a 1-inch (25) length of 1-inch (25) diameter dowel rod and glue it into the socket. Drill a shallow socket, ¾ inch (20) in diameter (or to match the size of the lower end of the smokestack you purchased), near the front of the Boiler.
7. If you did not purchase a smokestack, shape the 2-inch (51) diameter rod as shown in **Figure G.** The Smokestack should be 1¾ inches (45) in diameter at the widest point, and ¾ inch (20) in diameter at the lower end.

Assembly   **1.** Attach the Underbed and Cowcatcher to the bottom of the Bed, as shown in the assembly diagram **(Figure G).** Trim the front edges evenly, at an angle. Attach the Front and Rear Wheel Supports and the Connector where indicated.
2. Turn the bed assembly right side up and attach the 2 Boiler Supports to the top of the Bed as shown. Glue the Boiler to the Boiler Supports. (Be sure that the Smokestack socket is facing upward when you glue the Boiler to the Supports, or you will have a very funny-looking Engine and very little credibility as a train builder.)

Figure G

Figure H

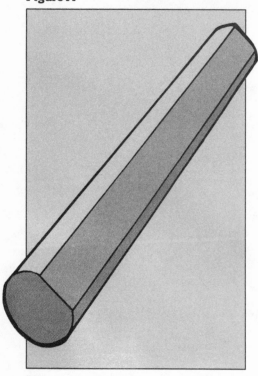

3. Glue the Cab Front to the Bed and Boiler. Attach the Cab Floor between the 2 Cab Sides,, with lower edges even. Attach this assembly to the Engine Bed and Cab Front, as shown. Add the Cab Roof. Cut a 6-inch (152) length of cove molding (optional), and attach it along the center line of the Roof. Cut, and attach a 6-inch (152) length of stripping along each edge of the Cab Roof.

4. To make the Piston Pegs, cut 2 shanks, each 1¼ inches (32) long, from the ¼-inch (6.35) diameter dowel rod. Glue a ⅜-inch (10) diameter plug over 1 end of each shank.

5. Cut a very thin slice from the length of each Piston, as shown in **Figure H.** Drill a shallow ¼-inch (6.35) diameter socket into 1 end of each Piston, placing the socket in the center. Glue an assembled Piston Peg into each hole, and apply glue to the long, flat edge of each Piston. Attach 1 Piston to each side of the Engine Bed above the Front Wheel Support as shown in **Figure G.** Make sure that the Piston Pegs are facing the rear of the Engine.

6. Insert 3¼-inch (83) long Axles through the holes in the Front Wheel Support and add small wheels and plugs as you did for the other cars. For the Rear Wheel Support, use 4-inch (102) long axles and the larger wheels and plugs.

7. Cut eight 2½-inch (64) lengths of stripping. Attach them vertically to the front of the Cowcatcher, evenly spaced, as shown in **Figure G.**

8. Cut a 1¼-inch (32) length of ¼-inch (6.35) diameter dowel rod for the Whistle peg. Drill a shallow socket of the same diameter into the Cab Roof, close to the the front edge. Glue the Whistle peg into the socket, and glue a Whistle Plug over the end of the peg.

Waddling Ducks – page 10

Rabbit, Fox, and Turtle – page 15

Tumbling Trio – page 25

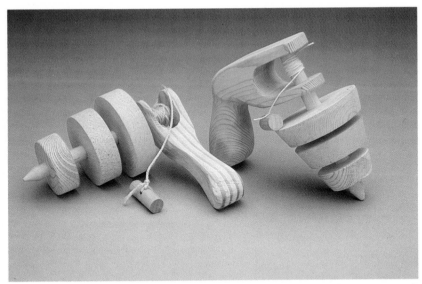

Spinning Tops – page 22

Tell-Time Clock – page 50

99

Alphabet Train – page 44

Size & Shape Box – page 47

Country Puzzle Picture – page 42

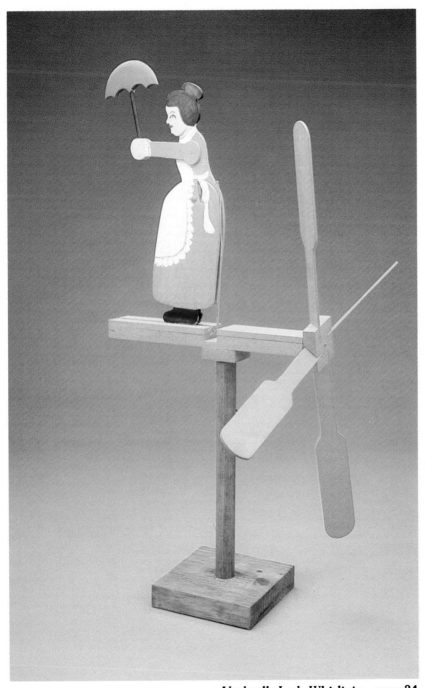

Umbrella Lady Whirligig – page 34

Drum Box & Whistle Flute – page 38

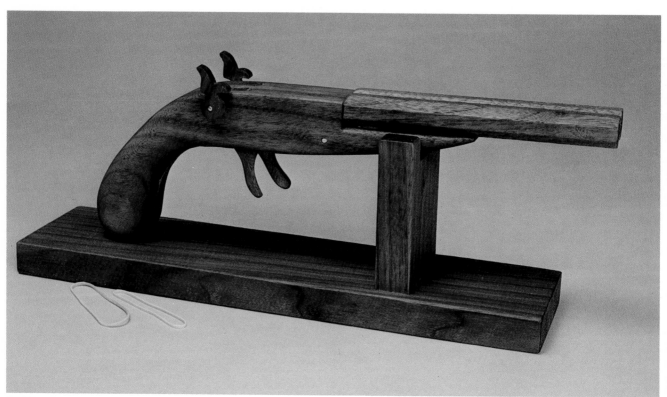

Rubber Band Shooting Iron – page 30

Sailing Sloop – page 58

Noah's Ark – page 65

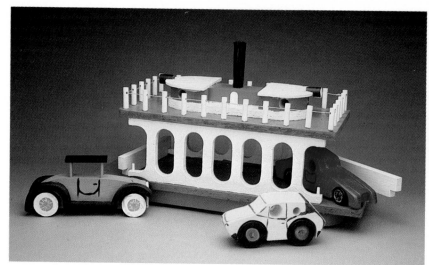

Ferryboat & Cars – page 69

Paddle Wheel Steamer – page 54

Biplane Flying Machine – page 80

Hook & Ladder Truck – page 116

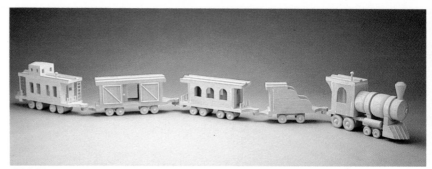

Old-Time Iron Horse – page 87

Stick Stallion – page 84

Scrap Wood Toys – page 121

Victorian Mansion Doll House – page 128

Rocking Doll Cradle – page 148

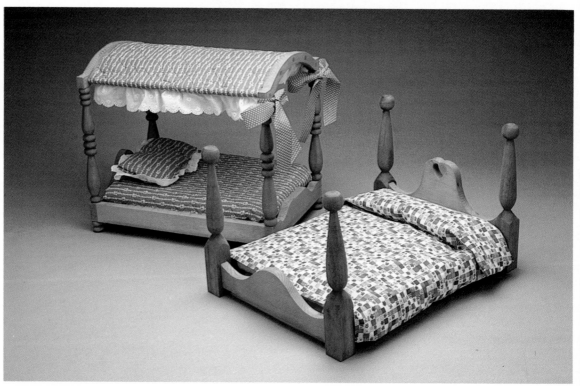

Antique Doll Beds – page 152

108

Spoon Dolls – page 158

Old Fashioned Rocking Horse – page 162

Fire Engine – page 168

Tin Lizzie Racer - page 178

Four-Wheel Horsey – page 194

Double-Duty Wagon – page 186

111

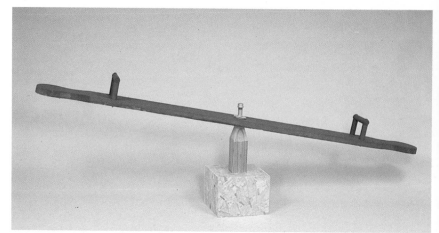

Whirling Seesaw – Page 190

Country Rocking Horse – page 199

Caboose
Cutting the pieces   **1.** Scale drawings for some of the Caboose parts are given in **Figure I**. Enlarge the drawings to full-size patterns on kraft paper.
2. Cut the following pieces from the ½-inch (13) thick lumber: 2 Sides; 2 End Walls; 2 Cupola Sides; 2 Cupola Front Walls (1 will be used as the Cupola Rear Wall); 1 Bed, using the Passenger Car Bed pattern; 1 Connector, using the Coal Car Connector pattern; 1 Roof, 3½ x 12 inches (89 x 305); and 1 Cupola Roof, 2¾ x 3½ inches (70 x 89). Cut the window openings where indicated on the scale drawings. Use a wood rasp followed by sandpaper to shape the Cupola Roof as shown in the end view pattern, **Figure I**.
3. Cut 2 Wheel Supports, using the Passenger Car Wheel Support pattern, from the pine 2 x 6 (38 x 140).
4. Cut the following parts from the ¼-inch (6.35) diameter dowel rod: 4 Axles, each 3¼ inches (83) long; and 8 Gate Posts, each 1¼ inches (32) long. Cut the following parts from the ⅛-inch (3) diameter dowel rod: 4 Ladder Sides, each 4 inches (102) long; 12 Rungs, each ¾ inch (19) long; and 2 Gate Crossbars, each 3¼ inches (83) long.

Figure I

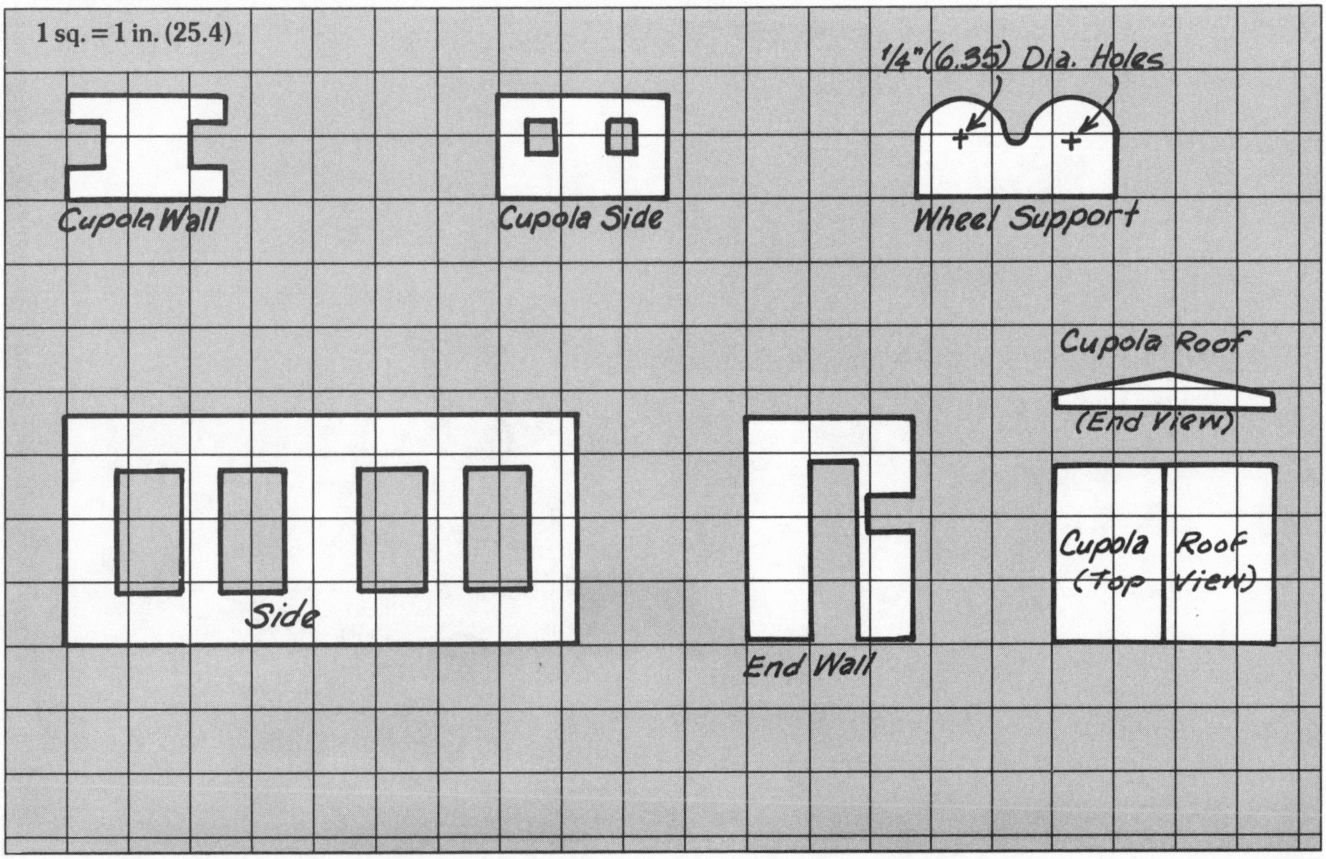

1 sq. = 1 in. (25.4)

Cupola Wall

Cupola Side

¼" (6.35) Dia. Holes

Wheel Support

Cupola Roof (End View)

Cupola Roof (Top View)

Side

End Wall

5. Drill two ¼-inch (6.35) diameter holes through each of the Wheel Supports where indicated on the scale drawing. Drill a ⅜-inch (10) diameter hole through the tongue portion of the Bed and Connector, as shown.

6. Drill 4 shallow sockets, ¼ inch (6.35) in diameter, near each end of the Bed, to accommodate the Gate Posts. Drill 2 shallow sockets, ⅛ inch (3) in diameter, near each end of the Bed, and near each end of the Roof, to accommodate the Ladder Sides. Refer to the assembly diagram, **Figure J,** for placement. Drill a ⅛-inch (3) diameter hole through each Gate Post, near 1 end.

Assembly **1.** Attach the Connector and Wheel Supports to the underside of the Bed, as shown in **Figure J.** Turn the assembly right side up, and attach the Sides, End Walls, and Roof, as shown.

Figure J

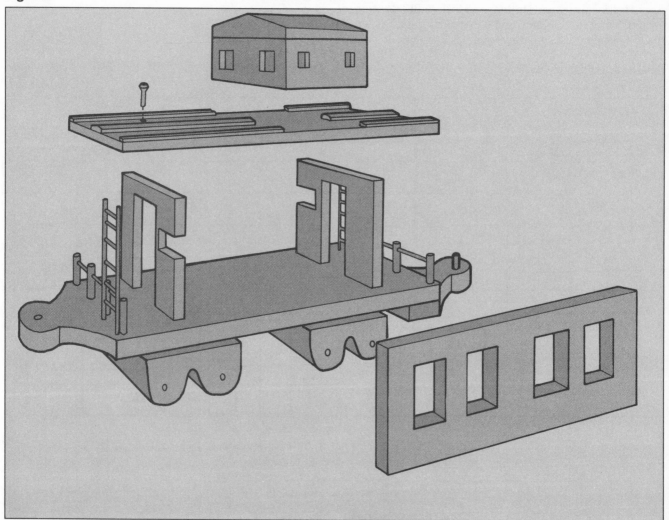

2. Assemble the Cupola, glueing the Front and Rear Walls between the Cupola Sides, and attach this structure to the Caboose Roof where indicated. Add the Cupola Roof.

3. To assemble the Ladders, make a small notch in both ends of each Rung. Glue 6 Rungs between the Sides of each Ladder, spacing the rungs evenly.

4. Insert the Ladders into the sockets in the Bed, and add the Caboose Roof, guiding the tops of the Ladders into the sockets in the Roof.

5. To assemble the gates, glue the Gate Posts into the sockets in the Caboose Bed, so that the holes near the upper ends of the Posts are aligned. Slide the Gate Crossbars through the aligned holes.

6. Insert an Axle through each of the axle holes, leaving equal extensions on each side. Install 8 Wheels (1 on each end of each Axle), and glue a wooden plug to each axle end.

7. Cut 1 length of cove molding (optional), and 2 lengths of stripping, each 6½ inches (165) long. Cut an additional length of cove molding and 2 additional lengths of stripping, each 2¾ inches (70) long. Attach the cove molding along the center line of the Roof, and the lengths of stripping along the edges of the Roof, on either side of the cupola, as shown.

8. Cut 1 chimney peg shank, 1 inch (25) long, from the ¼-inch (6.35) diameter dowel rod. Glue a contoured chimney plug over 1 end of the shank. Drill a shallow ¼-inch (6.35) diameter socket into the Caboose Roof, about 3 inches (76) from the rear edge, midway between the cove molding and 1 of the wood strips. Glue the Chimney into the socket.

Connecting the cars   **1.** Cut 4 Connector Peg shanks, each 1¼ inches (32) long, from the ¼-inch (6.35) diameter dowel rod. Glue a ⅜-inch (10) diameter plug over 1 end of each shank.

2. Place the train cars in a straight row, so that the hole in the Connector tongue of 1 car is aligned with the hole in the Bed tongue of the car behind it. Place the Engine in the front, of course, followed by the Coal Car, Box Car, Passenger Car, and Caboose, in that order. Insert a Connector Peg through each set of aligned holes.

Practice up for the unveiling ceremony by memorizing the oft-quoted line attributed to Casey, the famous old-time railroad engineer, "All aboard! If you can't get aboard, get a plank." Practice running away quickly if you plan to use this line in public.

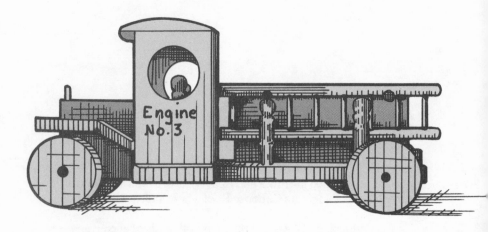

Hook & Ladder Truck

Back in the good old days, a hook and ladder truck was the ultimate in high-tech fire fighting equipment. Our model, complete with 6 firemen and 2 removable ladders, will keep all of your toddlers entertained for hours on end.

Metric equivalents in millimeters are indicated in parentheses.

Materials

3-foot (914) length of 1 x 12-inch (17 x 286) clear white pine.

10-inch (254) length of 2 x 4-inch (38 x 89) clear white pine.

Wooden dowel rod: 25-inch (635) length of ¾-inch (19) diameter; 4-foot (1219) length of ½-inch (13) diameter; 16-inch (406) length of ⅜-inch (10) diameter; 3-foot (914) length of ¼-inch (6.35) diameter.

3½-inch (89) length of soft metal rod, approximately ⅛ inch (3) in diameter.

4 metal washers, each ¾-inch (19) or larger in diameter, with a ½-inch (13) diameter center hole. (Or, you can make wooden washers quite easily by drilling a hole through the center of a short length of dowel rod, and cutting thin slices from the drilled rod.)

Handful of 1¼-inch (32) long finishing nails.

Small quantities each of red, black, and white non-toxic paint (or other colors of your choice).

Carpenter's wood glue, kraft paper, medium and fine sandpaper, and a small quantity of wood filler.

Tools

Hammer, nailset, wood rasp, compass, small paint brush, artist's fine-tipped paint brush, saber saw (or hand crosscut and coping saws), and an electric or hand drill with bits of the following diameters: ⅛-inch (3), ¼-inch (6.35), ⅜-inch (10), and ¾-inch (19). In addition, you will need a ⁷⁄₁₆-inch (11) diameter bit that is at least 5 inches (127) long, to drill the axle holes. A circle-cutting drill attachment will speed up the wheel-cutting process, but it is not necessary to complete the project.

Cutting the pieces   1. Enlarge the scale drawings given in **Figure A** to full-size patterns on kraft paper.

Figure A

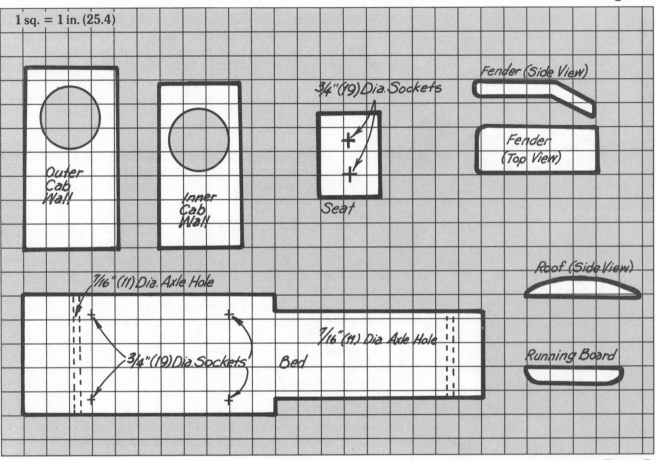

1 sq. = 1 in. (25.4)

Outer Cab Wall

Inner Cab Wall

3/4"(19)Dia.Sockets

Seat

Fender (Side View)

Fender (Top View)

Roof (Side View)

Running Board

7/16"(11)Dia. Axle Hole

3/4"(19)Dia.Sockets

7/16"(11)Dia. Axle Hole

Bed

Figure B

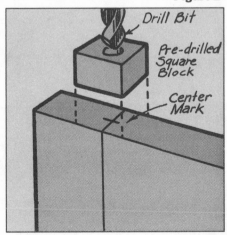

Drill Bit

Pre-drilled Square Block

Center Mark

2. Cut the following pieces from the pine board: 1 Center Panel, 4 x 9 ½ inches (102 x 241); 1 Firewall, 3½ x 3½ inches (89 x 89); 1 Roof, 4¾ x 4⅞ inches (121 x 124); 4 Wheels, each 3½ inches (89) in diameter; 1 Bed; 2 Outer Cab Walls; 1 Inner Cab Wall; 2 Running Boards; and 1 Seat.

3. Cut the window openings in the Outer and Inner Cab Walls, where indicated on the scale drawings. Drill 4 shallow sockets into the Bed, and 2 into the Seat (indicated by cross marks on the scale drawings), to accommodate the Firemen. Drill a ⅜-inch (10) diameter hole through the center of each Wheel. Use a wood rasp followed by sandpaper to contour the Roof, as shown in the side view drawing, **Figure A.**

4. Drill 2 axle holes through the Bed, where indicated by dotted lines on the drawing. Drill as straight as possible, or the truck will roll in a peculiar manner, if at all. (If you are not an experienced driller, you might find it helpful to use a pre-drilled, perfectly right-angled block as a guide, as shown in **Figure B.**)

Figure C

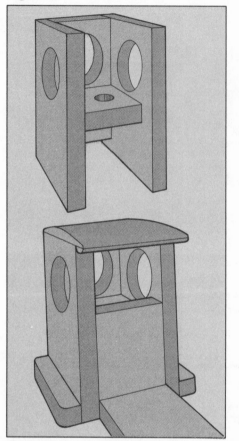

5. Cut a 4½-inch (114) length of the 2 x 4-inch (38 x 89) pine, for the Hood. To make the 2 Fenders, cut the remaining 5½-inch (140) length of 2 x 4 (38 x 89) in half lengthwise, so that you have two 5½-inch (140) lengths of 2 x 2 (38 x 38). (These will not actually measure 2 x 2 inches, because a 2 x 4 does not actually measure 2 x 4 inches, but we won't go into that now. And we didn't put the metric equivalents into the last sentence because that would just confuse things.) Refer to the scale drawing for the Fender (side view) in **Figure A**, and cut 1 Fender from each of the 2 x 2's (38 x 38's).

6. Sand all of the pieces to eliminate splinters, rough spots, and sharp edges.

Assembly Use glue and nails for all assembly steps, unless otherwise specified. Recess all nails, and fill the holes with wood filler.

1. Attach the Inner Cab Wall between the 2 Outer Cab Walls, with upper edges flush (**Figure C**). Add the Seat, placing it just below the window opening in the Inner Cab Wall. Attach this assembly to the Bed, and add the Firewall. Attach the Cab Roof over the walls with rear edges flush, so that it extends about ¾ inch (19) beyond the front edge. Cut a 4⅞-inch (124) length of ¾-inch (19) diameter dowel rod. Split the rod in half the long way, and attach 1 half underneath the roof overhang. Add the 2 Running Boards flush with the lower edges of the Outer Walls.

2. Drill two ⅜-inch (10) diameter holes through the Center Panel to accommodate the Ladder Hooks. Each of the holes should be ½ inch (13) from the upper edge of the Panel, and 1 to 2 inches (25 to 51) from the front or rear edge, respectively (**Figure D**). Cut two 2-inch (51) lengths of ⅜-inch (10) diameter dowel rod for the Ladder Hooks. Contour each of the Hooks as shown in the enlarged drawing, **Figure D**. Glue the Ladder Hooks in place, and attach the Center Panel to the Bed, with rear edges flush.

3. Cut a 6¾-inch (172) length of ⅜-inch (10) diameter dowel rod for the Rear Axle. Insert the axle through the rear axle hole, leaving equal extensions on each side. Add a washer to each side of the axle, and glue a Wheel flush with each axle end. Cut a 5-inch (127) length from the same dowel rod for the Front Axle, and repeat the assembly process with washers and Wheels.

Figure D

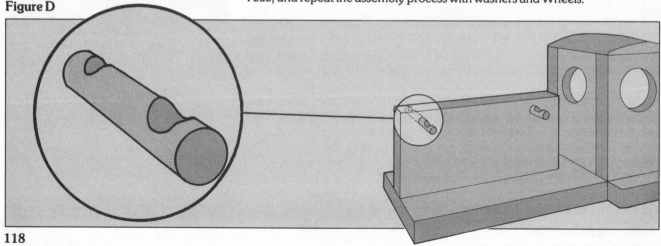

Figure E

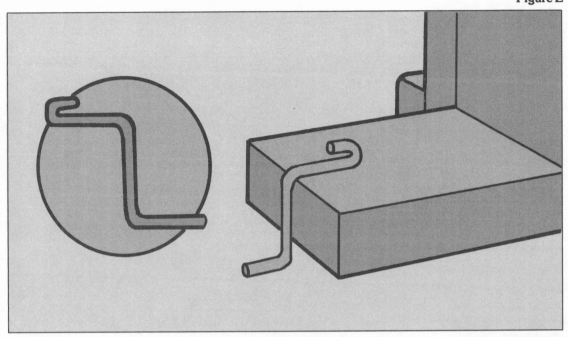

Figure F

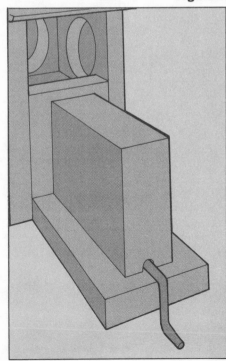

4. To create the Crank (no electric ignition in this baby!), bend the length of soft metal rod as shown (full size) in **Figure E**. Place the Crank over the front edge of the Bed, extending along the center line, as shown. Carefully center the Hood over the Bed, flush against the Firewall, and press down on it, so that the curled end of the Crank will leave indentations on the Bed and Hood. Drill a shallow ½-inch (13) diameter socket into the Bed, and another into the Hood, at the indentations. (The sockets will allow the curled end of the Crank to turn as the handle end is rotated.) Drill a ⅛-inch (3) diameter groove along the center line on the lower edge of the Hood, from the front end all the way to the socket. (The groove will accommodate the Crank shaft.) Put the Crank back in place, and attach the Hood to the Bed (**Figure F**).

5. Attach the Fenders to the sides of the Hood. Drill a shallow ⅜-inch (10) diameter socket into the Hood, to accommodate a hood ornament. Cut a short length of ⅜-inch (10) diameter dowel rod for the ornament. Glue it into the socket as is, or use a wood rasp and sandpaper to contour the ornament before gluing it in place. As a unique alternative to the wooden hood ornament, you can substitute a small metal character from a child's board game (e. g., the dog from a Monopoly game). If you choose this alternative, we suggest that you first get permission from the game's owner, because you'll need to attach the purloined metal ornament with epoxy cement. And it will never more travel the circuit of its home board.

6. Allow all glued sections to dry for several hours before sanding and painting the Hook & Ladder Truck.

Figure G

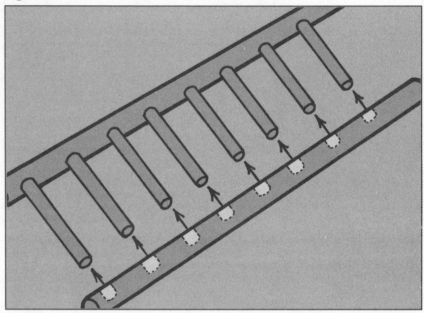

Figure H

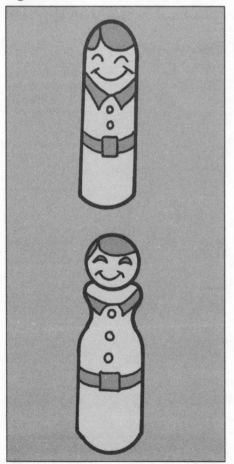

7. To make the 2 ladders, cut four 12-inch (305) lengths of ½-inch (13) diameter dowel rod for the Ladder Sides. Cut sixteen 2¼-inch (57) lengths of ¼-inch (6.35) diameter dowel rod for the Rungs. Drill 8 sockets, each ¼ inch (6.35) in diameter, in a straight line along each Ladder Side. Space the sockets as shown in **Figure G**. Glue the Rungs into the sockets, and allow several hours for the glue to dry before you paint the ladders. When the paint has dried, hang the ladders on either side of the Center Panel.

Firemen   There are 2 ways to create a Fireman. The easiest method is to cut a length of ¾-inch (19) diameter dowel rod and round off 1 end. Paint facial features and hair on the rounded "head" end, and clothing on the body portion of the dowel.

If you want to get a little fancier, cut a length of dowel, and contour it as shown in the second drawing, **Figure H**. Attach a spherical wooden drawer pull or finial to the top, for the head, and paint in facial features, hair, and clothing.

Make 4 Firemen, each approximately 3½ inches (89) tall, to ride on the back of the Fire Truck. Make 2 additional Firemen, each approximately 2½ inches (64) tall, to ride in the cab.

Present your finished Hook & Ladder Truck to a small, aspiring fire fighter. We suggest that you caution him or her against exceeding the speed limit, or someone's bound to ask, "Where's the fire?"

Scrap Wood Toys

Materials

Scrap wood. The body for each vehicle is cut from standard 2-inch (38) thick lumber (which is actually only 1½ inches thick). The fenders are cut from standard 1-inch (17) thick lumber (actually only ¾ inch thick), and the axles are lengths of ⅜-inch (10) diameter wooden dowel rod. You probably have enough scrap wood around to build all 10 vehicles, as the largest body part requires only a 15-inch (381) length of lumber, and the longest axle requires only a 5-inch (127) length of dowel. If you purchase the wood to make all 10 cars, you'll need 10 feet (3048) of 2 x 8-inch (38 x 184) pine, 13½ feet (4115) of 1 x 8-inch (17 x 184) pine, and 8 feet (2438) of dowel rod.

Wheels. Purchase pre-made wheels, or make them from standard 1-inch (17) thick wood. You'll need 49 wheels, each 2¼ inches (57) in diameter, with a ⅜-inch (10) diameter axle hole.

46 metal washers, 1½ inches (38) in diameter, with ½-inch (13) diameter center holes.

Non-toxic paint or stain (optional) in the colors of your choice.

Carpenter's wood glue, kraft paper, several C-clamps, medium and fine sandpaper, and carbon paper.

Tools

Saber saw, wood rasp, and an electric or hand drill with ½-inch (13), and ⅜-inch diameter bits.

This entire fleet of vehicles can be made from the collection of scrap wood that's been threatening to take over your shop. The vehicles are simple to cut, easy to assemble, and will be loads of fun for the kids.

Metric equivalents in millimeters are indicated in parentheses.

Figure A

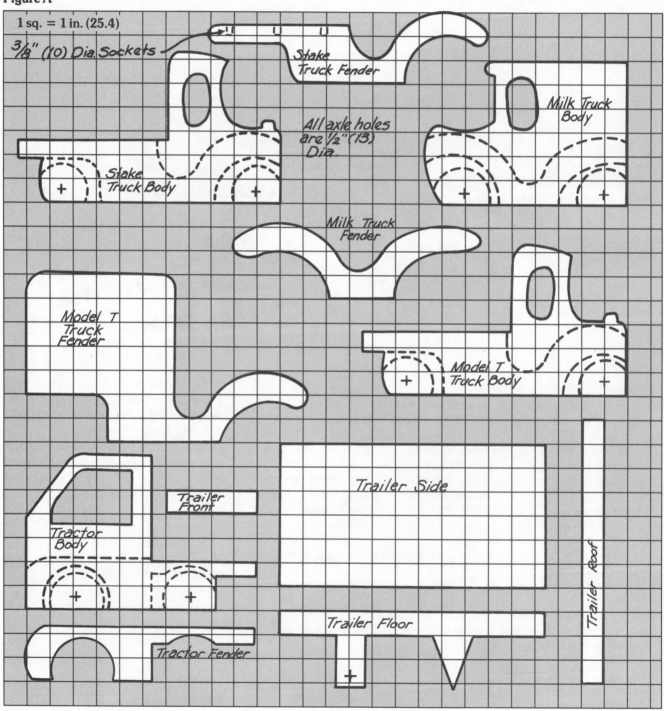

1 sq. = 1 in. (25.4)

3/8" (10) Dia. Sockets

Stake Truck Fender

Milk Truck Body

All axle holes are 1/2" (13) Dia.

Stake Truck Body

Milk Truck Fender

Model T Truck Fender

Model T Truck Body

Tractor Body

Trailer Front

Trailer Side

Trailer Roof

Tractor Fender

Trailer Floor

1 sq. = 1 in. (25.4)

Sports Coupe Body

All axle holes are ½" (13) Dia.

Touring Car Body

Sports Coupe Fender

Sports Car Fender

Touring Car Fender

Sports Car Body

Model A Fender

Van Body

Van Fender

Model A Body

Pickup Truck Fender

Pickup Truck Body

Cutting the pieces Each of these vehicles is put together like a sandwich. Each has a Body (the baloney, if you will) and 2 identical Fenders (the bread), attached with wood glue (the mayonnaise).

1. Make full-size, kraft paper patterns by enlarging the scale drawings given in **Figure A**. Cut the Body pieces (1 for each vehicle) from 2-inch (38) thick lumber, and the Fenders (2 identical pieces for each vehicle) from 1-inch (17) thick lumber. The Tractor/Trailer has some additional pieces: cut 1 Roof, 1 Front, and 1 Floor from 2-inch (38) thick stock, and 2 Sides from 1-inch (17) thick stock. Label each piece.

2. Use carbon paper and a pencil to transfer the fender placement lines, window outlines, axle hole positions, and other markings to the pieces.

3. Cut out the windows and drill the axle holes in each of the Body pieces. (Don't panic if your aim is not quite true and some of the holes come out a bit off kilter. The resulting movement will probably draw more interest from the kids.) Drill 3 shallow sockets into the upper edge of each Stake Truck Fender to accommodate the Stakes, where indicated on the scale drawing.

4. If you are a true glutton for woodworking, and are determined to make your own wheels, you'll need to cut 49 circles, each 2¼ inches (57) in diameter, from 1-inch (17) thick stock. Drill a ⅜-inch (10) diameter axle hole through the center of each wheel.

5. Cut 10 Axles, each 3½ inches (89) long, from the ⅜-inch (10) diameter dowel rod. Cut six 3-inch (76) lengths for the Stake Truck Stakes. You'll also need to cut two 5-inch (127) long Axles for the Tractor/Trailer.

6. Thoroughly sand the pieces to eliminate sharp edges. Don't sand off the fender placement lines, or you'll have to go back and retrace them.

Figure B

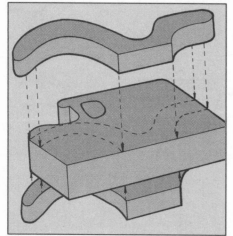

Figure C

Assembly The assembly of these vehicles is outrageously simple, so you might as well let your apprentices handle it while you supervise from the comfort of your favorite chair or hammock. The Tractor/Trailer is a bit different than the others, and will be explained separately. Find the Body and Fender pieces for any 1 of the vehicles, and start making sandwiches.

1. Spread a thin coat of glue on the inner sides of the 2 Fenders (mayonnaise really won't work very well), between the fender placement lines. Put the Fenders in place (**Figure B**).

2. Clamp the assembly or place it under a heavy weight and let the glue dry.

3. Insert 3½-inch (89) Axles through the axle holes, leaving equal extensions on each side. On each Axle end, place 1 washer and 1 wheel, attaching the wheel with a spot of glue.

4. The Van, Sport Coupe, and Sports Car each have a spare tire attached to the back. Refer to **Figure C**, and drill a shallow, ⅜-inch (10) diameter socket in the center back of each of these vehicles. Glue a short piece of dowel rod into the hole. Slip a wheel over the dowel, glue in place, and trim the dowel flush with the wheel.

5. Glue a Stake into each of the sockets in the Stake Truck Fenders.

Figure D

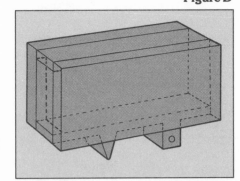

Tractor/Trailer **1.** Assemble the Body and Fenders of the tractor (front) portion as you did for the other vehicles.
2. To assemble the trailer (rear) portion, glue the Front, Roof, and Floor between the 2 Sides with edges flush, as shown in **Figure D**. This will look like an empty "box" with an open back. Apply C-clamps or a weight, and let the glue dry.
3. The Tractor/Trailer has 3 Axles; 2 on the tractor and 1 on the trailer. For the front tractor Axle, use a 3½-inch (89) length of dowel. For the rear tractor Axle and the trailer Axle, use the 5-inch (127) lengths. Install the Axles and washers, and attach the wheels as you did for the other vehicles. Add a second washer and wheel to each end of the 5-inch (127) axles (**Figure E**).

Figure E

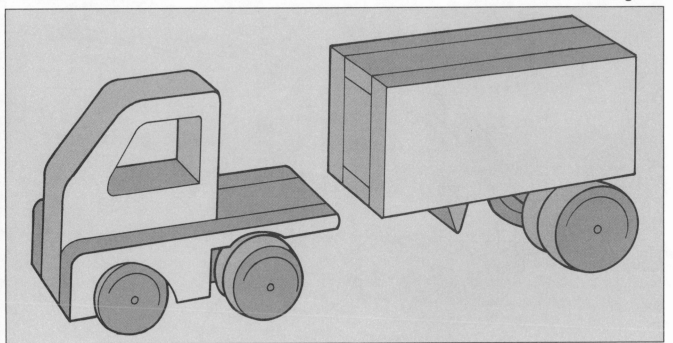

4. To make the coupling assembly (**Figure F**) drill a ½-inch (13) deep socket into the underside of the trailer Floor near the front edge, centering it between the sides. Glue a 2-inch (51) length of dowel rod into this hole. Drill a hole through the tractor Body near the rear edge, centered between the sides. To hitch the 2 sections together, insert the dowel rod extension into the hole in the tractor. Do not use glue, as the hitch should swivel freely.

Finishing   Leave the toys with a natural finish or add color with non-toxic paint or stain.

Now that you know how to do it, put on your automotive engineer's hat and design some other styles. It's sure to keep the little sandwich makers busy for a few days, at least!

Figure F

"Rock-a-bye baby, in the tree top"
Toys for doll lovers

Victorian Mansion Doll House

From 1837 until 1901 Queen Victoria ruled the British Empire and stylish elegance became the standard for every element of Western culture, particularly for the field of architecture. Throughout the modern world, countless numbers of graceful Victorian structures still stand.

Here's an opportunity to add a little Victorian style to your own corner of the world. To build the doll house, you'll need a good measure of patience, but you need not be a woodworking virtuoso. If you have basic abilities with a few tools (power saw, router, miter box), you can complete the structure in about a week's time.

Metric equivalents in millimeters are indicated in parentheses.

Materials

50 to 60 square feet (4.7 to 5.5 sq. m.) of ¼-inch (6.35) veneer-core plywood. Baltic Birch or another high-quality plywood will look best.

8-foot (2438) length of 1 x 12-inch (17 x 286) clear white pine.

Wooden dowel rod: 6 feet (1829) of 1-inch (25) diameter, 8 feet (2438) of ¼-inch (6.35) diameter.

12 feet (3658) of decorative railing, 1½ to 2 inches (38 to 50) in height, for the porches and roof. You can usually find this material in the shelving section of most home improvement centers.

1,200 miniature wood shingles or 600 tongue depressors. If you prefer to cut your own shingles, you'll need a 7-foot (2134) length of 1 x 4-inch (17 x 89) pine. A simple method for cutting the shingles is described in the "Finishing" section of the instructions below.

12 miniature metal door hinges, with screws or nails.

Piano hinge, 18 to 22 inches (457 to 559) long, 1½ to 2 inches (38 to 50) wide, with screws (optional).

600 square inches (3870 sq. cm.) of clear acetate or other thin transparent plastic material.

8 x 10-inch (203 x 254) sheet of white, self-adhesive label paper.

Box of ¾-inch (19) finishing nails, carpenter's wood glue, small paint brushes, and non-toxic paint in your choice of colors.

Tools

Fine-tooth hand saw, saber saw, and circular saw.

Electric or hand drill with ¼-inch (6.35) diameter bit, and a router with ogee (or quarter round) and rabbet (or dado) bits.

Hammer, chisel, T-square, miter box, carpenter's rule, razor knife, and a very small screw driver.

Glue gun and hot-melt adhesive (optional).

Tips

We'd like to offer a few words of encouragement at this point. The doll house is really not difficult to build, but it will take some time. Read through the instructions completely before you begin.

We have divided the construction process into 8 units. Since there are so many pieces to the puzzle, we've combined the cutting and assembly directions for each unit, instead of having you cut all the pieces for the entire doll house at the beginning. This way, we hope you'll be whistling as you work, not muttering strong oaths as you shuffle through a mass of pieces to find an elusive wall or stair tread.

If you work slowly and carefully, taking 1 unit at a time, you'll be surprised at how smoothly the work will go. The construction of each unit is arranged in a logical manner, so follow the steps as they are written.

Because measurements are, in some cases, as small as ⅛ inch (3), we suggest that you check each measurement against the portion of the house you are assembling. The width of a saw cut or a loosely-glued joint can throw off the fit. Perform temporary assembly wherever possible to make sure of the fit before permanently attaching the part on which you are working.

Many of the trim pieces are cut from the pine board. If you are truly a beginner in the woodshop, you may wish to purchase smaller-sized wood from which to cut these parts. For instance, all of the wall-to-floor and wall-to-ceiling joints are reinforced with ⅛-inch (3) wide corner-round molding. To cut the molding from the pine board, it is necessary to rout and cut to very small dimensions. As an alternative, you can purchase ¼-inch (6.35) diameter dowel rod, and split it into quarters.

You may, understandably, wish to forego entirely the pleasure of this process. If so, many of these small trim pieces can be purchased at hobby shops or stores that specialize in miniatures. As you read through the directions, make a note of the trim pieces you wish to purchase ready-made, or of the smaller sizes of wood you'll need to buy.

It will save a great deal of tedious painting if you will assemble the entire house and paint it (it can be spray painted) before adding the trim. Cut, assemble, and paint the trim pieces before you attach them to the house.

If you follow these suggestions, we know you'll breeze right through this project. Good luck, and have fun!

Back Section   You'll begin by cutting all of the exterior and interior walls and floors for the back half of the doll house. All parts are cut from plywood, unless otherwise specified. The interior walls and floors are joined together by a system of interconnecting, ¼-inch (6.35) wide slots.

1. Cut 1 Exterior Back as shown in **Figure A.** Transfer the placement markings for the First and Second Floors and Interior Walls. Cut the window and door openings as shown.

2. Cut 2 Exterior Side Walls **(Figure B).** Transfer the placement markings for the First and Second Floors and Interior Walls. Cut the window openings where indicated on the drawing.

3. Cut 2 Interior Walls as shown in **Figure C.** Transfer the placement markings for the First and Second Floors and cut two ¼-inch (6.35) wide slots, each 5 inches (127) long, where indicated.

4. Cut 2 Interior Floors **(Figure D).** Transfer the placement markings for the Interior Walls and cut two ¼-inch (6.35) wide slots, each 5 inches (127) long, as shown. On the Second Floor only, cut the opening for the staircase.

5. Cut 1 Attic Floor **(Figure E)** with a staircase opening as shown.

Figure A

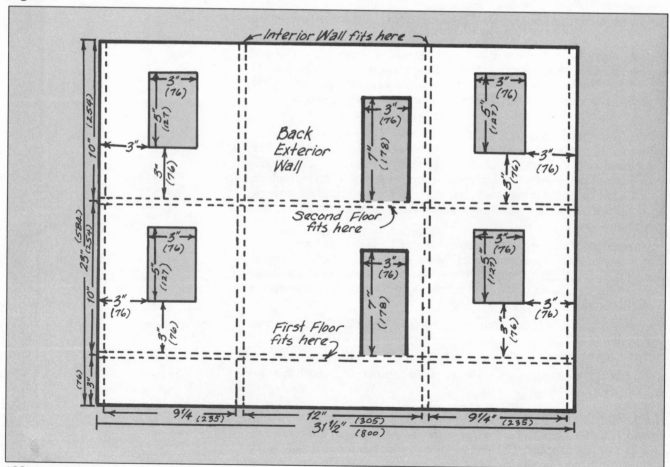

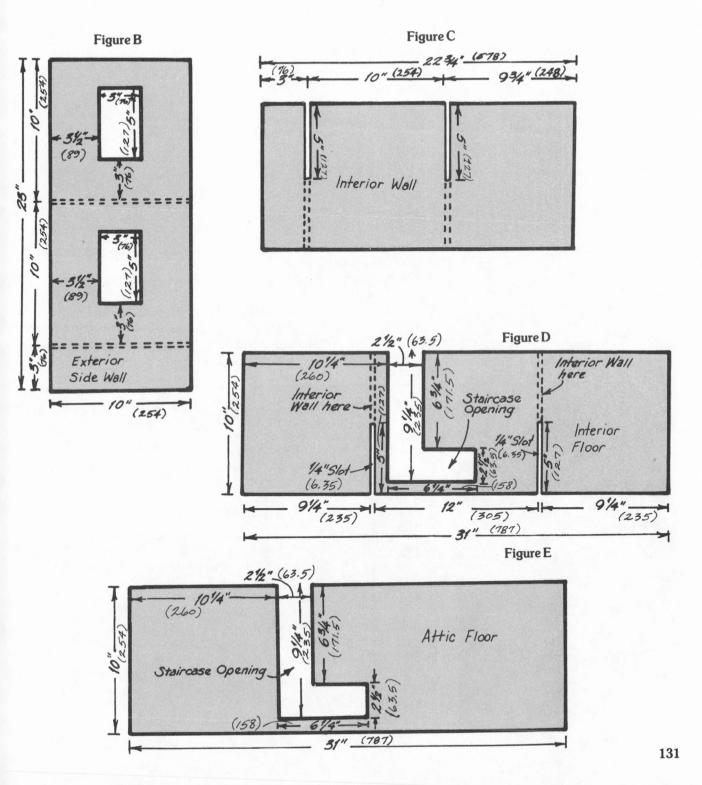

Figure B

Figure C

Interior Wall

Figure D

Interior Wall here

Interior Wall here

Staircase Opening

Interior Floor

Figure E

Staircase Opening

Attic Floor

Exterior Side Wall

Figure H

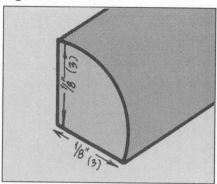

6. Connect the First and Second Floors to the Interior Walls **(Figure F)** by fitting the proper slots together.

7. Nail the Attic Floor to the tops of the Interior Walls **(Figure G).** Add the Exterior Side and Back Walls as shown.

8. Cut ⅛-inch (3) wide corner molding **(Figure H)** from the pine board or from ¼-inch (6.35) diameter dowel rod. You'll need 30 pieces, each 10 inches (254) long. Glue 1 length of molding along each wall-to-floor and wall-to-ceiling joint on the inside, as shown in **Figure G.**

Figure F

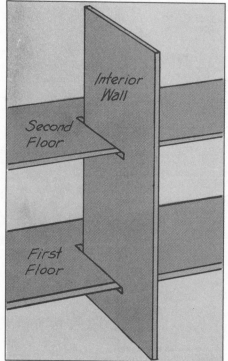

Figure G

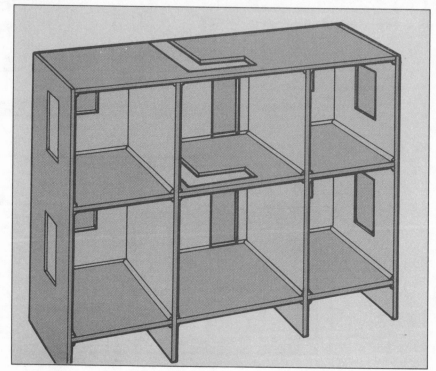

9. Cut 3 Roof Brace Supports to fit flush with the tops of the Exterior Side and Back Walls. A full-size pattern (end view) is given in **Figure I.** Cut 2 Supports each 11 inches (280) long and 1 Support 33 inches (839) long. Attach them to the Exterior Walls as shown in **Figure J.** You can miter the corners where the Brace Supports meet, or butt them together and trim the ends to fit flush.

10. Cut 11 Roof Braces, each ⅝ x 7 inches (16 x 178), from the pine board. Miter the ends as shown in **Figure K.** Install the Roof Braces on top of the Brace Supports **(Figures J and L),** placing 7 Braces along the Back Support and 1 Brace at each end of the Side Supports. You may wish to glue a small block of wood to the Attic Floor at the end of each Brace, to add stability.

Figure I

Figure J

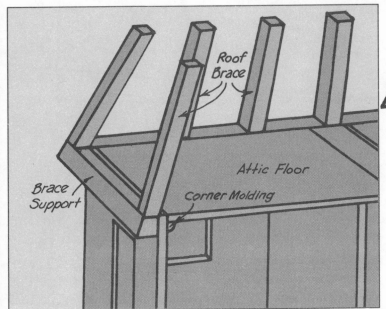

Figure K

Figure L

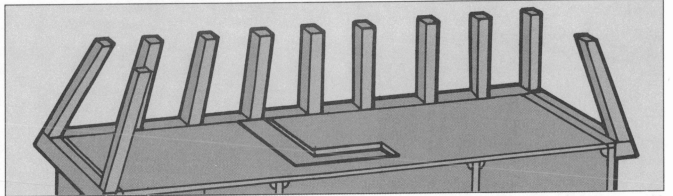

11. Cut 1 Roof, 2 Side Roofs, and 1 Back Roof as shown in **Figure M**. Attach the Roof over the tops of the Roof Braces, trimming or sanding the Braces until the Roof is level. Attach the Back and Side Roofs to the angled Roof Braces **(Figure N)**. It may be necessary to trim the edges of the Back and Side Roofs to achieve a good fit. Don't panic if there are slight gaps, as the Roof will be covered later with shingles and joint trim.

Figure M

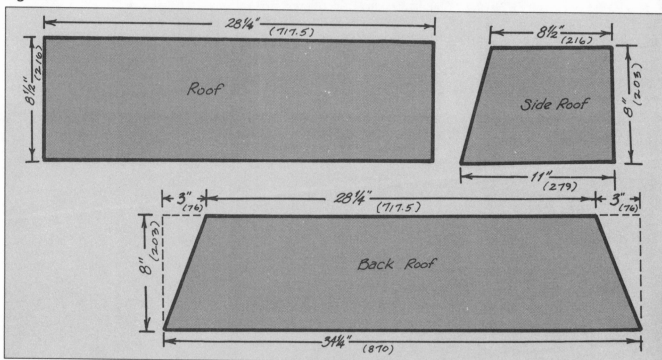

Figure N

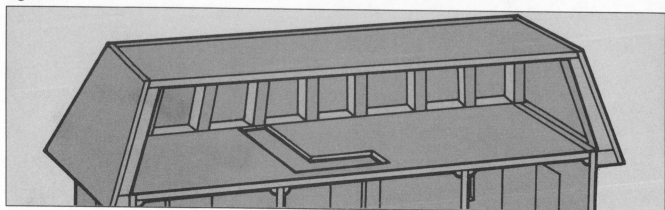

Front section   Each bay at the front of the doll house has 4 walls; 1 Center Bay Wall, 2 Side Bay Walls, and 1 Inner Bay Wall.

1. Cut 4 Side Bay Walls and 2 Center Bay Walls, as shown in **Figure O.** Transfer the placement markings for the First and Second Floors and cut the window openings where indicated.

2. The Inner Bay Walls extend into the doll house to become interior walls. Cut 2 Inner Bay Walls as shown in **Figure P.** Transfer the placement markings for the First and Second Floors and Center Walls. Cut the window openings and two ¼-inch (6.35) wide slots, each 4 inches (102) long, as shown.

Figure O

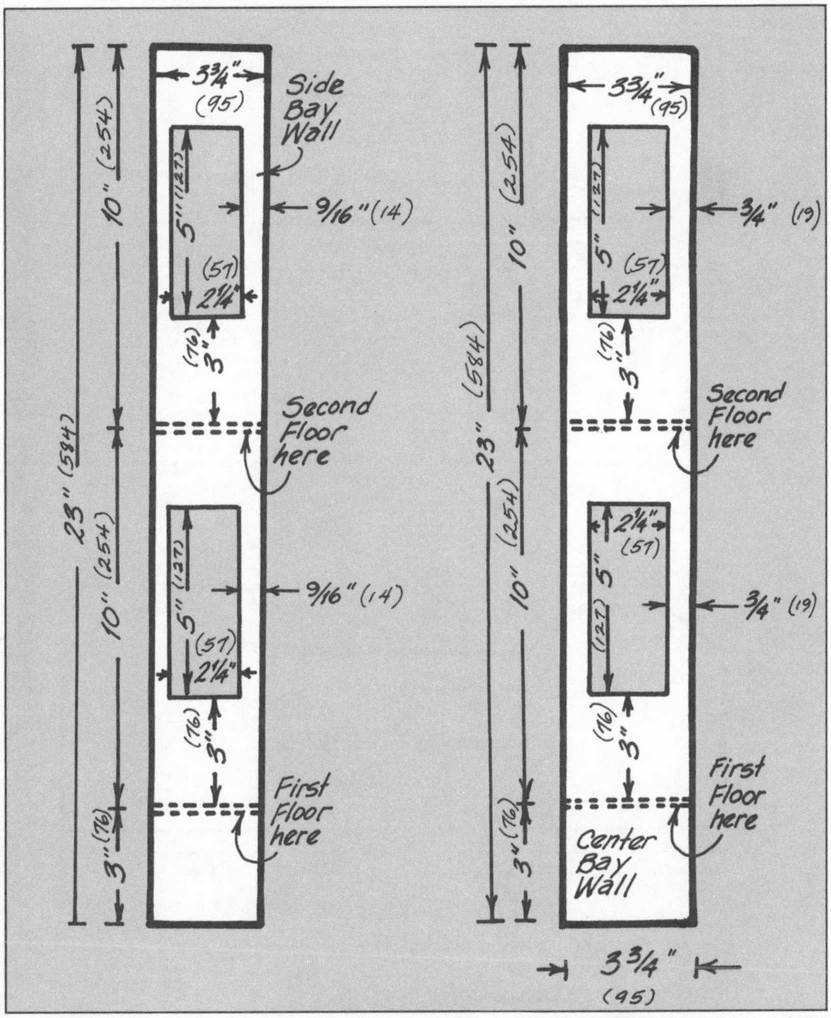

Figure P

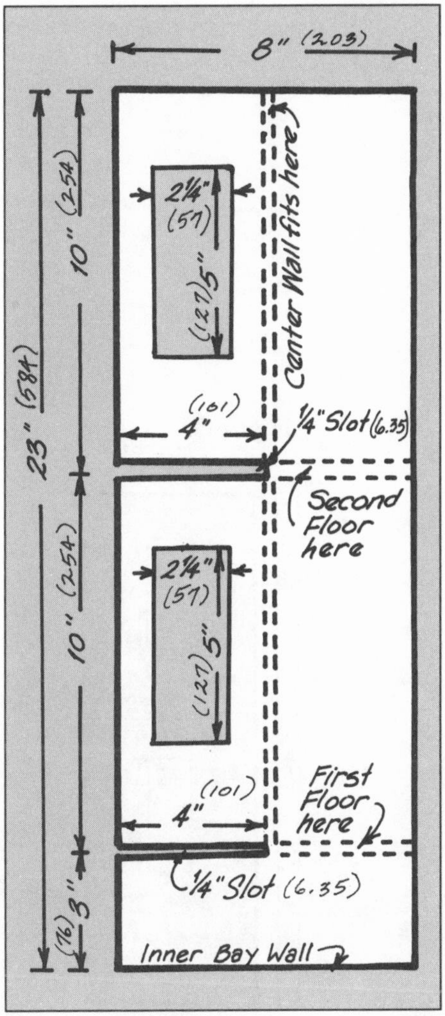

3. Cut 2 Exterior Side Walls **(Figure Q).** Transfer the placement markings for the First and Second Floors and cut the window openings where indicated.

4. Cut the First and Second Floors as shown in **Figure R.** Transfer the placement markings for the Interior and Center Walls. Cut two ¼-inch (6.35) wide slots, each 4 inches (102) long, along the Interior Wall markings, as shown.

Figure R

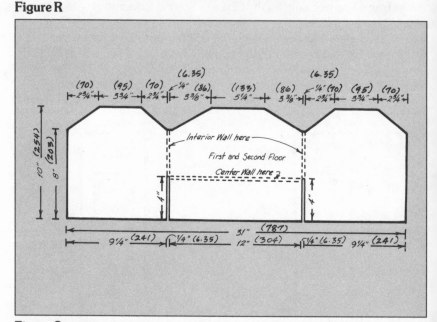

Figure S

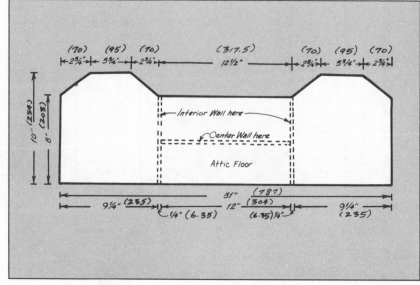

Figure Q

Figure T

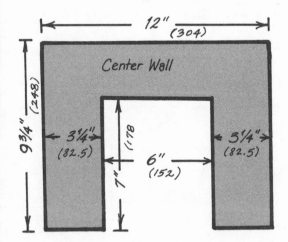

Center Wall

12" (304)

9¾" (248)

3¼" (82.5)

7" (178)

6" (152)

3¼" (82.5)

Figure U

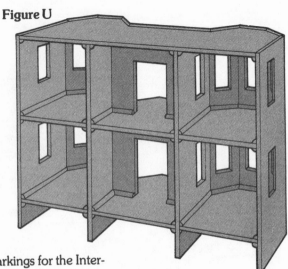

5. Cut 1 Attic Floor **(Figure S)**. Transfer the placement markings for the Interior and Center Walls.

6. Cut 2 Center Walls **(Figure T)**. Cut the door openings where indicated.

7. Figure U shows the floor and wall assembly. Connect the First and Second Floors to the Inner Bay Walls, matching the slots as you did for the back section of the doll house (see **Figure F**). Add the 2 Center Walls, and nail the Attic Floor over the tops of the Inner Bay Walls. Attach the Exterior Bay and Side Walls, as shown.

8. Cut about 30 feet (9144) of ⅛-inch (3) wide corner molding, as you did for the doll house back (see **Figure H**). Glue a length of the molding along each wall-to-floor and wall-to-ceiling joint, as shown in **Figure U.** (Yes, that does include all of those short bay-wall joints. Just breathe deeply and consider it a meditation on the importance of detail work.)

9. Cut Roof Brace Supports to fit flush with the tops of the Exterior Walls, using the end view pattern given in **Figure I.** Bear in mind that the Roof Brace Supports for the doll house front will not be cut to the same lengths as those for the back section, because of the bays. Cut each Brace Support a little longer than the top of the wall it will be attached to, so that you can miter or trim the ends to fit together. If necessary, refer back to **Figure J,** which shows Brace Support assembly for the doll house back.

10. Cut 13 Roof Braces, each ⅝ x 7 inches (16 x 178), as you did for the back roof. Miter the ends, using the pattern given in **Figure K.** Install the Roof Braces over the Brace Supports, placing them as shown in **Figure V.**

11. Scale drawings for the front roof sections are given in **Figure W.** Cut l Roof, and the following vertical roof pieces: 1 Center Roof, 2 Side Roofs, and 2 each of Roof Sections 1 through 4.

12. Attach the Roof over the Roof Braces, trimming or sanding the Braces as necessary, so that the Roof is level. Install the vertical roof pieces as shown in **Figure X,** trimming the edges to fit.

Figure V

Figure W

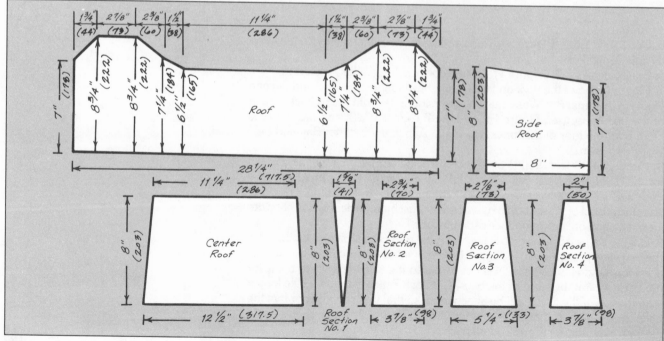

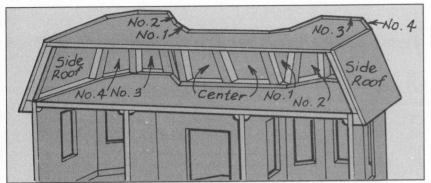

Figure X

Front porches and steps

1. Cut 2 Side Enclosures and 1 Center Enclo-sure **(Figure Y).** Miter the side edges of the Center Enclosure, and install the Enclosures underneath the lower porch floor **(Figure Z).**

2. Cut 4 Side Railings, each 4¼ inches (108) long, and 1 Center Railing, 5¾ inches (147) long, from the purchased decorative railing material. Cut 2 Porch Posts, each 9 ¾ inches (248) long, from the 1-inch (25) diameter wooden dowel rod.

3. Cut out the lower portion of each Porch Post to accommodate the Side Rail-ing, as shown in **Figure AA.** Trim 2 of the Side Railing sections to fit between the Posts and the Inner Bay Walls on the lower porch. Attach the Posts and Side Railings to the lower porch floor. Attach the tops of the Posts to the under-side of the upper porch floor.

4. Trim, fit, and attach 1 Center and 2 Side Railing sections to the edge of the upper porch floor **(Figure AA).**

Figure AA

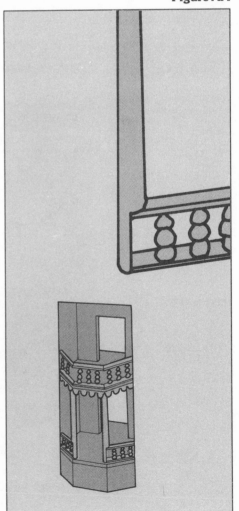

Figure Y

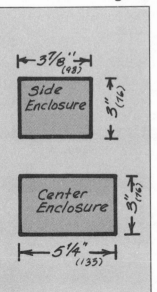

Figure Z

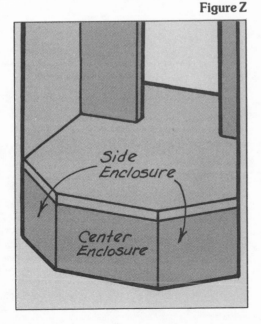

5. Patterns for the scalloped Upper Porch Trim are given in **Figure BB.** Cut 1 Center section and 2 Side sections. Trim the edges to fit, and attach them under the upper porch floor. Refer to **Figure AA** for placement.

6. Drawings are given in **Figure CC** for the parts required to build the front steps. Cut 2 Side Supports, 1 Back Support, 1 Upper Tread, 3 Lower Treads, and 4 Risers. Assembly of the stairs is shown in **Figure DD.** Attach the Back Support and Risers between the 2 Side Supports. Round off the front edges of the Treads before adding them to the assembly. Glue the assembled stairs to the front porch of the doll house.

Doors and windows   You'll need to make 2 complete double doors for the doll house front, to the dimensions given in the assembly diagram, **Figure EE.** To create the single doors for the doll house back, make 2 Frames, each ½ the width of the Frame for the double doors.

Figure BB

Figure CC

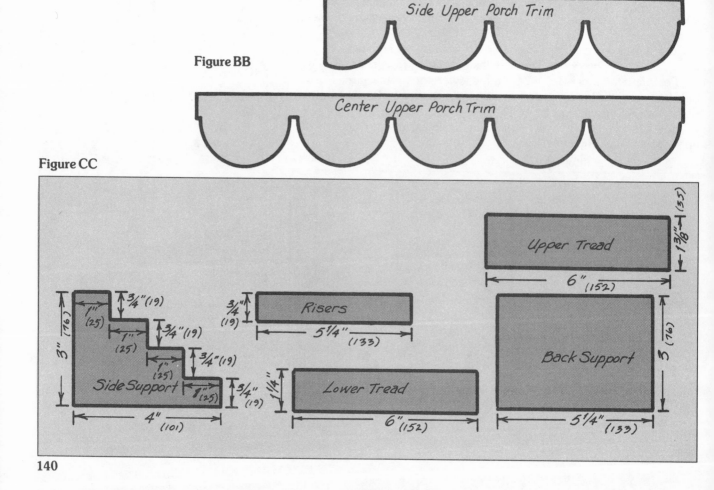

1. To make the Frames, start with ½ x ½-inch (13 x 13) wood stripping (purchased, or cut from the pine board). Rout a long piece of the stripping with a rabbet or dado bit to remove a quarter section. The Frame pictured in the assembly diagram (**Figure EE**) shows what the stripping looks like when it has been routed correctly.

2. Cut 3 lengths of the routed strip for each Frame; 1 a little longer than the length of the Frame top, and 2 a little longer than the length of the Frame side. Miter the strips at the upper corners, and glue the pieces together. Be sure that the routed edges are on the outside of the assembled frames.

3. Cut a ⅛ x ¼-inch (3 x 6) strip of wood to fit across the bottom of each door Frame, between the side pieces.

4. Install 1 Frame in each of the door openings in the doll house, placing the wider portion of each Frame on the outside of the wall.

5. Make 6 Doors to the dimensions given in **Figure EE.** Use the same technique as you did for the Frames to create the routed stripping, but place the routed edges toward the center, as shown, when assembling the Doors.

Figure DD

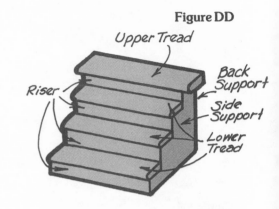

Figure EE

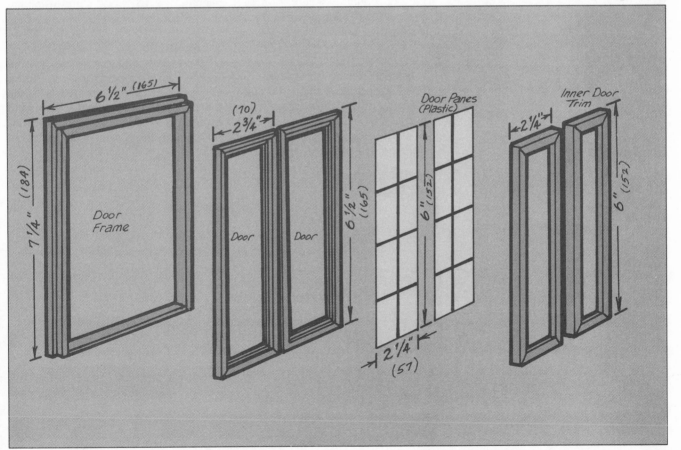

6. Cut lengths of ¼ x ¼-inch (6 x 6) wood stripping for the Inner Door Trim. Miter the ends and assemble the strips as shown to fit the routed inner edges of the Doors. The Trim will hold the Door Window Panes in place.

7. Cut 6 Door Window Panes from the clear plastic, following the dimensions given in **Figure EE**. Cut Window Pane Molding strips, ⅛ inch (3) wide, from the self-adhesive label material. Cut the Molding strips to the proper lengths to create the criss-cross patterns, as shown in **Figure EE**. Apply the molding strips to the Door Window Panes.

8. Fit the Door Window Panes into the Doors, and secure them in place with the Inner Door Trims. Install the assembled Doors in the Frames. Attach 2 small hinges to each door/frame joint, on the exterior side.

9. There are 2 different window sizes for the doll house. You'll need to make 8 large windows and 20 small windows. Dimensions for the Window Frames, Panes, Moldings, and Trims are given in **Figure FF**. The windows are cut and assembled like the doors.

10. Cut and assemble the Window Frames as you did the Door Frames, routing out a quarter section of a ½ x ½-inch (13 x 13) wood strip. Install the Frames in the window openings with the wider portion of each Frame on the inside of the wall.

11. Cut and assemble the Panes and Pane Moldings as you did for the doors.

12. Window Trim is used to secure the Panes in place and to cover the exterior sides of the window openings. The Window Trim pieces are shown in **Figure FF**. The decorative top and bottom sections of the Window Trim can be easily made by routing the edges of a board which has been cut to the proper width, and slicing off thin pieces, as shown in **Figure FF**. When you have cut the Window Trim sections, place the Window Panes on the outside of the window openings, and secure them in place with the Trim.

Figure FF

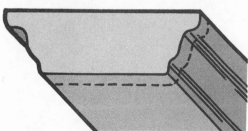

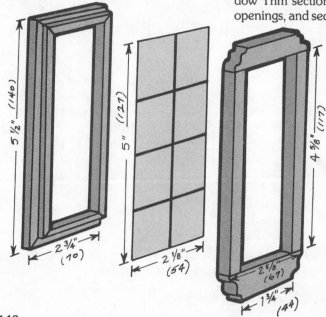

For Larger Windows:

Frame	3½ x 5½ inches (89 x 140)
Panel	3 x 5 inches (76 x 127)
Vertical Trim	4⅝ x ⅜ inches (117 x 9.5)
Horizontal Trim	3¾ inches (95) long

Figure GG

Staircases   There are 2 inner staircases; 1 from the first to the second story, and 1 from the second story to the attic. Each staircase has an upper and lower section. We have provided directions for 1 complete staircase, so when you've finished building 1, take a deep breath and make another.

1. Drawings for the staircase pieces are given in **Figure GG.** Cut out the 7 pattern pieces in the following quantities: 2 Upper Frames, 1 Lower Outside Frame, 1 Lower Inside Frame, 1 Landing Tread, 1 Upper Tread, 11 Treads, and 13 Risers.

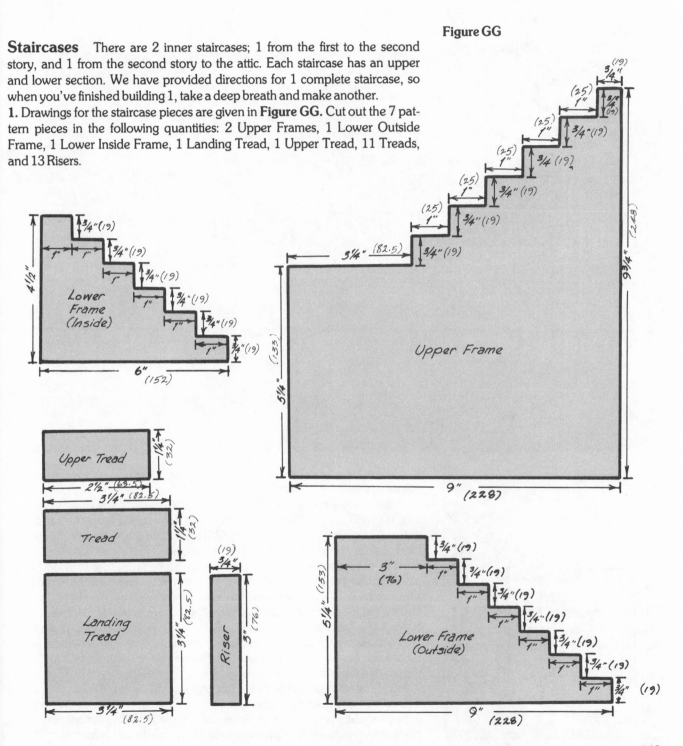

Figure HH

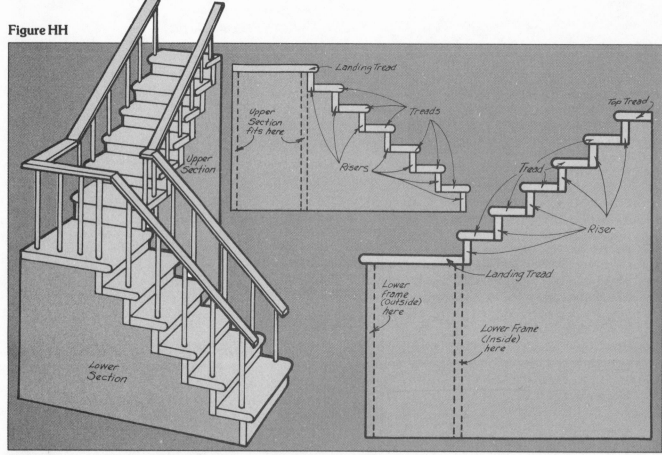

Figure II

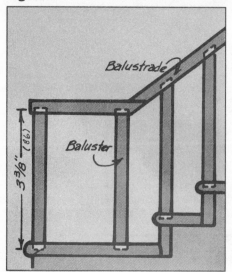

2. Assemble the upper and lower staircase sections as you did the front steps, following the diagram given in **Figure HH.**

3. Drill 2 shallow sockets, ¼-inch (6.35) in diameter, in each Tread to accommodate the Balusters. Placement of the holes is shown in **Figures HH and II.**

4. Cut 28 Balusters, each 3⅜ inches (86) long, from the ¼-inch (6.35) diameter dowel rod. Glue 1 Baluster into each of the holes in the stair Treads.

5. Refer to **Figure HH,** and cut 6 lengths of ½ x ⅜-inch (13 x 10) wood stripping to make a Balustrade, which will fit on top of the Balusters. Measure each separate section of your staircase carefully to determine the lengths of stripping you'll need to cut, and be sure to allow a little extra for mitering the ends.

6. Mark the spots where the tops of the Balusters will fit into the Balustrade. Drill a shallow socket, ¼ inch (6.35) in diameter, into the underside of the Balustrade at each mark, and glue the Balusters into the holes, trimming the tops so that the Balustrade fits evenly.

7. Install the staircase between the first and second stories. Repeat the cutting and assembly procedures to make the second staircase. We know that repeating a procedure is not as much fun as doing it the first time, but grit your teeth and persevere. As Mom (Mum) was fond of saying, it builds character.

Figure JJ

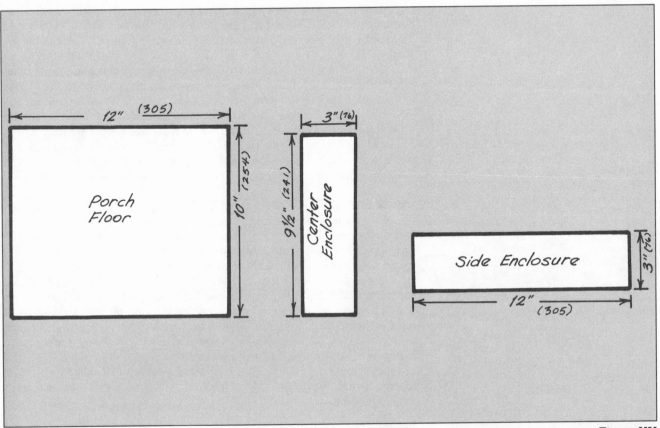

Back porch and steps **1.** Refer to **Figure JJ,** and cut the following porch pieces: 2 Floors, 1 Center Enclosure, and 2 Side Enclosures. Cut 4 Posts, each 9¾ inches (248) long, from 1-inch (25) diameter dowel rod.

2. Figure KK shows the back porch assembly. Install the 3 Enclosure sections underneath the Floor, flush with the edges. Attach the 4 Posts, 1 at each corner, leaving enough room between the Posts and the edges of the Floor to fit the railings. Use the remaining Floor piece as a Roof, trimming the tops of the Posts so that the Roof is level.

3. Cut lengths of the purchased decorative railing to fit around the 3 outer edges of the Floor and Roof. Leave a 5-inch (127) gap in the railing on 1 side of the Floor, as shown in **Figure KK.** Miter the ends of the railing pieces to fit together at the corners.

4. Cut and assemble the back steps exactly as you did the front steps, referring back to **Figures CC, DD,** and the instructions for making the front steps in the "Front porches and steps" section above. Attach the steps to the back porch at the gap in the side railing.

5. Attach the completed back porch to the doll house back, placing it so that the back doors open onto the porch.

Figure KK

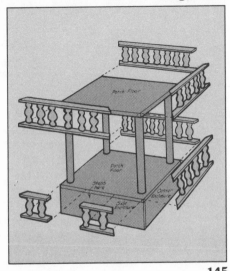

Fireplace **1.** You can add a fireplace to any room you wish. For each fireplace, cut 2 Sides, 1 Inner Top Wall, 2 Inner Side Walls, 1 Front, 1 Floor, and 1 Mantel from plywood, to the dimensions given in **Figure LL**. Assemble the pieces as shown.

2. Decorative molding is used to hide the raw edges of the wood on the fireplace structure. The Mantel Molding (shown already attached to the Mantel in the assembly diagram) is ⅝-inch (16) wide, cut to fit beneath the front and sides of the Mantel. The ends should be mitered to fit at each corner. Any size molding may be substituted, and you may trim the width of the Mantel.

3. The Front Trim and Floor Trim pieces are cut from ¼-inch (6.35) molding. Cut 3 pieces to fit around the fireplace opening, and 3 additional pieces to cover the front and side edges of the Floor. Miter all ends to fit at the corners.

Finishing **1.** You'll need about 1,200 shingles for the doll house roof. Miniature shingles are available in many hobby shops, or you may wish to make your own. There are 2 methods you can use to make the shingles. The first is to purchase tongue depressors (you'll need 600). Cut a 1½-inch (38) length from both rounded ends of each depressor. As an alternative, you can cut the shingles from a 7-foot (2134) length of pine 1 x 4 (17 x 89) using the routing and slicing technique described for making the Window Trim. In this instance, use a corner round bit to completely round off both long edges of the pine board. Cut the routed board into ⅛-inch (3) thick slices and cut each slice in half to create 2 shingles. A full-size pattern and placement guide is given in **Figure MM**. The shingles can be smaller than the size shown in the diagram, but they should not be any larger. Attach the first row of shingles so that it slightly overlaps the lower edge of the roof. Add subsequent rows as shown, overlapping each row.

Figure LL

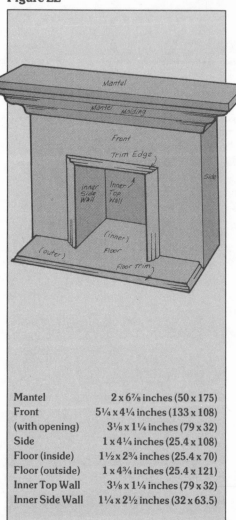

Mantel	2 x 6⅞ inches (50 x 175)
Front	5¼ x 4¼ inches (133 x 108)
(with opening)	3⅛ x 1¼ inches (79 x 32)
Side	1 x 4¼ inches (25.4 x 108)
Floor (inside)	1½ x 2¾ inches (25.4 x 70)
Floor (outside)	1 x 4¾ inches (25.4 x 121)
Inner Top Wall	3⅛ x 1¼ inches (79 x 32)
Inner Side Wall	1¼ x 2½ inches (32 x 63.5)

Figure MM

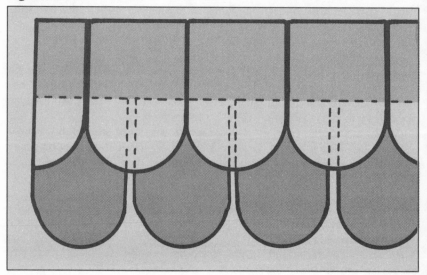

Figure NN

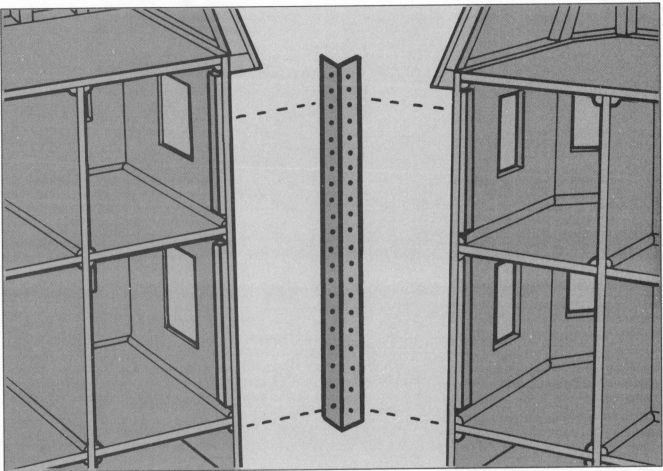

Figure OO

2. Cut sections of the decorative railing to fit straight across the front and sides of the roof. Miter the ends, and install the railing sections.

3. If you are going to hinge the 2 halves of the doll house, cut 4 Hinge Supports, each ¾ x 1 x 9¾ inches (17 x 25 x 248) from the pine board. Glue the strips to the inside of the Exterior Side Walls (**Figure NN**). Attach the piano hinge to the outside of the walls as shown, using small screws.

4. Look closely at the drawing of the finished doll house and you will see that all of the exterior wall and roof joints are covered by trim. The trim serves to hide any gaps or uneven edges. Cut long strips of wood, each ⅛ x ¼ inch (3 x 6). Miter 1 long edge of each strip as shown in **Figure OO**. Glue the trim pieces over the wall and roof joint angles.

Heave a monstrous sigh of relief and treat yourself to something refreshing while you collect pats on the back and an "attaboy!" or "attagirl!" as the case may be.

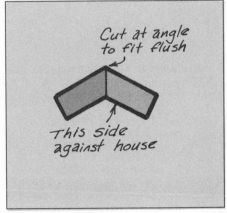

Cut at angle to fit flush

This side against house

Rocking Doll Cradle

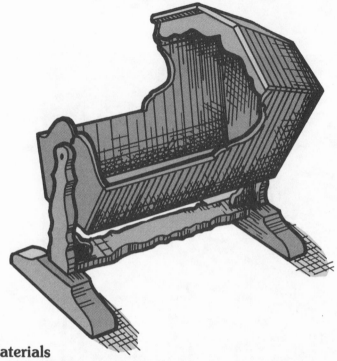

Rocking wooden cradles like this doll-size model have remained popular for centuries. The canopy originally served to keep cold drafts away from sleeping babies. When your children outgrow their dolls, you'll have an attractive magazine rack or planter.

Metric equivalents in millimeters are indicated in parentheses.

Materials

4 x 4-foot (1219 x 1219) piece of lumber-core plywood, ¼ inch (6) thick.
12-foot (3658) length of 1 x 3-inch (17 x 64) lumber, preferably hardwood.
5½-inch (140) length of 1 x 4-inch (17 x 89) lumber, preferably hardwood.
6-inch (152) length of ½-inch (13) diameter wooden dowel rod.
Handful each of ½-inch (13) long and 1¼-inch (32) long finishing nails.
Carpenter's wood glue, medium and fine sandpaper, kraft paper, and a small quantity of wood filler.
1 quart (1 liter) of non-toxic paint or stain in the color of your choice.

Tools

Saber saw (or coping saw), hammer, miter box, nailset, paint brush, and an electric or hand drill with ⅝-inch (15) and ½-inch (13) diameter bits.

Cutting the pieces　**1.** Scale drawings for the Cradle pieces are given in **Figure A.** Enlarge the drawings to full-size patterns on kraft paper.
2. Cut the following pieces from plywood: 1 Headboard, 1 Footboard, 2 Sides, 2 Canopy Sides, 1 Canopy Trim, and 1 Canopy Center. In addition, cut 1 Floor, 5 x 21¾ inches (127 x 553). Drill a ⅝-inch (15) diameter hole through the Headboard and Footboard where indicated on the scale drawing.
3. Cut the following pieces from the 1 x 3-inch (17 x 64) lumber: 1 Headboard Support, 1 Footboard Support, 4 Outer Legs, 4 Inner Legs, and 1 Lower Support. Cut 2 Corner Supports from the 1 x 4-inch (17 x 89) lumber.
4. Drill a ½-inch (13) diameter hole through the Headboard Support and Footboard Support where indicated on the scale drawings.
5. Cut the wooden dowel rod into two 3-inch (76) lengths. Sand all of the pieces to eliminate sharp edges.

Figure A

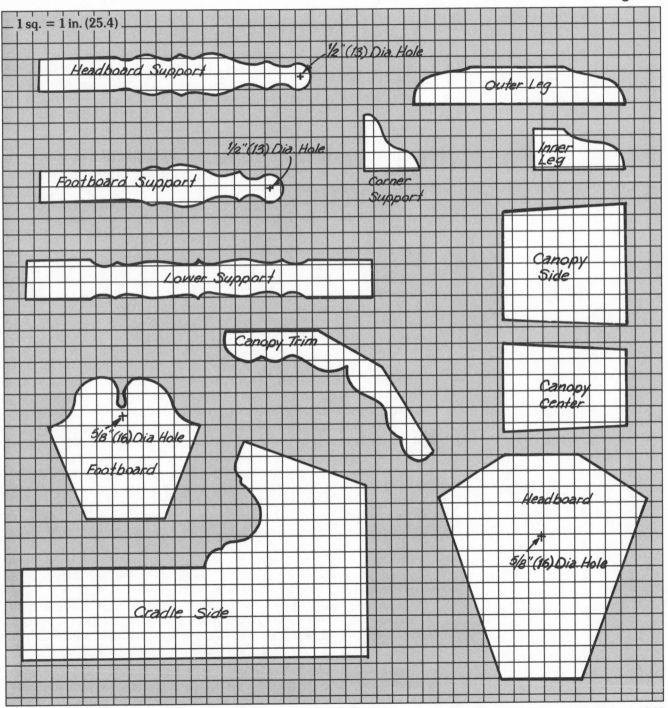

1 sq. = 1 in. (25.4)

Headboard Support

½" (13) Dia. Hole

Outer Leg

Inner Leg

½" (13) Dia. Hole

Footboard Support

Corner Support

Canopy Side

Lower Support

Canopy Trim

Canopy Center

5/8" (16) Dia Hole

Footboard

Headboard

5/8" (16) Dia Hole

Cradle Side

Assembly   The assembly is divided into 2 units: the cradle box and canopy, and the cradle support assembly. Because some trimming and fitting will be necessary, we suggest that you perform temporary assemblies on all units before you apply glue or recess the nails. (For a good lesson in frustration, try extracting a recessed finishing nail. We had plenty of practice at that in our early woodworking days, and let me tell you, we have frustration down to a real science!)

Cradle box and canopy   1. **Figure B** shows the assembly of the cradle box and canopy. Form the cradle box by temporarily nailing the Headboard, Footboard, and Floor between the 2 Sides.
2. Add the Canopy sides and Center so that they cover the raw edges of the Headboard and Sides. It will be necessary to miter the long upper edges of the Canopy Sides and both long edges of the Canopy Center so that they fit together properly, as shown in **Figure C.**
3. Install the Canopy Trim underneath the canopy, between the cradle Sides. The Canopy Trim should be flush with the front raw edges of the canopy and the cradle Sides.
4. Permanently assemble the cradle box and canopy using glue and recessing the nails. Fill the nail holes and any slight gaps between the pieces with wood filler, and sand the resulting lumps. (It is one of Murphy's Woodworking Laws that wood filler, however carefully applied, always leaves lumps.)

Cradle support assembly   1. An assembly diagram for the cradle supports is given in **Figure D.** Begin by assembling the legs. Sandwich the Headboard Support between 2 Inner Legs (as shown in the enlarged detail drawing, **Figure D**), and attach all 3 pieces to 1 Outer Leg. Attach another Outer Leg to the opposite side of the assembly. Form another leg assembly using the Footboard Support and the remaining Outer and Inner Legs.
2. Attach the Lower Support between the 2 leg assemblies as shown in **Figure D.** Add Corner Supports to the angles where the Lower Support meets the Headboard and Footboard Supports.
3. Permanently assemble the cradle support system using glue and nails. Recess the nails, fill the nail holes with wood filler, and sand the resulting lumps.

Finishing   1. Carefully sand all of the sharp edges and inspect the Cradle and support assembly for splinters or rough spots. Paint or stain both assemblies and the 2 short lengths of dowel rod.
2. Hold the Cradle between the upright supports, aligning the hole in the Headboard with the hole in the Headboard Support. Insert a length of dowel rod through the 2 holes. Insert the remaining length of dowel rod through the aligned holes in the Footboard and Footboard Support.

Place a soft blanket in the Cradle, find a toddler with a doll who needs rocking, and show 'em how it's done. If the dolls are otherwise employed, do what our kids do — rock the family kitten or puppy — gently.

Figure B

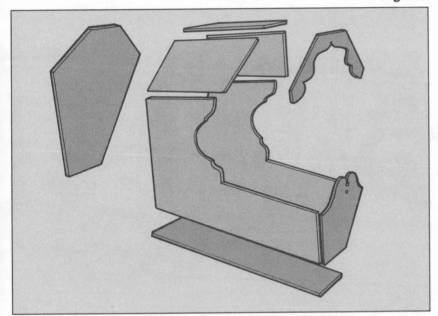

Figure C

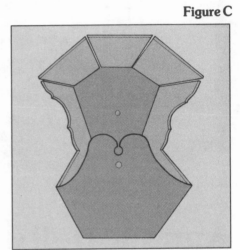

Figure D

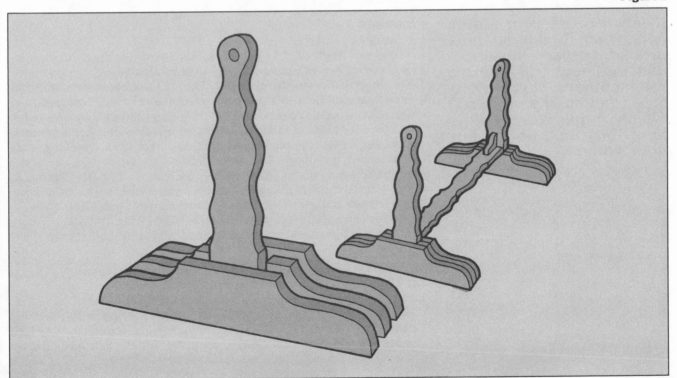

Antique Doll Beds

If the dolls in your family fuss when bed time rolls around, perhaps these elegant doll beds will improve their tempers. This is a perfect beginner's project, which requires very little know-how and only a few hour's time.

Metric equivalents in millimeters are indicated in parentheses.

Materials

For the Canopy Bed:

2½-foot (762) length of 1 x 12-inch (17 x 286) clear white pine.

11 x 17-inch (279 x 432) piece of ⅛-inch (3) thick plywood.

Three 3-foot (915) lengths of ⅜-inch (9.5) diameter wooden dowel rod. (You'll have half of 1 rod left over, but you can use it for the Poster Bed.)

4 decorative wooden posts, each 11 to 12 inches (280 to 305) long and ¾ to 1 inch (19 to 25) in diameter. These are usually sold in home improvement centers as shelving components, and have plain dowel-like ends, which should be no larger than ½-inch (13) in diameter.

4 wooden drawer pulls or finials, each 1 to 2 inches (25 to 51) long and ¾ to 1 inch (19 to 25) in diameter. These are also available in home improvement centers, and are usually manufactured with screws already in them.

10½ x 16½-inch (267 x 419) piece of 2-inch (51) thick foam rubber.

16 finishing nails: eight ¾ inch (19) long, and eight 1½ inches (38) long.

For the Poster Bed:

31-inch (788) length of 1 x 10-inch (17 x 235) clear white pine.

13 x 18-inch (330 x 457) piece of ⅛-inch (3) thick plywood.

1-foot (305) length of ⅜-inch (9.5) diameter wooden dowel rod (or use the length of dowel rod that will be left over from the Canopy Bed). The dowel rod will be used to assemble the bed frame (see the Assembly instructions in the Poster Bed section below). If you opt for the alternate method of assembly, you'll need 8 small gauge, flat head wood screws, each 2 inches (51) long, or 8 thin finishing nails, each 2 inches (51) long.

4 decorative wooden posts, each 13 to 15 inches (330 to 381) long and 1½ inches (38) square at the lower end. The exact size is not critical, as long as the posts have straight lower sides, at least 4½ inches (114) long, to which the bed frames can be attached.

13 x 18-inch (330 x 457) piece of 2-inch (51) thick foam rubber.

Medium and fine sandpaper, carpenter's wood glue, a small quantity of wood filler, kraft paper, carbon paper, and wood stain in the color of your choice.

Tools

Saber saw or coping saw, hammer, and an electric or hand drill with a ⅜-inch (9.5) diameter bit and a bit to match the diameter of the Canopy Bed post ends. If you choose not to use the doweling technique described below for assembly of the Poster Bed, you'll also need a drill bit to match the head diameter of the wood screws, and a bit slightly smaller than the shank diameter of the screws.

Canopy Bed

Cutting the pieces   **1.** Scale drawings for the Canopy Bed Headboard, Footboard, and Canopy Frame are given in **Figure A.** Enlarge the drawings to full-size patterns on kraft paper.

Figure A

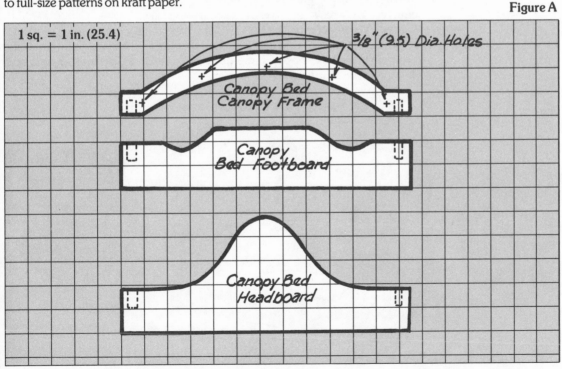

2. Cut 1 Headboard, 1 Footboard, and 2 Canopy Frames from the pine board. Cut the following additional pieces from the same material: 2 Sides, each 1¾ x 17 inches (44 x 432), and 2 Mattress Support Strips, each 1 x 17 inches (25 x 432). Sand all of the pieces.

3. Cut each of the dowel rods in half, so that you have six 18-inch (457) lengths. (You'll only use 5 — put 1 aside to use for the Poster Bed.)

4. Drill 5 holes through 1 Canopy Frame using the ⅜-inch (9.5) diameter bit. Placement of the holes is shown in the scale drawing, **Figure A.** Since a misaligned canopy would be highly disturbing to any well-bred dolly, use the drilled Canopy Frame as a guide to drill the holes in the remaining Frame.

5. Drill a shallow socket near each end of the Canopy Frames, Headboard, and Footboard, using the drill bit that matches the diameter of the post ends. The sockets should be drilled into the lower edges of the Canopy Frames, and into the upper edges of the Headboard and Footboard. Placement is indicated by dotted lines on the scale drawings.

Assembly   **1.** Center and glue a Mattress Support Strip to each bed Side, flush with the inside bottom edge. Secure the Strips with the shorter finishing nails. (You can see 1 of the Strips in **Figure B**.)

2. Assemble the bed frame (Headboard, Footboard, and Sides), butting the ends as shown in **Figure B.** Use glue and 2 of the longer finishing nails at each joint, recess the nails, and fill the holes with wood filler.

3. Attach 1 drawer pull to the bottom of the bed frame at each corner.

4. Spread a thin coat of glue on both ends of each dowel rod and insert the rod ends into the Canopy Frame holes **(Figure B).** Push the rod ends only ½ inch (13) into the holes.

Figure B

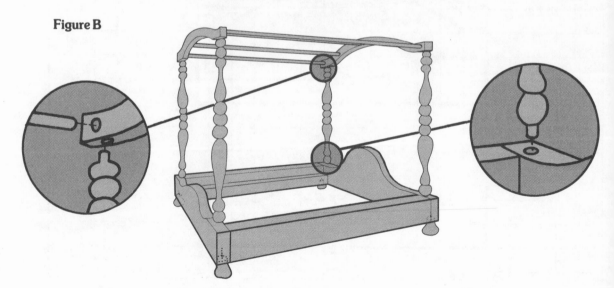

5. Insert the lower ends of the 4 bed posts into the Headboard and Footboard sockets. If the dowel ends are too long for the sockets, remove them and trim the ends. Perform the same testing procedure for the upper ends of the posts, which should fit into the sockets in the Canopy Frames. When you have achieved a good fit all around, glue the posts into the sockets.

6. Let the glue dry for a few hours. Inspect the bed for sharp edges, splinters, or rough spots, and sand wherever necessary. Stain the assembled bed.

7. Trim the small sheet of plywood so that it will fit inside the frame, resting on the Support Strips. Place the mattress on top of the plywood.

8. You can use any combination of fabric remnants, large cloth dinner napkins, and lace antimacassars for the bed spread and canopy cover. (In case you didn't know, antimacassars are decorative covers used to protect the back and arms of a chair or sofa. They are usually made of heavy lace or embroidered fine cotton and were popular for many generations, up until the early 1950's when streamlined, modern home decor became the vogue. The name "antimacassar" was derived from a commonly used hair oil called Macassar.)

Poster Bed
Cutting the pieces   **1.** Scale drawings for the Poster Bed Headboard and Footboard are given in **Figure C**. Enlarge the drawings to full-size patterns on kraft paper. Transfer the heart-shaped design to the Headboard pattern.

Figure C

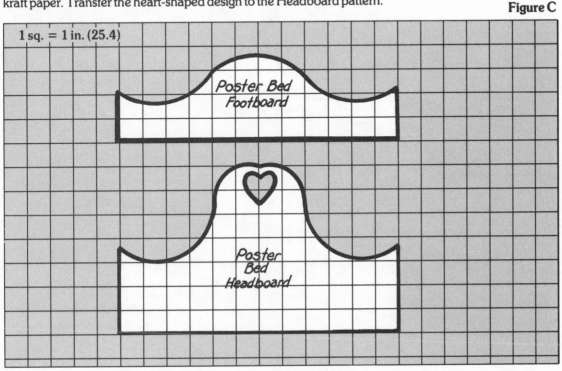

1 sq. = 1 in. (25.4)

Poster Bed
Footboard

Poster
Bed
Headboard

2. Cut the following pieces from the pine board: 1 Headboard, 1 Footboard, 2 Sides, each 2 x 18 inches (51 x 457), and 2 Mattress Support Strips, each 1 x 18 inches (25 x 457).

3. Use carbon paper to transfer the heart-shaped design from the paper pattern to the wooden Headboard. Drill a hole through the center of the design, insert the saw blade through the hole, and cut around the outline.

4. Sand all of the pieces to eliminate sharp edges. Don't forget to sand the inner edge of the heart-shaped cut out.

Figure D

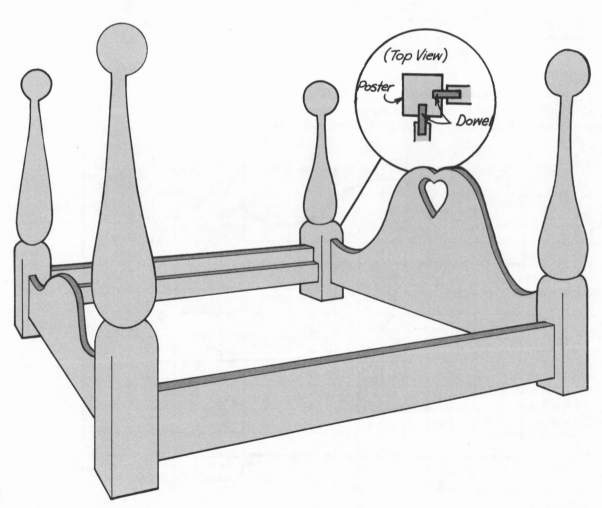

Figure E

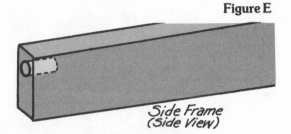

Side Frame (End View)

Side Frame (Side View)

Assembly **1.** Glue a Mattress Support Strip to each bed Side, flush with the lower inside edge. Secure the Strips with the smaller finishing nails.

2. Assembly of the Poster Bed is shown in **Figure D.** As you can see, the frame pieces (Headboard, Footboard, and Sides) are attached to the lower ends of the posts, not to each other. The preferred technique for connecting the pieces is called "doweling," shown in the enlarged detail drawing, **Figure D**. If you do not wish to use this technique, skip to step **5**, below.

3. To assemble the bed using the doweling technique, you'll need to cut eight 1½-inch (38) lengths from the wooden dowel rod. Drill a ¾-inch (19) deep dowel socket into each end of both bed Sides, ½ inch (13) from the upper edge and centered between the side edges **(Figure E)**. Drill a dowel socket into each end of the Headboard and Footboard, ½ inch (13) from the lower edge and centered between the side edges. Glue a dowel into each socket.

4. Arrange the frame sections and posts in the proper configuration and mark the positions where dowel sockets will be drilled in the posts. (Don't forget that the frame sections should be about ¾ inch [19] up off the floor.) Drill the sockets into the posts, spread glue on the exposed surfaces of the dowels, and assemble the bed. Skip to step **6** below.

5. For those of you who are not up to doweling today, there is an alternate method of assembling the Poster Bed. It will not look as professional as doweling, but it will take less time. When you have arranged the frame sections and posts into the proper configuration, with the frame sections raised to the correct height, simply drive long finishing nails or wood screws through the posts and into the frames. (If you use wood screws, pre-drill the holes, using the bit that is slightly smaller than the diameter of the screw shanks, to avoid splitting the posts and frames. You'll also need to drill a shallow socket for each screw head, using the matching-sized bit.) Recess the nails or countersink the screws, and fill the resulting holes with wood filler.

6. Inspect the bed for sharp edges, splinters, or rough spots, and sand wherever necessary. Stain the assembled bed.

7. Trim the small sheet of plywood to fit inside the bed frame. Insert it so that it rests on the Mattress Support Strips. Place the foam rubber mattress on top of the plywood.

8. Refer back to the final assembly instructions in the Canopy Bed section for suggestions on bed coverings. It is also quite simple to stitch up a small quilt to serve as a bed spread for the Poster Bed.

Congratulations! You've made your own beds. But we can't guarantee their continued existence if you try to lie in them.

Spoon Dolls

Trade your woodworking
equipment for a sewing
machine, and dress up a
pair of wooden kitchen
spoons to make these
charming dolls. No one
knows for certain who in-
vented the Spoon Doll, but
the concept serves to re-
mind us of a time when
people were short of ready-
made entertainment and
long on ingenuity.

Metric equivalents in millimeters are indicated in parentheses.

Materials

2 wooden kitchen spoons, each 10 inches (254) long.
10 x 21-inch (254 x 533) piece of calico fabric.
5 x 6-inch (127 x 152) piece of white fabric.
26-inch (660) length of 2½-inch (64) wide, white eyelet trim.
29-inch (737) length of ½-inch (13) wide, white lace trim.
8-inch (203) length of ⅛-inch (3) wide, white satin ribbon.
14-inch (356) length of ⅛-inch (3) wide satin ribbon, to match the calico.
½ yard (457) of unbleached muslin.
Small quantities of triple-strand yarn in 2 colors of your choice, for the hair.
6 x 7-inch (152 x 178) piece of brown felt.
6 x 11-inch (152 x 280) piece of checkered fabric for the boy's knickers.
9 x 10-inch (229 x 254) piece of cotton fabric for the boy's shirt.
2½ x 9-inch (64 x 229) piece of dark cotton fabric for the boy's suspenders.
1 x 2½-inch (25 x 64) piece of white felt for the boy's collar.
8-inch (203) length of ⅜-inch (10) wide striped trim, for the boy's bow tie.
Small quantities of non-toxic black, blue, and red paint, or non-toxic felt tip
    markers in those colors.
White glue, white thread, thread to match the boy's knickers, kraft paper or
    dressmaker's pattern paper, and a small quantity of polyester fiberfill.

Tools

Scissors, sewing needle, artist's fine paint brush (if you will be using paint in-
    stead of markers), and a tape measure.
A sewing machine will speed the costume-making, but all of the stitching can
    be done by hand quite easily.

Cutting the pieces   **1.** Enlarge the scale drawings given in **Figure A** to
full-size paper patterns.
2. For the girl's costume cut 2 Dresses and 1 Hat from the calico. Cut 1 Apron
from the white fabric. When cutting the Dress and Apron pieces, double the
fabric and place the designated edge of each pattern along the fold, so that
the resulting pieces are twice as large as the paper patterns.
3. Cut the following pieces for the boy's costume: 1 Hat and 1 Hat Bill from
brown felt; 1 Collar; 2 Shirts (using the shortened Dress pattern); and 2 Knickers. Note that the Shirt pattern should be placed on a fold.

Figure A

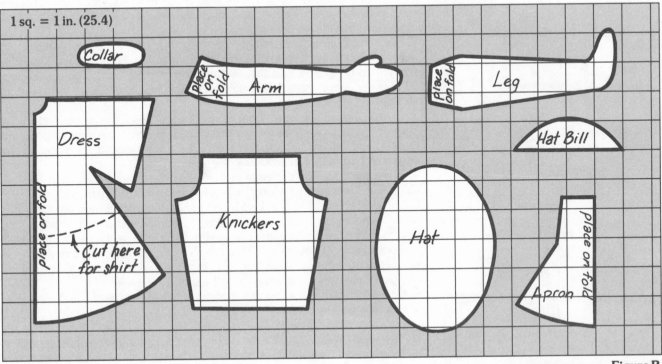

1 sq. = 1 in. (25.4)

Collar

Place on fold — Arm

Place on fold — Leg

Dress

Hat Bill

place on fold

Cut here for shirt

Knickers

Hat

place on fold

Apron

Figure B

4. Cut 4 each of the Arm and Leg patterns from unbleached muslin. Once again, place the designated edge of each pattern along a fold of doubled material each time you cut.

Assembly   **1.** Paint or draw facial features on the back of the bowl section of each wooden spoon. Our designs for the faces are shown in **Figure B**, but you can alter them to suit yourself.

2. Stitch 2 Arm pieces together, in 1 continous seam, near the raw edges (**Figure C**). Leave a 2-inch (51) opening at the center of 1 edge, as shown. Repeat, using the remaining 2 Arm pieces.

3. Stitch 2 Leg pieces together, as you did for the Arms, leaving an opening at the center of 1 edge. Repeat, using the remaining 2 Leg pieces.

4. Turn each of the stitched leg and arm pieces right side out. (Insert a pencil or other long, thin object to turn the thumbs and toes.) Stuff with fiberfill, carefully pushing the stuffing down into the hands and feet. Whipstitch the openings together, so that the dolls won't lose their stuffing, and place 3 lines of stitching through each hand, to create the fingers (**Figure C**). Use black paint or marker to color in a shoe on each foot.

5. Lay 1 arm assembly across the front of 1 spoon, just below the bowl (**Figure D**), and glue it in place. Attach 1 leg assembly near the end of the handle, on the same side of the spoon. Repeat this step to attach the remaining arm and leg assemblies to the remaining spoon.

Figure C

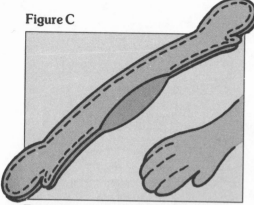

Figure D

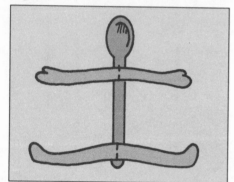

Figure E

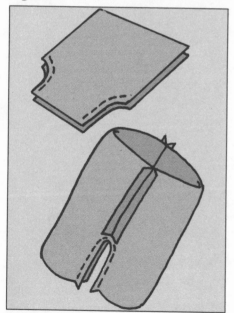

Girl's costume   **1.** Stitch a narrow hem around the entire Apron, and add eyelet trim to the lower edge. Sew a short length of white ribbon to each upper corner, for the straps. Center, and attach the remaining length of white ribbon across the waistline.

2. Place the 2 Dress sections right sides together, with the Apron sandwiched between. Stitch the shoulder seams, catching in the Apron straps. Stitch the side/underarm seams, catching in the Apron sashes, but keeping the lower edge of the Apron free of the seam lines. Add lace trim to each sleeve edge, and gather with basting stitches.

3. Cut a 2-inch (51) long slit from the neck edge, down the center back of the Dress. Slip the Dress over the girl doll's head, inserting the arms through the sleeves, and adjust the gathers to fit. Glue the slit closed, overlapping the edges, and glue a lace ruffle around the neck.

4. Baste stitch around the edge of the calico Hat. Gather, and stuff the Hat lightly with fiberfill. Stitch a length of eyelet trim around the gathered edge.

5. The doll's hair consists of braids and bangs. Cut nine 8-inch (203) lengths of yarn, and weave them into 1 long braid. Tie off the ends with short lengths of yarn. Stitch the center of the braid to the eyelet trim on the Hat, so that each end points slightly downward. Tie a length of narrow ribbon in a bow at each braid end. Cut approximately thirty 2½-inch (64) lengths of yarn for the bangs, and glue them over the upper edge of the spoon.

6. Glue the Hat in place. Make a bow from leftover strips of calico, and glue or stitch it to the lower edge of the Hat.

Boy's costume   **1.** Place the 2 Shirt pieces right sides together, and stitch up the shoulder and underarm/side seams. Hem the sleeve edges. Use a contrasting thread to make 2 straight lines of stitching, approximately ½ inch (13) apart, down the front of the Shirt.

2. Place the 2 Knicker pieces right sides together, and stitch the curved front and back seams (**Figure E**). Align and stitch the inner leg seam. Hem the waist and leg edges. Gather each leg edge slightly.

3. Slit the back neck edge of the Shirt, as you did for the Dress, and slip the Shirt over the boy's doll head. Insert the arms into the sleeves, and glue the slit closed. Cut 2 Suspender pieces, each 1¼ x 8 inches (32 x 203). Fold each piece in half lengthwise, and stitch close to the long edge. Turn right side out. Slip the Knickers onto the doll, and sew the Suspender ends in place.

4. Glue the Collar around the neck. Tie the striped trim into a bow, and glue it to the center front of the Collar.

5. Cut 3-inch (76) lengths of yarn for the boy's hair, and 2-inch (51) lengths for his bangs. Glue the hair to the back of the head, and the bangs over the upper edge.

6. Gather the edge of the Hat, and stuff lightly with fiberfill. Glue the Bill to the gathered edge. Glue the Hat to the boy doll's head, with the bill pointing slightly sideways.

Bestow these dolled-up spoons on your most exemplary family toddlers. Or, as the late Rev. William A. Spooner would probably have put it, "Bespoon these stowed-up dolls on your most toddley family exemples." (Consult a good dictionary if you don't know about the Rev. Spooner and his famous spoonerisms.)

"Oh, what fun it is to ride!"
Toys to ride

Old-Fashioned Rocking Horse

This enchanting plaything is similar to an heirloom rocking horse made in 1850, and now on display at the Ford Museum. Our original model was made by Ed's great-grandfather. The project can be completed in a weekend and is a delightful, long-lasting toy your children will enjoy.

Metric equivalents in millimeters are indicated in parentheses.

Materials

45-inch (1143) length of 1-inch (25) diameter wooden dowel rod.

4 x 8-foot (1219 x 2438) sheet of ¾-inch (19) thick veneer-core plywood.

2 wood blocks, each ¾ x 1 x 6 inches (17 x 25 x 152).

Handful of 1½-inch (38) long, flat head wood screws; several 1½-inch (38) long common nails; handful each of 1¼-inch (32) and 1½-inch (38) long finishing nails; and 4 small brass tacks.

Carpenter's wood glue, wood filler, wood plugs to cover the screw holes, sandpaper, kraft paper, and carbon paper.

5 x 9-inch (127 x 229) piece of leather or heavy canvas for the horse's ears.

Paint. Use durable, non-toxic paint in the colors of your choice. We painted our horse burnt orange, with a brown mane and facial features. The folk art design on the side of the rockers was done in brown, white, yellow, and green. You need about a quart of the burnt orange, and minimal amounts of the other 4 colors.

Figure A

1 sq. = 1 in. (25.4)

Figure A

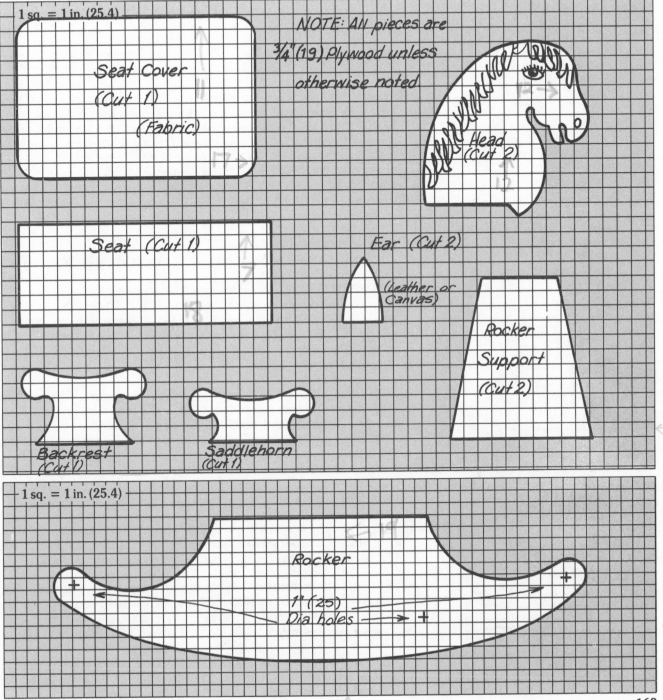

1 sq. = 1 in. (25.4)

Seat Cover
(Cut 1)

(Fabric)

NOTE: All pieces are
3/4"(19) Plywood unless
otherwise noted

Head
(Cut 2)

Seat (Cut 1)

Ear (Cut 2)

(Leather or
Canvas)

Rocker
Support
(Cut 2)

Backrest
(Cut 1)

Saddlehorn
(Cut 1)

1 sq. = 1 in. (25.4)

Rocker

1" (25)
Dia holes

Tools

Carpenter's rule, hammer, 1 large and 1 small paint brush, scissors or sharp razor knife, screwdriver, nailset, saber saw or coping saw, and an electric or hand drill with bits of the following diameters: 1-inch (25), a bit slightly larger than the diameter of the screw heads and a bit slightly smaller than the diameter of the screw shanks.

Optional tools

Router and corner-round bit. If you don't have a router, use a wood rasp to round off the edges.

Optional materials

Upholstering the seat is optional, but is extremely simple to do. You need the following materials and tools:

11 x 17-inch (279 x 432) piece of heavy upholstery fabric.

2 yards (1829) of decorative upholstery tape.

10½ x 16½-inch (267 x 419) piece of 2-inch (51) thick foam rubber.

Staple gun and ⅜-inch (10) long staples (or substitute small upholstery tacks and a tack hammer).

50 decorative upholstery tacks.

Figure B

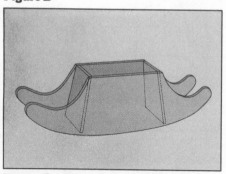

Figure C

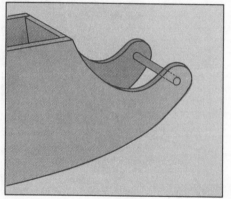

Cutting the pieces **1.** Enlarge the scale drawings given in **Figure A** to full-size patterns on kraft paper. Cut 2 Rockers, 2 Rocker Supports, 1 Seat, 1 Backrest, 2 Heads, and 1 Saddlehorn from the plywood. To cut 2 pieces exactly alike, use the enlarged paper pattern to cut the first piece. Use the wooden piece as your cutting pattern for the identical twin. Round off 1 long curved edge of each Rocker. These will be the inner edges.

2. Use carbon paper and a pencil to transfer the facial features to opposite sides of the 2 Head pieces, and to mark the positions where holes will be drilled.

Assembly The assembly is simple, and should be performed in 3 stages: first, assemble the lower section; second, the upper section; and finally, join the 2 sections. Use the smaller finishing nails, unless otherwise specified.

Lower section assembly **1.** We suggest that you perform a temporary assembly on the Rockers and Rocker Supports (**Figure B**). Carefully align the Rocker Supports at the top edges of the Rockers, as shown. When the Rocker Supports are at the correct angle, they will fit flush with the bottom edge of the Rockers.

2. Drive a few temporary holding nails through the Rockers, into the edges of the Rocker Supports. If you hammer the nails completely flush with the wood, you'll be gnashing your teeth when you try to remove them later.

3. Place the assembled lower section on level ground and check the rocking action. If necessary, reposition the pieces so that the unit rocks evenly.

4. When the rocking action is smooth and even, mark the positions of the pieces, and permanently attach the Rockers to the Rocker Supports with glue and screws. Countersink the screws, and glue wood plugs over the openings.

5. Drill 3 dowel rod holes in each Rocker, using the 1-inch (25) diameter bit. Placement of the holes is indicated by cross marks on the scale drawing. Bear in mind that the Rockers are assembled at an angle, so it may be necessary to enlarge portions of the holes to accommodate the rods.

6. Connect the Rockers with sections of the 1-inch (25) wooden dowel rod, placing 1 through the front of the Rockers and 1 through the back **(Figure C)**. Both of these rods should be cut flush with the outer sides of the Rockers.

7. Cut an 18-inch (457) length of dowel rod for the Footrest. Insert it through both Rockers, with equal extensions on each side. Use wood filler to secure the rods in the holes.

Upper section assembly   **1.** Carefully align the 2 Heads, placing blank sides together. Glue and nail the pieces together **(Figure D)**.

2. Round off both edges along the top and sides of the glued Head piece. Do not round off the bottom edges, as they will fit flush with the Seat.

3. The assembled Head fits over the front of the Seat **(Figure D)**. Use the Head piece as a guide to mark and trim the front edge of the Seat at an angle, so that the Head will fit flush against the edge. Trim the back edge of the Seat to correspond to the front.

Figure D

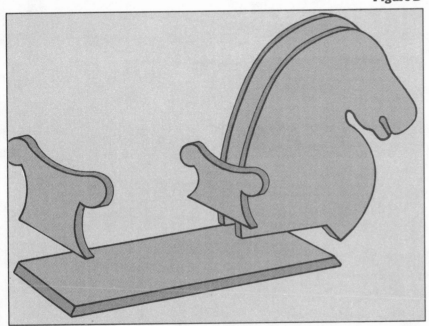

4. Trim the lower edge of the Backrest at about the same angle as used to trim the Seat. The exact angle is not important as long as it will allow the Backrest to tilt slightly to the rear of the horse, providing a comfortable support for even the littlest wrangler.

5. Position the Head, Backrest, and Saddlehorn on the Seat, as shown in **Figure D.** The Backrest fits flush with the trimmed back of the Seat. The Head fits over the front of the Seat, and the Saddlehorn fits flush against both the Seat and back of the Head. Use 2 screws to attach each piece (Backrest, Head, and Saddlehorn) to the Seat, inserting the screws from the bottom of the Seat, up into the other pieces. Use an additional screw to secure the Saddlehorn to the neck. Be sure to angle the screws that go into the Backrest.

6. For additional support, place a wood block on each side of the Head. Attach these to the Head and Seat with glue and nails **(Figure E).**

Figure E

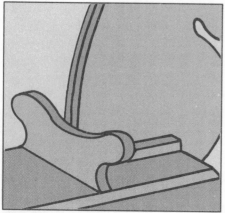

Joining lower and upper sections   **1.** Carefully center the upper section (Head, Seat, Backrest, and Saddlehorn) over the lower section (Rocker Supports and Rockers) as shown in **Figure F.** Fasten them together with glue and long finishing nails, or screws driven through the top of the Seat. Be sure to countersink nails or screws, and fill the holes, so that young riders will escape without a scratch.

2. Sand the long edges of the Seat to fit flush with the top of the Rockers.

3. Completely sand the assembled horse. Begin with medium sandpaper, and finish with fine.

Figure F

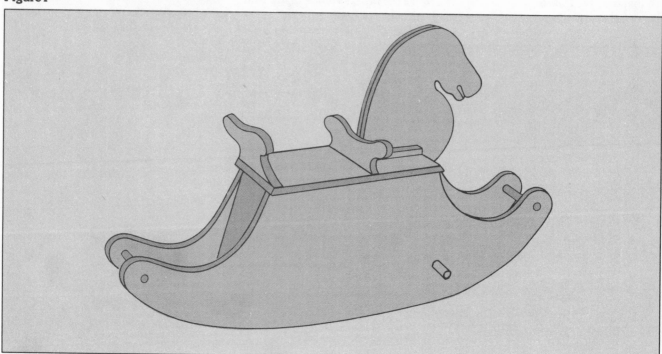

Figure G

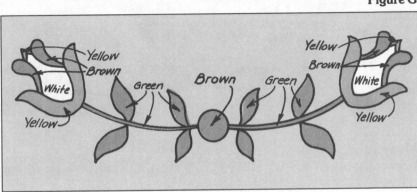

Figure H

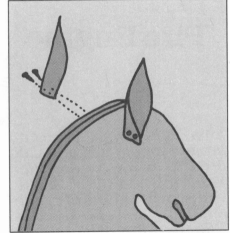

Figure I

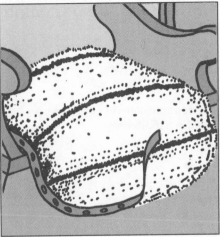

Painting 1. Enlarge the folk art design provided in **Figure A** to full size. Transfer the design to the outer side of each Rocker.
2. Paint the background color first. Add the mane, facial features and the folk art design. We followed the color scheme shown in **Figure G**.

Adding the ears 1. A scale drawing for the ears is given in **Figure A**. Cut 2 ears from soft leather or canvas.
2. Fold the ears in half lengthwise, and use small brass tacks to attach one ear to each side of the horse's Head **(Figure H)**.

Upholstering 1. Glue the foam rubber pad over the Seat between the Backrest and the Saddlehorn. Make sure that the side extensions over the Rockers are even.
2. Staple or tack the upholstery fabric over the foam rubber, starting on the Seat and working down each side, stretching the fabric as you work.
3. Glue upholstery tape over the staples and raw fabric edges. Secure with upholstery tacks placed about 2 inches (51) apart **(Figure I)**.

Install a budding cowpoke on the finished horse, and let'er rip.

Fire Engine

This is a great weekend project for parents and children to work on together. The finished Fire Engine will provide hours of excitement for young fire fighters. Although the diagrams are somewhat detailed, the Fire Engine is not complicated to build.

Metric equivalents in millimeters are indicated in parentheses.

Materials

Exterior plywood: 4 x 8-foot (1219 x 2438) sheet of ¾-inch (19); 2 x 18-inch (51 x 457) piece of ½-inch (13).

Clear pine lumber: 12-inch (305) length of 2 x 8-inch (38 x 184); 4-foot (1219) length of 2 x 4-inch (38 x 89); 8-foot (2438) length of 1 x 12-inch (17 x 286); 6-foot (1829) length of 1 x 2-inch (17 x 38).

Wooden dowel rod: 6-foot (1829) length of 1¼-inch (32) diameter; two 4-foot (1219) lengths of ¾-inch (19) diameter; two 3-foot (914) lengths of ½-inch (13) diameter.

Bolt: ½-inch (13) diameter, 6½ inches (165) long, with a nut and 3 washers.

2 small eyebolts, each about 1 inch (25) long, with ¼-inch (6) diameter eyes.

Flat head wood screws: four 1½-inches (38) long; four ⅝-inch (16) long.

Box of 1½-inch (38) long finishing nails; 2 small swivel pulleys; wood filler; carpenter's wood glue; carbon paper; kraft paper; and lubricant.

Non-toxic paint in the colors of your choice. We used red for the body, and white and black for the trim.

8-foot (2438) length of ⅛-inch (3) diameter nylon cord.

Several empty bleach bottles or other plastic containers.

Tools

Saber saw and circular saw; two 24-inch (610) pipe clamps; 1 wide and 1 narrow paint brush; hammer; screwdriver; carpenter's rule; wood rasp; sandpaper; compass; pliers; nailset; putty knife; and an electric or hand drill with bits of the following diameters: 1½-inch (38), 1¼-inch (32), ¾-inch (19), ⅝-inch (16), ½-inch (13), and ¼-inch (6).

Figure A

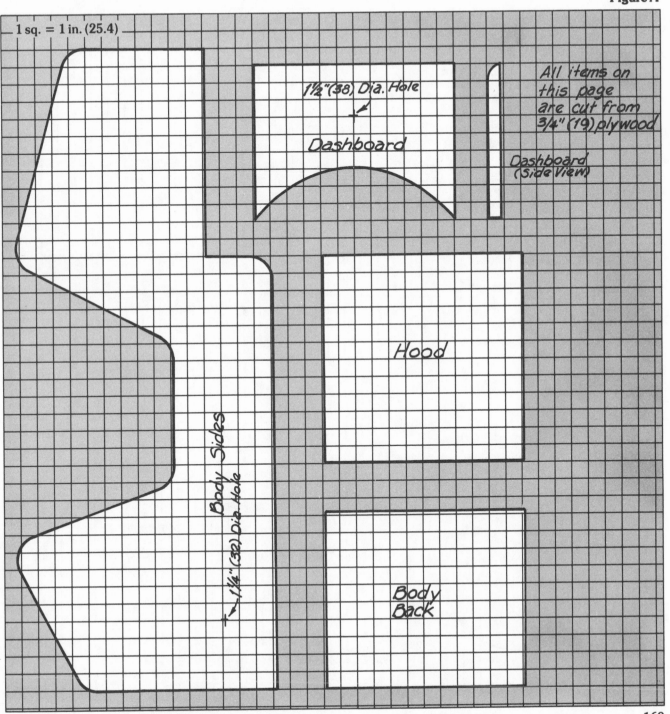

1 sq. = 1 in. (25.4)

1½"(38) Dia. Hole

Dashboard

Dashboard (Side View)

All items on this page are cut from 3/4"(19) plywood

Hood

Body Sides

1¼"(32) Dia. Hole

Body Back

Figure A

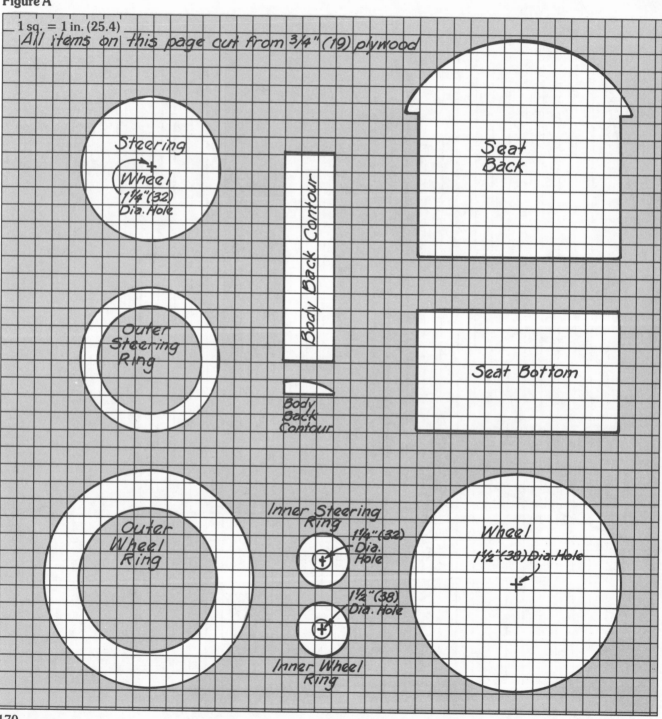

1 sq. = 1 in. (25.4)

All items on this page cut from 3/4" (19) plywood

Steering Wheel 1¼"(32) Dia. Hole

Outer Steering Ring

Body Back Contour

Body Back Contour

Seat Back

Seat Bottom

Outer Wheel Ring

Inner Steering Ring — 1¼"(32) Dia. Hole

Wheel 1½"(38) Dia. Hole

1½"(38) Dia. Hole

Inner Wheel Ring

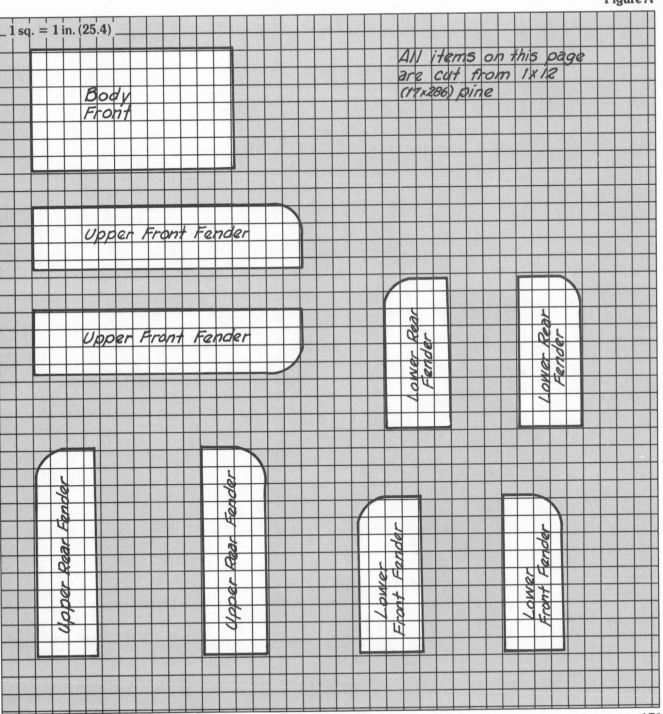

1 sq. = 1 in. (25.4)

Body Front

All items on this page are cut from 1 x 12 (17 x 286) pine

Upper Front Fender

Upper Front Fender

Lower Rear Fender

Lower Rear Fender

Upper Rear Fender

Upper Rear Fender

Lower Front Fender

Lower Front Fender

Figure A

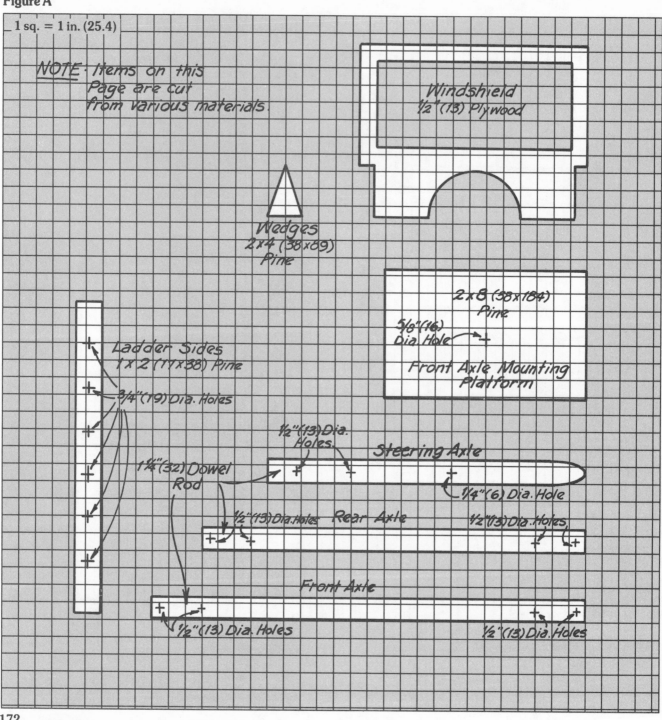

1 sq. = 1 in. (25.4)

NOTE: Items on this Page are cut from various materials.

Windshield
½" (13) Plywood

Wedges
2x4 (38x89)
Pine

2x8 (38x184)
Pine

5/8"(16)
Dia. Hole

Front Axle Mounting
Platform

Ladder Sides
1x2 (17x38) Pine

3/4"(19) Dia. Holes

1¼"(32) Dowel
Rod

½"(13) Dia.
Holes

Steering Axle

¼"(6) Dia. Hole

½"(13)Dia.Holes   Rear Axle   ½"(13)Dia.Holes

Front Axle

½"(13) Dia. Holes   ½"(13) Dia. Holes

Cutting the pieces

1. Refer to the scale drawings in **Figure A,** and make full-size kraft paper patterns. Some additional parts, not shown in **Figure A,** will be cut as they are needed in the assembly process.

2. Cut the pieces according to the quantities and materials specified on the scale drawings. Label each piece. Drill all the holes, which are marked for position and proper diameter in **Figure A.** To cut the 2 large Body Sides, we suggest that you temporarily nail 2 pieces of plywood together. Draw the outline, and cut out both pieces at once. Drill the Rear Axle hole through both pieces before removing the holding nails.

3. Cut 10 Dowel Pins, each 6½ inches (165) long, from the ½-inch (13) diameter dowel rod.

Assembly

Gather your young apprentices for help (and distraction) along the way. You might read through the assembly instructions to get a bird's-eye view of the project before you begin work. Use glue and nails for all assembly steps, except where otherwise specified. Holding on to your hat is helpful, but not required.

Steering wheel and axle

1. Insert the Steering Axle through the hole in the center of the Dashboard **(Figure B).** The Dashboard fits between the 2 holes at the blunt end of the Steering Axle. Glue a Dowel Pin in each of the holes, as shown in the illustration, but do not glue the Steering Axle to the Dashboard. Sand the rounded end of the Steering Axle smooth.

2. Apply glue liberally, and fit the Steering Wheel over the blunt end of the Steering Axle, letting the wheel sit flush against the Dowel Pin **(Figure B).** Place the Inner Steering Ring over the end of the Steering Axle. Cut or sand the blunt end of the Steering Axle even with the Inner Ring. Attach the Outer Steering Ring to the Steering Wheel and finish the open grain.

3. Attach the 2 Wedges to the back of the Dashboard, referring to **Figure D** for placement.

4. Cut a 2½-inch (64) length of the pine 2 x 4 (38 x 89) for the Pivot Block. Attach the Pivot Block to the Front Axle Mounting Platform, as shown in **Figure D,** using glue and the longer wood screws. Drill a 1½-inch (38) diameter socket into the Pivot Block. This socket will receive the rounded tip of the Steering Axle, and should be drilled at an angle **(Figure C).** Sand the socket smooth, and apply lubricant liberally inside the socket and at the tip of the Steering Axle, to produce "power steering."

Figure B

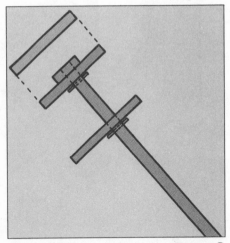

Figure C

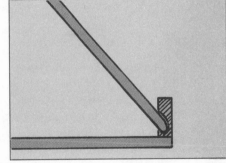

Figure D

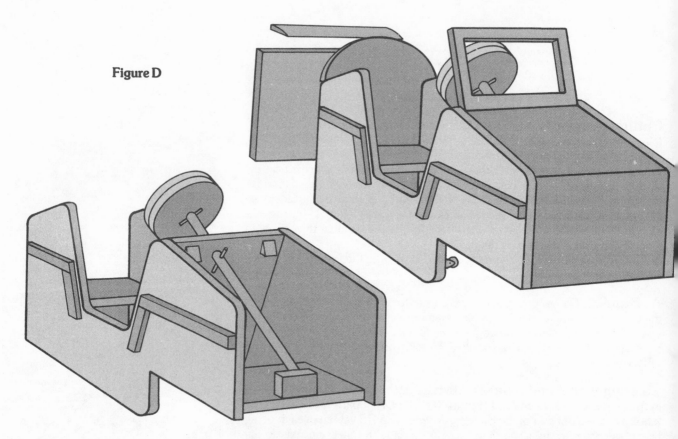

Body assembly **1.** Cut the following Fender Supports from the pine 1 x 2 (17 x 38): 2 Upper Front Supports, 1½ x 13 inches (38 x 330); 2 Upper Rear Supports, 1½ x 9 inches (38 x 229); and 4 Lower Supports, 1½ x 8 inches (38 x 203). Attach these to each Body Side piece **(Figure D)**.

2. Refer to **Figure D** as you position and glue the main body parts: Begin with the Body Sides, Seat Bottom, Dashboard (including the Steering assembly), and Front Axle Mounting Platform. Be sure that the lower end of the Steering Axle fits into the socket. It may be necessary to enlarge or adjust the angle of the socket to get a proper fit. Drive a few nails to hold the parts in place.

3. Refer to **Figure D** and add the Seat Back, Body Back Contour, Body Back, Windshield (set at an angle on the Wedges), Hood, and Front. Drive a few more holding nails, and pull the sides of the Fire Engine together with the pipe clamps. Finish nailing all parts in place, recess the nails, and let the glue dry for 24 hours.

4. Install the pulleys, using glue and the shorter screws **(Figure D)**.

Front Axle Assembly   **1.** Cut 2 Front Axle Holders, each 17½ inches (445) long, from the pine 2 x 4 (38 x 89). Using the circular saw, cut a V-shaped groove down the center of each, as shown in **Figure E.**

2. Sandwich the Front Axle between the 2 Front Axle Holders, so that the ends of the axle extend equally **(Figure F).** Glue and nail the 3 pieces together, install the eyebolts, and drill a ⅝-inch (16) diameter hole through the exact center of the entire axle assembly as shown.

3. Lubricate the Bolt and insert it through the Front Axle Mounting Platform and the Front Axle Assembly, placing the 3 Washers and Nut as shown in **Figure G.** This Bolt serves as a pivot for the Front Axle, and should be left loose enough to allow the assembly to swivel freely.

Figure E   **Figure F**

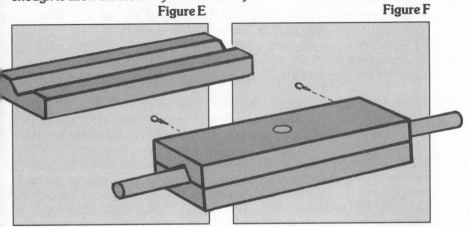

Figure G

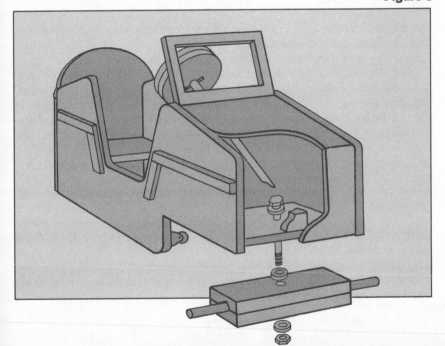

Rear axle and wheels **1.** Refer to **Figure H,** and glue the Rear Axle in place, making sure that it extends evenly on both sides of the body. Glue a Dowel Pin into the hole closest to the body on each end of the axle.

2. To assemble a Wheel (you'll need 5 — one will be a "spare"), glue and nail the Outer and Inner Wheel Rings to the Wheel, aligning the center holes and rims. Finish the open grain.

3. Lubricate the inside of the hole and the end of the axle. Cut 8 circular washers from the empty bleach bottles, each 3 inches (76) in diameter, with a 1½-inch (38) diameter center hole. Install the wheel on the axle, placing a plastic washer on each side of the wheel. Glue a Dowel Pin through the remaining hole in the axle. Repeat for the remaining wheels.

Trim **1.** Cut the following trim pieces from the pine 1 x 12 (17 x 286): 1 Upper Grille, 1½ x 15 inches (38 x 381); 2 Lower Grilles, 1½ x 13½ inches (38 x 343); and 6 circular Lights, each 3½ inches (89) in diameter. Use what's left of the 1¼-inch (32) diameter dowel rod for the Hood Ornament.

2. Attach the Upper and Lower, Front and Rear Fenders to the Body Sides over the corresponding Fender Supports. The Spare Wheel goes on the back, and Upper and Lower Grilles on the front. Glue 2 of the circles together for each Headlight, and attach to the Upper Grille. Taillights (the remaining 2 circles) go at the lower corners of the Body Back. Place the Hood Ornament at the front of the Hood.

Finishing Work **1.** Round off the Body Front and Body Back with a rasp, and sand flush with the sides and top.

2. Sand the entire Fire Engine, to eliminate rough edges.

3. Thread the nylon cord through the remaining hole in the Steering Axle (yes, it is now behind the Dashboard, but not difficult to get at), leaving equal amounts of cord on each side of the hole. Wrap one end of the cord clockwise around the Steering Axle 4 or 5 times, then thread it through the left-hand pulley, and attach it to the eyebolt on the left side of the Front Axle Assembly. Do the same with the other end of the cord, wrapping it counter-clockwise around the Steering Axle, passing it through the right-hand pulley, and tying it to the right-hand eyebolt.

4. Paint the Fire Engine red, with black and white trim, or in other colors of your choice.

Ladders **1.** Cut 12 Rungs, each 7 inches (178) long, from the ¾-inch (19) diameter dowel rod.

2. Glue the Rungs into the Ladder Side Pieces (which you already cut and drilled according to the scale drawings, and put aside where you could easily find them — right?) Let the glue dry overnight.

Figure H

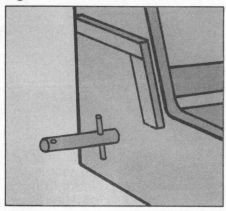

Figure I

3. Paint the ladders. When they are dry, nail them to the sides of the Fire Engine, as shown in **Figure I**.

Signs   **1.** Cut 2 rectangles, each 4 x 8 inches (102 x 203), from the pine 1 x 12 (17 x 286). Sand, and paint them white.
2. Full-size Letter Patterns are provided in **Figure J**. Trace, then use carbon paper to transfer the letter outlines to the dry Sign Boards. Paint the letters.

Fill the Fire Engine with Kid Power (an abundant, easy-to-find fuel), sit back, and enjoy the hoopla.

Figure J

ENGINE NO. 44

Tin Lizzie Racer

The design for this zippy little racer is loosely based on Henry Ford's Model T, which captivated the horse-and-buggy generation of 1908 America. Ford had great success with the Tin Lizzie, selling 15 million between 1908 and 1928, when he replaced the original with a new design — the Model A.

Metric equivalents in millimeters are indicated in parentheses.

Materials

Waferwood: 4 x 4-foot (1219 x 1219) piece of ¼-inch (6); 3 x 4-foot (914 x 1219) piece of ⁷⁄₁₆-inch (11).

Pine lumber: 36½ feet (1113 cm.) of 1 x 2-inch (17 x 38); 5-foot (1524) length of 1 x 6-inch (17 x 140); 5-foot (1524) length of 2 x 4-inch (38 x 89).

5-foot (1524) length of ½ x ¾-inch (13 x 19) parting stop molding.

2-foot (610) length of 1¼-inch (32) diameter wooden dowel rod.

A set of old lawn mower wheels: two 6 inches (153) in diameter, and two 8 inches (203) in diameter.

Two ½-inch (13) diameter steel rods, each 27 inches (686) long.

One ⅝-inch (16) diameter bolt, 6 inches (152) long, with a nut and 5 washers.

8 metal washers, 1¼ inches (32) in diameter, with a ⅝-inch (16) diameter or larger center hole.

2 eyebolts, about 1¼ inches (32) long; and 2 small swivel pulleys.

8-foot (2438) length of ¼-inch (6) diameter nylon cord.

Handful of flat head wood screws, 1 inch (25) long.

Carpenter's wood glue, lubricant, handful of 2½-inch (64) long nails, a box of 1¼-inch (32) long nails, handful of 1¼-inch (32) long finishing nails, and 4 cotter pins.

1½ x 5-inch (38 x 127) piece of rubber (from an inner tube or car floor mat).

Tools

Saber saw; hammer, screwdriver, carpenter's rule, sandpaper, compass, staple gun, a few staples with ½-inch (13) legs, and an electric drill with bits of the following diameters: 1⅜-inch (35), 1¼-inch (32), ¾-inch (19), ⅜-inch (10), and a ⅛-inch (3) bit capable of drilling through steel.

Cutting the pieces   **1.** Enlarge the scale drawings given in **Figure A** to full-size patterns on kraft paper.

2. Cut and label the parts, and drill the holes as specified on the scale drawings. We suggest that you cut the 2 Body Sides simultaneously. Put the pieces aside in your usual organized manner, so they won't get lost in the shuffle.

Assembly

There are 5 assembly stages. You will get good results using glue and nails for the pine frame, but use glue and wood screws to assemble the waferwood body pieces, except where otherwise indicated.

Frame   1. Cut Frame Supports from the pine 1 x 2 (17 x 38), of the following lengths: two 4 inches (102), two 6⅞ inches(175), one 15 inches (381), two 18¾ inches (476), one 19 inches (483), and two 36½ inches (927).
2. Refer to **Figure B,** and attach the Frame Supports to the Center Frame. Be sure to butt the ends of the Supports as shown in the diagram, so the pieces of the puzzle will fit correctly.
3. Install a pulley on each long edge of the Center Frame, about 6 inches (152) in front of the central Frame Support.
4. Cut a 5½-inch (140) length from the pine 1 x 6 (17 x 140) for the Clearance Block. Attach this block to the underside of the Center Frame, 2 inches (51) from the front edge, as shown in **Figure B.** Drill a ¾-inch (19) diameter hole through the Clearance Block, aligning it with the hole in the Center Frame.

Figure A

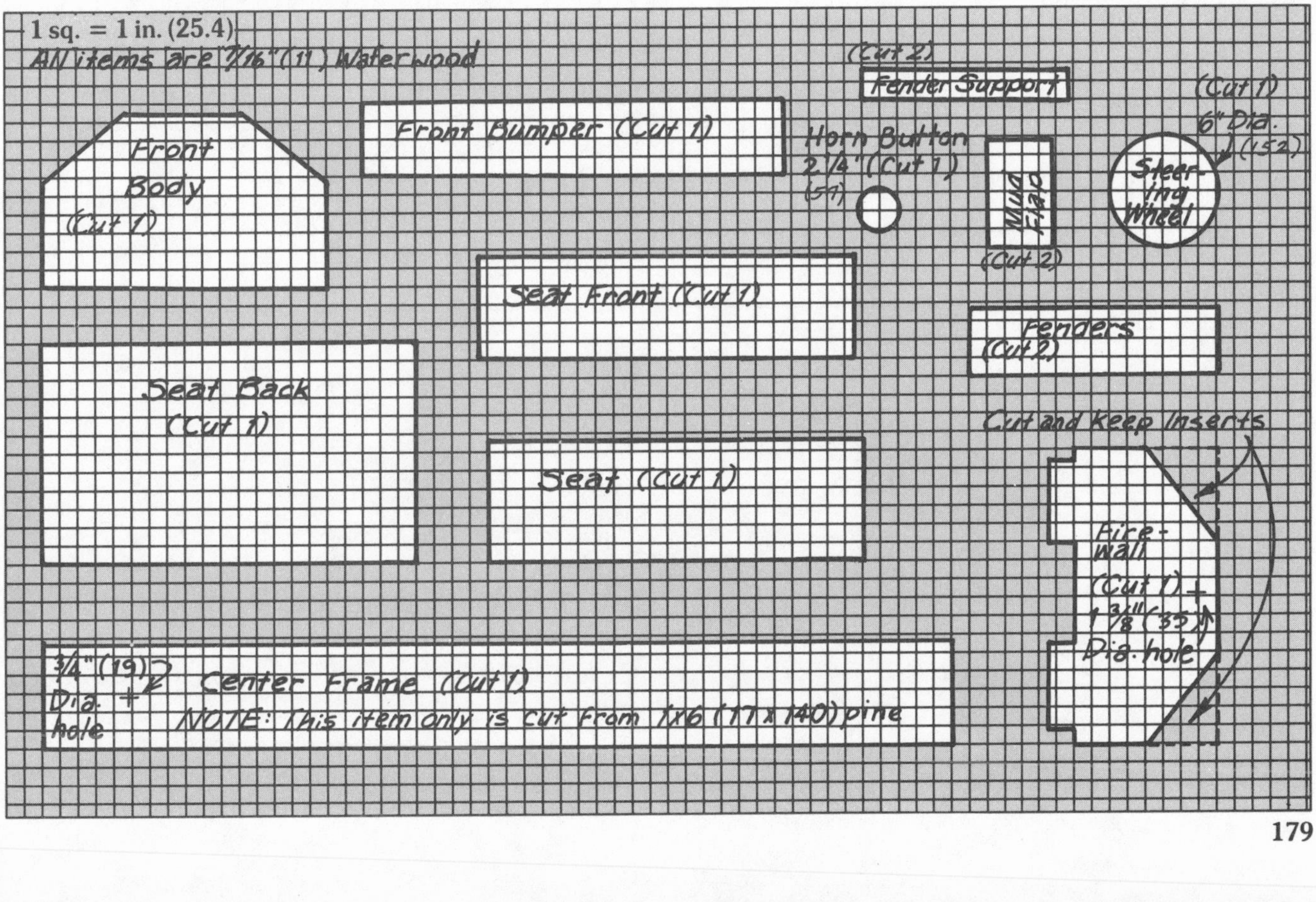

1 sq. = 1 in. (25.4)
All items are ⁷⁄₁₆" (11) Waferwood

Front Body (Cut 1)
Front Bumper (Cut 1)
Fender Support (Cut 2)
Horn Button 2¼" (Cut 1) (57)
(Cut 2) Mud Flap
Steering Wheel 6" Dia. (152) (Cut 1)
Seat Front (Cut 1)
Fenders (Cut 2)
Seat Back (Cut 1)
Cut and Keep Inserts
Seat (Cut 1)
Fire-wall (Cut 1) 1⅜" (35) Dia. hole
¾" (19) Dia. hole   Center Frame (Cut 1)
NOTE: This item only is cut from 1x6 (17 x 140) pine

Axles and wheels **1.** Cut 2 Axle Supports, each 22 inches (559) long, from the pine 2 x 4 (38 x 89). Cut the following parts from the pine 1 x 2 (17 x 38): 2 Rear Axle Holders, each 22 inches (559) long; and 4 Front Axle Holders, each 9¾ inches (248) long.

2. Glue and nail the 2 Rear Axle Holders to the Rear Axle Support, as shown in **Figure C.** Attach the rear axle assembly underneath the frame, about 6 inches (152) from the rear edge, using the longest nails **(Figure D).**

Figure A

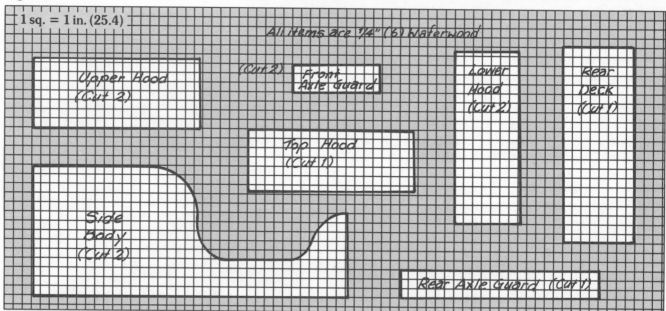

Figure B

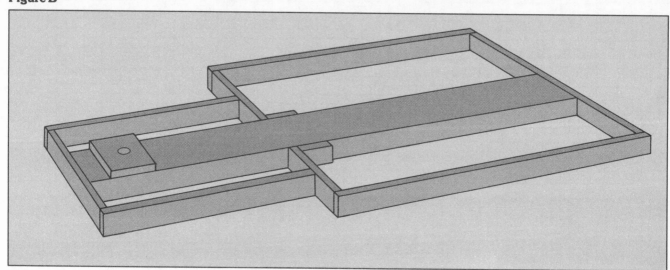

3. Drill a ¾-inch (19) diameter hole through the Front Axle Support, placing the center of the hole midway between the 2 ends, and 1⅛ inches (29) from 1 long edge. Attach the Front Axle Holders to the Axle Support with ends flush, leaving a 2½-inch (64) gap in the center (**Figure E**). Insert the axles into the slots, and add the Axle Guards. Install the 2 eyebolts (**Figure D**).

4. Lubricate the bolt, and insert it through the Center Frame and front axle assembly, placing the washers and nut as shown in **Figure E**. Leave the bolt loose enough to allow the axle assembly to pivot easily.

5. Drill a small hole through each metal axle, about ¾ inch (19) from each end. Lubricate the axle ends, install the 2 smaller wheels on the front axle, and the 2 larger wheels on the rear axle, placing a washer on both sides of each wheel. Insert cotter pins through the holes at the ends of the axles.

Figure C

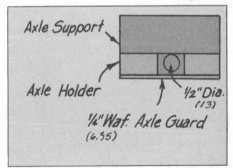

Figure D

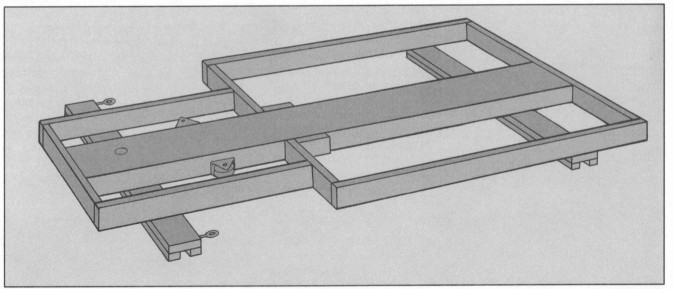

Figure E

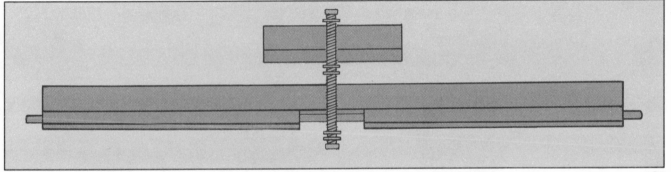

Figure F

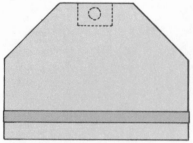

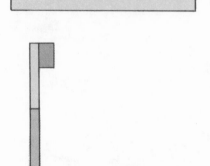

Steering Assembly **1.** Cut a Bumper Support, 16½ inches (419) long, from the pine 1 x 2 (17 x 38). Attach it to the Front Body, 1½ inches (38) from the lower edge, as shown in **Figure F**.

2. Cut a 3-inch (76) length from the pine 2 x 4 (38 x 89) for the Pivot Block. Drill a 1⅜-inch (35) diameter socket, about 1 inch (25) deep, into the Pivot Block, and attach the block to the inside of the Front Body **(Figure F)**. Connect the Front Body to the frame, with lower edges flush.

3. For the Firewall Block, cut another 3-inch (76) length from the pine 2 x 4 (38 x 89). Sand the corners smooth, and attach it to the Firewall at the top center. Drill a 1⅜-inch (35) diameter hole through the block, aligned with the hole in the Firewall. Attach the Firewall to the frame **(Figure G.)**

4. Cut a 19-inch (483) length of wooden dowel rod for the Steering Axle. Drill a ⅜-inch (10) diameter hole through the center of the Steering Axle, about 8 inches (203) from 1 end. This will be the end that holds the Steering Wheel. Sand the other end smooth, insert it through the holes in the Firewall Block and Firewall, and into the lubricated Pivot Block socket.

5. Thread the nylon cord through the hole in the Steering Axle, leaving equal amounts of cord on each side of the hole. Wrap 1 end of the cord clockwise around the Steering Axle 4 or 5 times, thread it through the left-hand pulley, and tie it to the eyebolt on the left side of the front axle assembly. Do the same with the other end of the cord, wrapping it counter-clockwise around the Steering Axle, threading it through the right-hand pulley, and attaching it to the right-hand eyebolt.

Figure G

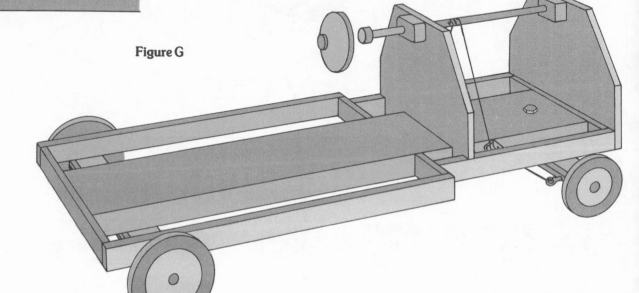

Figure H

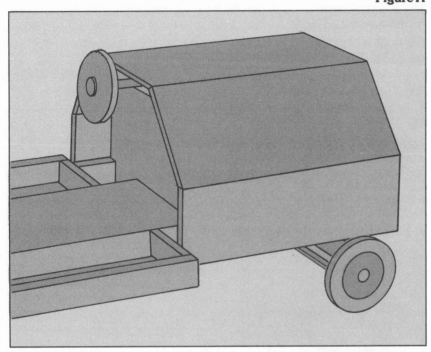

6. Cut a 2½-inch (64) diameter circle from the pine 2 x 4 (38 x 89) for the Steering Wheel Support Ring. Drill a 1¼-inch (32) diameter hole through the center. Apply glue, and install the Ring on the Steering Axle **(Figure G),** so that the ends are flush. Use 3 or 4 screws to secure the ring to the axle.

7. Glue the Steering Wheel to the end of the Steering Axle, matching the centers, and secure with 2 screws inserted off-center. Glue the Horn Button to the Steering Wheel, and secure with 1 screw through the exact center. You've earned a break, so install yourself in a comfortable lawn chair for a bit.

Figure I

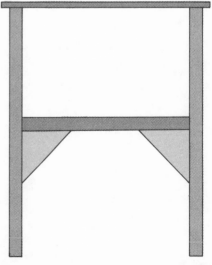

Body Assembly **1.** Attach the Lower Hood pieces to the frame with glue and screws **(Figure H),** positioning them so that the front edges are flush with the Front Body. Use glue and finishing nails to attach the other 3 Hood pieces to the top edges of the Front Body and Firewall.

2. To make the Windshield (we use the term loosely — it's actually a windshield frame, and does no shielding at all), cut the following lengths from the pine 1 x 2 (17 x 38): 1 Upper Strut, 23 inches (584); 1 Lower Strut, 17 inches (432); and 2 Side Struts, each 24 inches (610). Attach a Side Strut to the front of each central Frame Support, flush with the lower Hood piece. Glue the 2 triangular-shaped Inserts (previously cut from waferwood) between the Side Struts and the hood, as shown in **Figure I.** The Lower Strut goes above the hood and Inserts, and the Upper Strut is placed across the top edges of the Side Struts, extending equally on each side.

3. Assembly of the seat is shown in **Figure J.** Cut the following lengths from the pine 1 x 2 (17 x 38) for Supports: two 11¼ inches (286), and two 21 inches (533). Attach a 21-inch (533) Support to the frame, above the rear axle assembly. Miter the lower ends of the shorter Supports at a slight angle, and glue them along the edges of the Seat Back. Attach the remaining Support across the front of the Seat Back, 6 inches (152) from the upper edge (it will hold the Seat). Place this assembly on the frame, in front of the Support piece, with lower edges flush. Secure it in place with glue and screws. Add the Seat and install the Seat Front underneath.

4. Install the Body Sides **(Figure K),** using glue and screws to attach them to the Seat Back Supports, Windshield Side Struts, and frame. The Rear Deck is connected to the frame behind the seat assembly.

Figure J

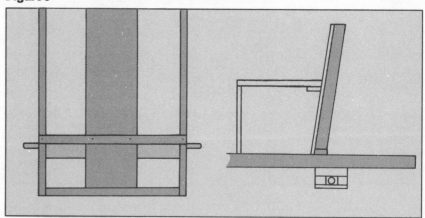

Figure K

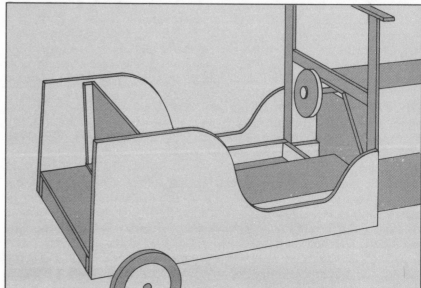

Figure L

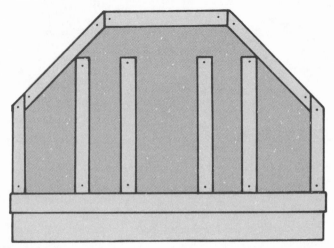

Figure M

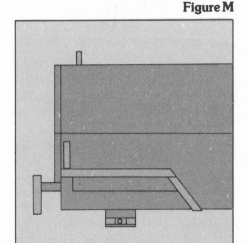

Figure N

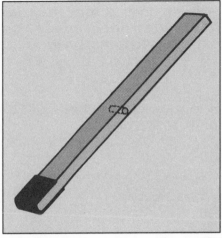

Trim and Hand Brake 1. Cut trim pieces from the parting stop molding to the following lengths: 4 Grilles, each 7½ inches (191); and 5 Front Trims, measured and mitered to fit on the front edges of the hood **(Figure L).** Cut 2 Headlights, each 3½-inches (89) in diameter, from the 2 x 4 (38 x 89).

2. Attach the Grilles and Front Trim as shown in **Figure L.** The Hood Ornament (the remaining short length of rod) is attached to the top of the hood. Front Bumper, Fender Supports, Fenders, and Mudflaps have already been cut from waferwood. Place them as shown in **Figure M**, and attach a Headlight on top of each Fender.

3. Cut a 15-inch (381) length of the pine 1 x 2 (17 x 38) for the Hand Brake. Glue and staple the small piece of rubber over 1 end, and drill a ⅜-inch (10) hole half-way through the width of the Brake **(Figure N.)** Attach the Brake to the right side of the racer, with a screw inserted into the hole you have just drilled. Position the Brake so that the lower, rubber-coated end will contact the wheel when the driver pushes forward on the upper end, but be sure that the lower end does not touch the ground when the Brake is in a vertical position. Check the screw Tension periodically when the racer is in use.

4. Sand all the sharp edges smooth. Waferwood has a built-in safety feature; the edges do not splinter, so your sanding job will be easy.

Select one pint-size driver and a gentle slope for the big test run.

Double-Duty Wagon

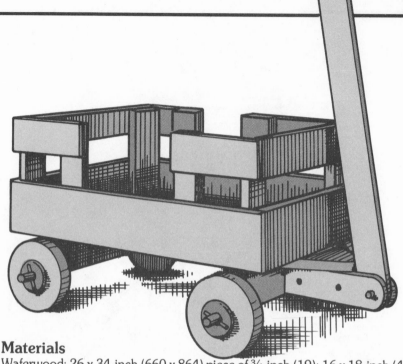

A spacious, sturdy wagon like this waferwood model will be more fun than the fabled barrel full of monkeys for children who like to transport their (and your) possessions to unlikely locations. It will also serve as an attractive, country-style planter for Mom when the kibosh has been put on further hauling activities. We enjoy working with waferwood, which has an interesting finish and is less expensive than plywood.

Metric equivalents in millimeters are indicated in parentheses.

Materials

Waferwood: 26 x 34-inch (660 x 864) piece of ¾-inch (19); 16 x 18-inch (406 x 457) piece of ¼-inch (6).

Pine lumber: 28-inch (711) length of 2 x 4-inch (38 x 89); 2-foot (610) length of 2 x 6-inch (38 x 140); 10-foot (3048) length of 1 x 3-inch (17 x 64).

Wooden dowel rod: 4 feet (1219) of 1-inch (25) diameter, 1 foot (305) of ¾-inch (19) diameter, 10 inches (254) of ¼-inch (6.35) diameter.

One ⅝-inch (16) diameter flat head stove bolt, 2½ inches (64) long, with a nut and 3 washers.

Nine ¾-inch (19) flat head wood screws; handful each of small, medium and large finishing nails (1 inch [25], 1¼ inches [32], and 1½ inches [38] long respectively); and a few 1½-inch (38) and 2½-inch (64) long common nails.

Carpenter's wood glue, sandpaper, kraft paper and lubricant.

Tools

Saber saw, and either a circular saw or router with a core box bit.

Electric or hand drill with bits of the following diameters: 1⅛-inch (29), ⅞-inch (22), ¾-inch (19), ½-inch (13), and ¼-inch (6.35).

Wood rasp, hammer, carpenter's rule, and screwdriver.

Cutting the pieces   **1.** Enlarge the scale drawings given in **Figure A** to full-size patterns on kraft paper. Cut the following pieces from ¾-inch (19) waferwood: 1 Hinge Support, 2 Ends, 2 Sides, and 1 Floor. Cut 2 Axle Supports from the pine 2 x 4 (38 x 89), and 4 Wheels from the pine 2 x 6 (38 x 140). Cut 8 Washers, 4 Side Rails, and 2 End Rails from ¼-inch (6) waferwood, and cut 1 Handle, 2 Hinges, and 8 Rail Supports from the pine 1 x 3 (17 x 64).

2. Drill the holes as specified on the scale drawings, and sand the solid wood pieces.

Figure A

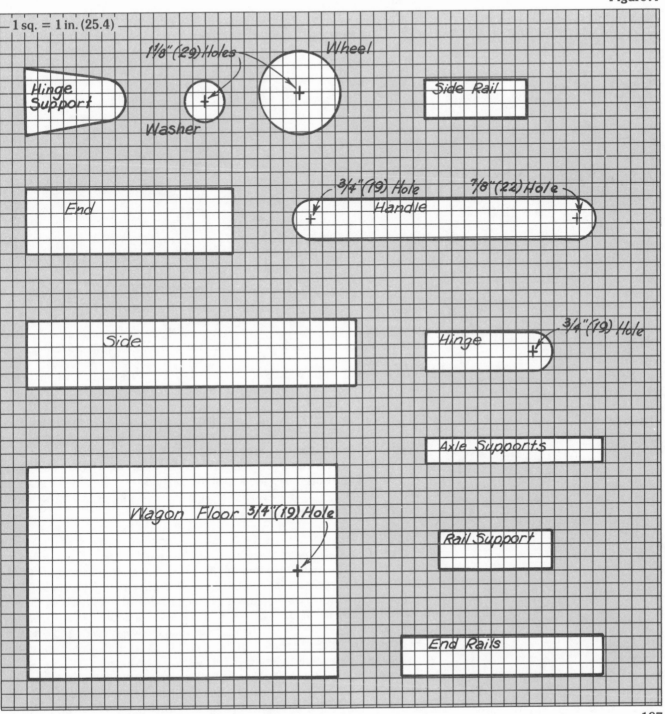

1 sq. = 1 in. (25.4)

Hinge Support

1⅛" (29) Holes

Washer

Wheel

Side Rail

End

¾" (19) Hole   ⅞" (22) Hole

Handle

Side

Hinge   ¾" (19) Hole

Axle Supports

Wagon Floor ¾" (19) Hole

Rail Support

End Rails

Figure B

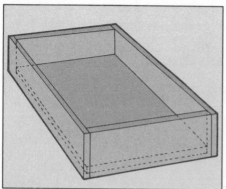

Figure C

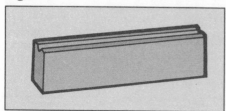

Figure D

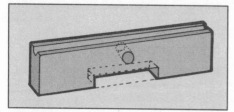

Figure E

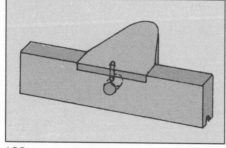

Figure F

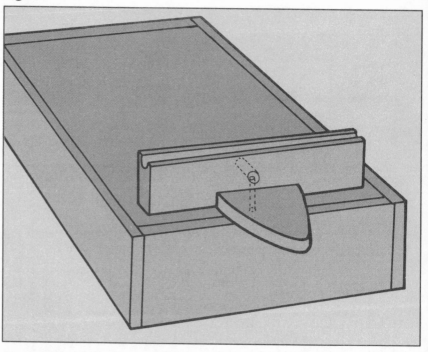

Wagon box and axle supports **1.** For the wagon box, use glue and long finishing nails to attach the Sides and Ends to the Floor, butting the pieces as shown in **Figure B**.

2. Cut a 1-inch (25) wide, full-length axle groove into one long edge of each Axle Support (**Figure C**). You can accomplish this in 1 pass with a router, or make 2 angled cuts with a circular saw to form a V-shaped groove.

3. On the Front Axle Support only, cut a rectangular slot 5 inches (127) long and ¾ inch (19) deep into the remaining long edge, as shown in **Figure D**. Drill a ¾-inch (19) diameter hole through the axle support, being careful to avoid the slot and axle groove.

Steering Assembly **1.** Fit the Hinge Support into the rectangular slot in the Front Axle Support, attaching it with glue and long nails (**Figure E**). Drill a ½-inch (13) diameter hole through the Hinge Support and continue drilling into the Axle Support until the drill bit emerges into the ¾-inch (19) hole.

2. Position the Front Axle Support on the underside of the wagon box, aligning the holes. Insert the stove bolt through the hole in the floor (**Figure F**), placing 1 metal washer under the bolt head, 1 between the wagon floor and axle support, and 1 washer and the nut at the end of the bolt. Tighten the nut so that it will hold the assembly together, but allow it to swivel freely.

3. Glue the 2 Hinges to the Hinge Support, leaving a 1-inch (25) space between them as shown in **Figure G.** Secure with nails driven through the Hinge Support and additional nails driven through the axle support.

4. You have already drilled a hole near each end of the Handle. Insert the end with the larger hole between the Hinges, aligning all 3 holes (**Figure G**). Cut a 5-inch (127) length of the ¾-inch (19) diameter dowel rod, and insert it through the holes, leaving equal extensions on each side. Do not use glue, for if you do, the handle action will be permanently frozen. Do use glue to secure the remaining 7-inch (179) length of ¾-inch (19) diameter dowel rod through the hole in the other end of the Handle.

Axles and wheels   **1.** Position the Rear Axle Support underneath the wagon floor, about 3 inches (76) from the rear edge, centered between the sides. Attach it with glue and screws.
2. Cut 2 Axles, each 20 inches (508) long, from the 1-inch (25) diameter dowel rod. Drill a ¼-inch (6.35) diameter hole, ¾ inch (19) from each end of the 2 axles. Cut 4 Dowel Pins, each 2½ inches (64) long, from the ¼-inch (6.35) diameter dowel rod.
3. Glue the axles to the axle supports, leaving equal extensions on each end. Refer to **Figure H,** and pre-drill screw holes half-way through each axle, using the ¼-inch (6.35) diameter bit. Insert screws through the holes and into the axle supports.
4. Figure H also shows the wheel assembly. Slip 1 wooden washer over 1 end of an axle, pushing it all the way up to the axle support. Lubricate the end of the axle and add the Wheel, followed by another wooden washer. Secure with a dowel pin glued into the hole near the end of the axle. Repeat this procedure for the other 3 wheels.

Upper rail assembly   **1.** Use glue and short finishing nails to attach 2 Side Rails to each End Rail, butting the pieces as shown in **Figure I**. Attach the Rail Supports to the Side and End Rails, using the same size nails.
2. Secure the rail assemblies to the wagon box with medium finishing nails.
3. Sand wherever necessary to eliminate rough edges.

Turn the finished wagon over to your resident small fry and batten down everything you don't want hauled away!

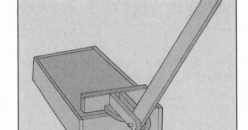
Figure G

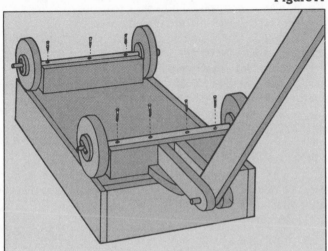
Figure H

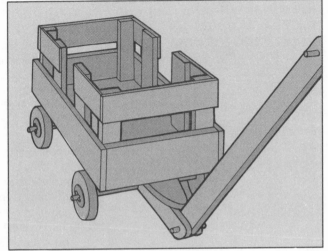
Figure I

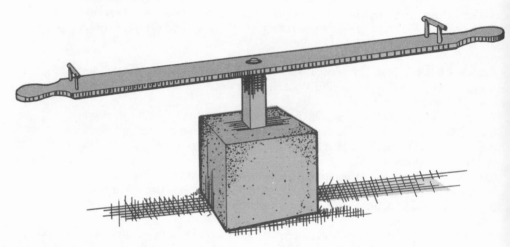

Whirling Seesaw

The seesaw may have risen
and fallen (ahem!) in popu-
larity over the centuries,
but it is one of the world's
oldest known inventions
for amusement. Our Whirl-
ing Seesaw gives a new
twist to the old form, and
does just what its name im-
plies — it spins as well as
teeters and totters.

Metric equivalents in millimeters are indicated in parentheses.

Materials

8-foot (2438) length of 2 x 8-inch (38 x 184) pine.

A length of 4 x 4-inch (89 x 89) pine. The actual length that you'll need will
    depend on whether you intend to bury the concrete base in the ground, or
    leave it above ground for a portable seesaw. We have designed the structure
    to work either way. If you intend to bury it, purchase a 33-inch (838) length.
    If not, purchase a 21-inch (533) length.

2 x 3-foot (610 x 914) piece of ¼-inch (6) thick exterior plywood or wafer-
    wood. This material will be used to make a form for the concrete base, and
    will be discarded, so don't bother trying to find a piece that looks good.

31-inch (787) length of 1¼-inch (32) diameter wooden closet rod.

12-inch (305) length of ¾-inch (19) diameter galvanized pipe, threaded on
    1 or both ends. In the plumbing trade, this is known as a "¾ x 12-inch (19
    x 305) nipple," and is a standard part which you can purchase at any plumb-
    ing supply center. (In case you didn't know, pipe diameter measurements
    are made on the inside of the pipe.)

¾-inch (19) pipe cap (to fit the threaded pipe).

4 hex bolts, each 7 inches (178) long and ⅜-inch (10) in diameter, with match-
    ing nuts.

80-pound (36 kg.) bag of instant concrete mix. This is a "just add water" prod-
    uct, which contains cement, sand and gravel in pre-measured proportions.

Small quantity of epoxy cement. We used approximately 1 fluid oz. (30 ml.).

Medium and fine sandpaper, kraft paper, and carpenter's wood glue.

Handful of 1-inch (25) long nails.

1 quart (1 liter) of non-toxic paint, stain, or waterproof wood sealer, in the color
    of your choice.

Tools

Saber saw or coping saw, carpenter's rule, hammer, table clamp or vise, wood rasp, paint brush, and an electric or hand drill with ⅜-inch (10), 1-inch (25), and 1¼-inch (32) diameter bits. Instead of the wood rasp, you may wish to use a rotary rasp drill attachment, or a router with a small chamfer bit. An electric sander or sanding attachment for your drill will be helpful, but is not necessary.

Cutting the pieces   **1.** You will need to contour a 1-foot (305) length at each end of the pine board to create the classic seesaw seat shape. A scale drawing for the contoured ends of the seesaw board is given in **Figure A.** Enlarge the drawing to full size on kraft paper.

2. Transfer the contour outlines to each end of the pine board, and cut around them. Sand the entire board, rounding off the sharp edges and eliminating all splinters and rough spots. Remember that any splinters you miss will eventually be embedded in a small person with a loud voice, so sand with care!

3. Drill a 1¼-inch (32) diameter hole through the exact center of the board. Use a rasp or router with chamfer bit to flare the upper and lower portions of the hole, as shown in **Figure B.** (This will allow the finished Seesaw to teeter on its mount as it whirls.) The outer edges should be flared to a finished diameter of about 1¾ inches (45), but the diameter measurement at the middle of the hole should not be altered. Sand the hole.

4. The handle assemblies are made from the wooden closet rod. Cut one 7-inch (178) length and two 4-inch (102) lengths from the rod. Drill a ⅜-inch (10) diameter hole about ⅝ inch (16) from each end of the longer piece. Drill a hole of the same diameter through the length of each of the shorter pieces. To drill through the length, clamp the rod in a vise or table clamp, place the tip of the bit at the exact center of 1 end of the rod, and drill in as straight a line as possible. Repeat this entire step to create pieces for the second handle.

5. Contour 1 end of each of the shorter rods, as shown in **Figure C,** to create a seat for the longer rod. You can use your saber or coping saw to make a simple V-shaped groove. If you have access to a band saw, you can create a semi-circular groove that will fit the side of the longer rod exactly. Sand all of the rods.

6. Cut the following pieces from plywood for the concrete form: 2 Sides, each 11¾ x 12 inches (298 x 305); 2 Wide Sides, each 12 x 12 inches (305 x 305); and 1 Floor, 11 x 12 inches (279 x 305). In addition, cut 1 circular washer, 3 inches (76) in diameter, with a 1⅛ inch (29) diameter center hole.

7. The 4 x 4-inch (89 x 89) piece of lumber will serve as the Seesaw Support. Drill a 1-inch (25) diameter socket, 8 inches (203) long, into 1 end of the Support. (This will be the upper end.) Drill the socket as straight as possible, down through the center of the Support.

8. Use a saw to taper the upper portion of the Support **(Figure D).** Start about 4 inches (102) from the end, and cut each side equally, so that the tapered upper end measures 1½ inches (38) square.

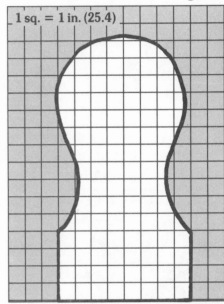
Figure A

1 sq. = 1 in. (25.4)

Figure B

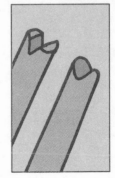
Figure C

Figure D

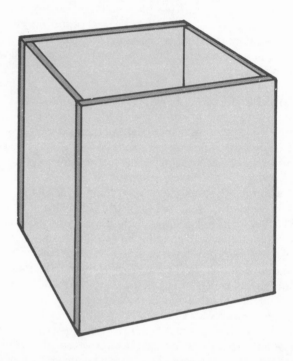

Figure E

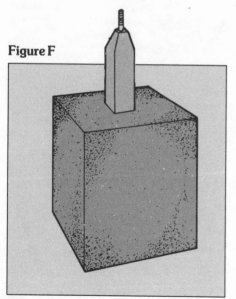

Figure F

Assembly **1.** Build a form for the concrete, using the 5 plywood squares (actually, only 2 of them are mathematically correct squares, but the others are close enough to fit the name for our purpose here). The form will be a box with 4 sides and a floor, but without a top. Assembly of the box is shown in **Figure E.** Use the 11 x 12-inch (279 x 305) piece as the floor of the box. Nail the 4 sides over the raw edges of the floor, butting the pieces as shown.

2. Mix the concrete according to the manufacturer's instructions on the bag. Place the 4 x 4-inch (89 x 89) Support in the center of the plywood box, drilled end up, and pour the concrete into the box, around the Support. Let it cure as long as the instructions recommend before you remove the plywood form.

3. Mix the epoxy cement, and spread it over the lower (or unthreaded) end of the length of pipe. Insert the pipe into the socket, threaded end up, as shown in **Figure F.** (If you bought a pipe with 2 threaded ends, it obviously won't matter which end is up. Sometimes, that's the way we feel around here.) Let the epoxy dry as long as the instructions recommend.

4. Figure G shows how the handles are assembled. For each handle, glue a 7-inch (178) rod across the tops of 2 shorter rods, aligning the holes. Insert a bolt through each set of aligned holes.

5. Attach 1 handle approximately 17 inches (432) from each end of the Seesaw board. To do this, place each handle assembly on the board where it will be attached, and press down on the bolts to mark their positions with indentations on the board. Drill a ⅜-inch (10) diameter hole straight through the board at each mark. Spread glue on the lower rod ends, reposition the handles, push the bolts through the board, and install the nuts. Tighten them securely, as they will be subjected to quite a bit of strain if your teeter-totterers are anything like ours. The nuts should be checked periodically, once your Whirling Seesaw is in use. (We mean the inanimate nuts that hold the handles on — not the extremely animated nuts who will be whooping it up on the seesaw — although it's a good idea to check them periodically, too.) Paint, stain, or seal the board.

6. When the cement has thoroughly cured, and the epoxy is dry, place the board over the support assembly, inserting the pipe end through the hole in the center of the board. Slip the plywood washer over the pipe end, and install the pipe cap tightly. Final assembly is shown in **Figure H.** The pipe cap should also be checked periodically, and tightened if necessary.

7. If you opted for the longer Support, now is the time to bury the concrete base in the ground.

Invite the neighborhood kids over to see the Seesaw you sawed yourself, and to see your self-sawed Seesaw swing!

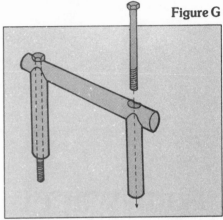

Figure G

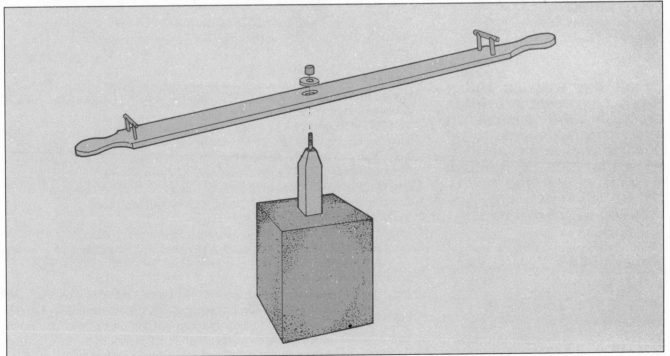

Figure H

Four-Wheel Horsey

Of all the wooden riding toys we've designed, this is probably the easiest to make. It also seems to be one of the most popular with the kids, if raucous squeals of joy and hearty "Hi-Ho Silver's" are any basis on which to judge.

Metric equivalents in millimeters are indicated in parentheses.

Materials

Wooden dowel rod: 36-inch (914) length of ¾-inch (19) diameter; 8-inch (203) length of ¼-inch (6.35) diameter.

8-foot (2439) length of 1 x 12-inch (17 x 286) pine lumber.

4 wheels, each 5 inches (127) in diameter, with a ⅞-inch (22) diameter center hole. You can use replacement lawn mower wheels, or cut wooden wheels from a 40-inch (1016) length of 1 x 6-inch (17 x 140) pine.

4 x 8-inch (102 x 203) piece of ¼-inch (6) waferwood or plywood.

4 metal bolts, each 1¾ inches (45) long, with washers and nuts.

Handful of 1½-inch (38) long finishing nails.

14 small-gauge, flat head wood screws, each 1¾ inches (45) long.

Sandpaper, wood glue, carbon paper, kraft paper, and wood filler.

Tools

Saber saw or coping saw, carpenter's rule, hammer, screwdriver, nailset, and an electric drill with bits of the following diameters: ¾-inch (19), ⅞-inch (22), ¼-inch (6.35), a bit slightly smaller than the diameter of the wood screw shanks, and a bit slightly larger than the diameter of the bolt shanks. A router with a corner-round bit will be helpful, but is not required.

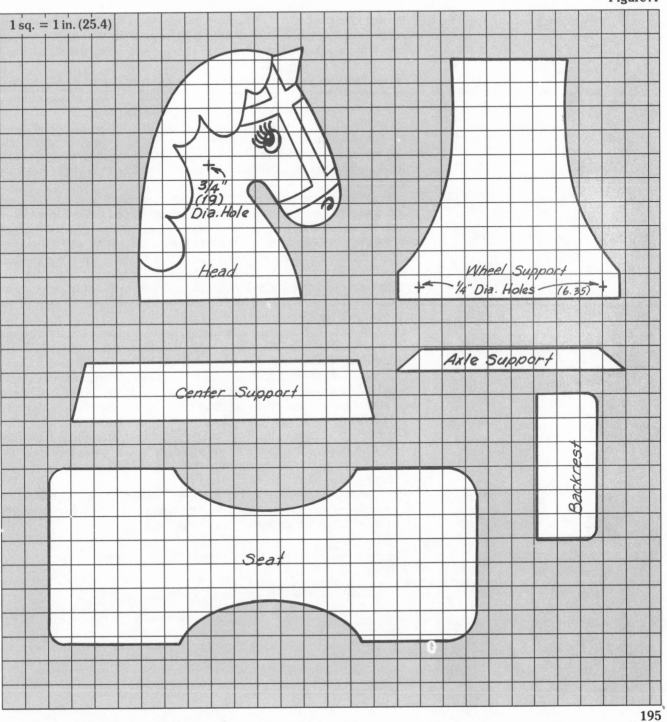

1 sq. = 1 in. (25.4)

Head

3/4"
(19)
Dia. Hole

Wheel Support
1/4" Dia. Holes — (6.35)

Axle Support

Center Support

Backrest

Seat

Cutting the pieces **1.** To make your job easier (which is no mean feat, considering the simplicity of this project), we suggest that you sand the whole length of the pine board before you start drawing and cutting the pieces. Sand first with medium sandpaper and finish with fine.

2. Scale drawings for the pattern pieces are given in **Figure A.** There are 6 pattern pieces: Head, Wheel Support, Center Support, Seat, Axle Support, and Backrest. Enlarge the patterns to full size on kraft paper.

3. Draw the outline of each piece on the pine board, following the suggested placement diagram in **Figure B.** (See how easy this is? We even tell you where to put the pattern pieces.) Cut 2 Wheel Supports, 2 Axle Supports and 1 each of the remaining pieces. Cut 2 Axles, each 14 inches (356) long, from the larger dowel rod.

4. Use carbon paper and a pencil to transfer the facial features, halter, and mane outlines to both sides of the wooden head. If you will put 2 pieces of carbon paper together (non-carbon sides together) as you trace the outlines onto the first side of the wooden Head, it will automatically transfer the reverse image of the outlines to the back of the kraft paper pattern. Then you can use the back of the pattern and a single sheet of carbon paper to transfer the outlines to the remaining blank side of the Head. (Frankly, the most difficult part of this project, for us, has been figuring out how to write coherent instructions for procedures like this one. Just try it—you'll see.)

5. Drill a ¾-inch (19) diameter hole through the Head where indicated on the scale drawing. This hole will accommodate the dowel-rod handle, which will be added later. Drill 2 holes through each of the Wheel Supports where indicated on the scale drawing, using the drill bit that is slightly larger than the diameter of the bolt shanks. Use the same bit to drill a hole 4⅛ inches (105) from each end of each Axle. Drill an additional hole ¼ inch (6) from each end of each Axle, using the ¼-inch (6.35) diameter bit.

6. Round off the edges of the Seat, the curved sides of the Wheel Supports, the top and sides of the Backrest, and all edges of the Head, excluding the straight bottom edge. You can accomplish this with sandpaper, or use a router with a quarter-round bit.

7. Cut 8 wheels, as specified in the "Materials" section above. Cut 8 washers from waferwood or plywood. Each washer should be a 2-inch (51) diameter circle with a ¾-inch (19) diameter center hole.

Figure B

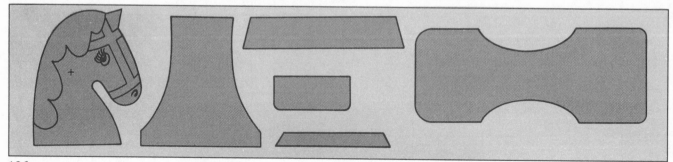

Assembly   Use wood screws for all assembly operations, except where nails are specified. Use glue with both nails and screws. To avoid cracking the wood, pre-drill all screw holes.

1. Carefully center each of the Wheel Supports at the top edges of the Center Support as shown in **Figure C**. Fasten the pieces together using 2 screws on each side.

2. Notice that the outer corner of each Wheel Support extends above the top of the Center Support **(Figure D)**. Trim the tops of both Wheel Supports so that they are flush with the Center Support.

3. Trim the bottom edge of the Backrest at approximately the same angle as used to trim the Wheel Supports. The exact angle is not important, as long as it allows the Backrest to tilt slightly to the rear of the Horsey when attached to the Seat.

Figure C

Figure D

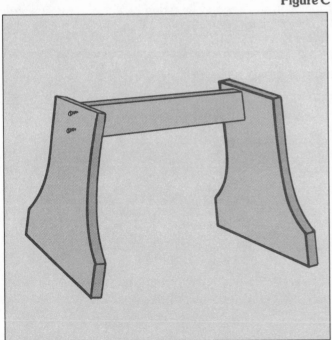

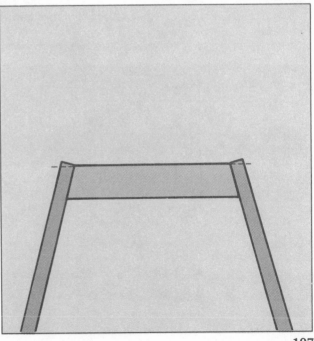

Figure E

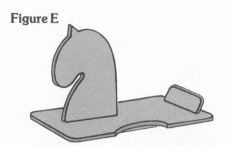

Figure F

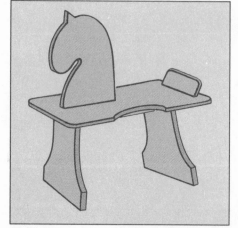

4. Position the Head and Backrest on the Seat (**Figure E**). Use 2 screws to secure each piece, as shown. Be sure to angle the screws that go into the Backrest. (Screws not inserted at the proper angle will produce complaints from the rider that will be heard throughout the entire neighborhood.)

5. If you foresee heavy-duty rodeo riding on the finished Horsey, you may want to add extra reinforcement to the sides of the Head. Cut 2 wooden support blocks, each ¾ x 6 inches (20 x 153), from the remaining pine scraps. Fasten them on either side of the Head with glue and small finishing nails.

6. Carefully center the top assembly (Head, Seat, and Backrest) over the support assembly (Wheel Supports and Center Support) as shown in **Figure F**. Fasten them together with glue, and drive 2 nails through the top of the Seat into each of the Wheel Supports. You may use screws instead of nails for extra stability. Recess the nails (or countersink the screws) and fill the holes with wood filler to avoid saddle rash, a common cowpoke's complaint.

Adding the wheels and handle **1.** Insert the bolts through the holes in the Wheel Supports and then through the Axles. Secure each bolt with a washer and nut **(Figure G)**.

2. Glue the 8 wheels together in pairs to create 4 wheels, each 1½ inches (38) thick. When gluing, place the wheels so that the grain of 1 is perpendicular to the grain of its mate.

3. Slip a wheel over each axle end, placing a washer on each side. Secure with a 2-inch (51) length of ¼-inch (6.35) diameter dowel rod (**Figure H**).

4. Nail and glue the Axle Supports over the Axles, as shown in **Figure H**.

When the paint is dry: call your favorite buckaroo, clean off his face, show him the Horsey, point in the general direction of the nearest downhill slope, and shout, "They went thataway!"

Figure G

Figure H

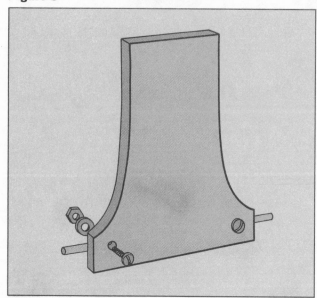

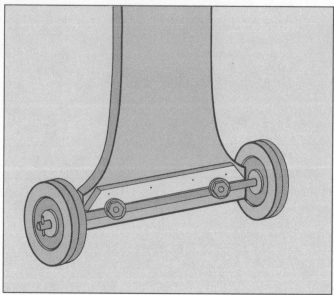

Country Rocking Horse

Materials

Pine lumber: 27-inch (686) length of 1 x 4-inch (17 x 89), 14 feet (4267) of 2 x 10-inch (38 x 235), 24-inch (610) length of 2 x 16-inch (38 x 387). The 2 x 16-inch (38 x 387) pine will be used for the horse's body. If your lumberyard can't supply this size wood, you can edge-glue 2 narrower boards, clamp them until completely dry, and then cut the piece.

36 square inches (232 sq. cm.) of walnut or other dark-colored hardwood, 3/8 inch (10) thick and at least 2½ inches (64) wide.

Wooden dowel rod: 25-inch (635) length of ¼-inch (6.35) diameter, 13-inch (330) length of ½-inch (13) diameter, 14-inch (356) length of ¾-inch (19) diameter, 27-inch (686) length of 1-inch (25) diameter.

White string-mop head.

8 flathead wood screws, 1½ inches (38) long.

Carpenter's wood glue, stain, sealer, medium and fine sandpaper, kraft paper.

Tools

Hammer, screwdriver, wood rasp, saber saw or coping saw, wood chisel, table saw, miter box or gauge, and an electric or hand drill with bits of the following diameters: ¼-inch (6.35), ¾-inch (19), 1-inch (25), a bit slightly smaller than the diameter of the screw shanks, and a bit slightly larger than the diameter of the screw heads.

This high-stepping steed will be a handsome addition to the playroom or corral. He'll give the toddlers an exciting ride, but is guaranteed not to buck, kick, or eat too much.

Metric equivalents in millimeters are indicated in parentheses.

Figure A

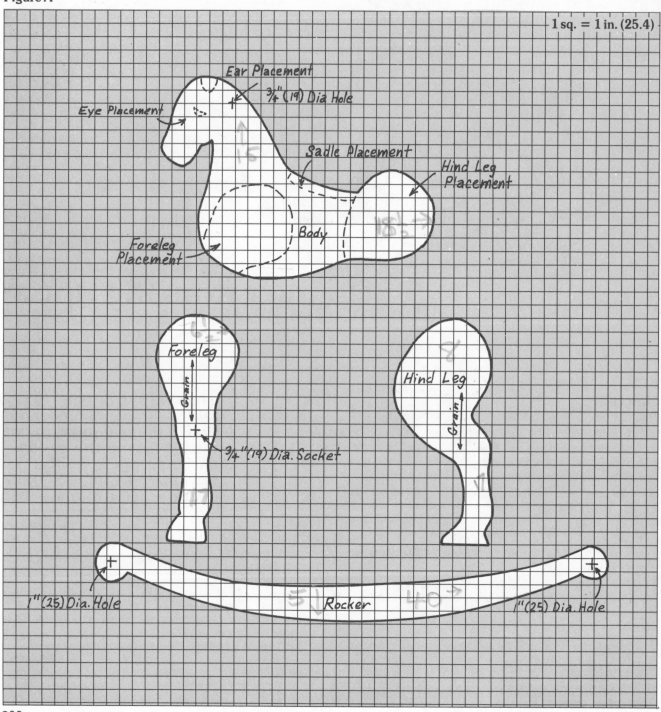

1 sq. = 1 in. (25.4)

Cutting the pieces   **1.** Scale drawings for the Body, Foreleg, Hind Leg, and Rocker are provided in **Figure A**. Scale drawings for the Ear and Saddle are provided in **Figure B**. Enlarge the drawings to make full-size paper patterns, and transfer the grain-alignment arrows and placement markings to the patterns. When cutting the pieces, align the arrows with the grain of the wood.
2. Cut the following pieces from the 2 x 10-inch (38 x 235) pine: 2 Forelegs, 2 Hind Legs, and 2 Rockers. Cut one Body from the 2 x 16-inch (38 x 387) pine. Transfer the placement markings to the wooden pieces.
3. Cut 2 Leg Supports, each 10½ inches (267) long, from the 1 x 4-inch (17 x 89) pine. Cut 2 Ears from the remaining 1 x 4-inch (17 x 89) pine, using the side view pattern. Use the front view pattern to contour the inner side of each Ear. The shaded areas on the drawings indicate portions that will be shaped later.
4. Cut 2 Saddles from the remaining 2 x 10-inch (38 x 235) pine, using the top view pattern. Cut the contours using the side view pattern.

Figure B

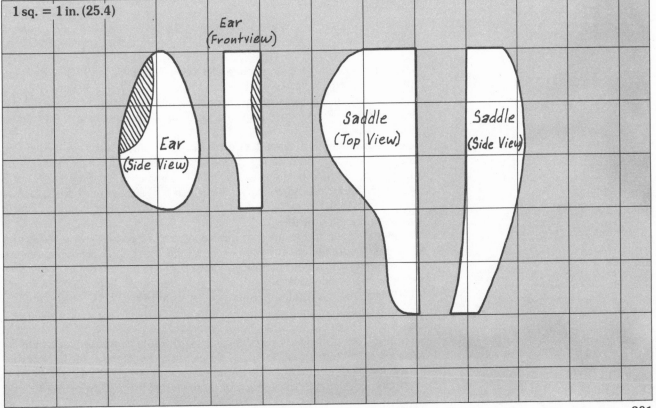

1 sq. = 1 in. (25.4)

Ear (Front view)

Ear (Side View)

Saddle (Top View)

Saddle (Side View)

Figure D

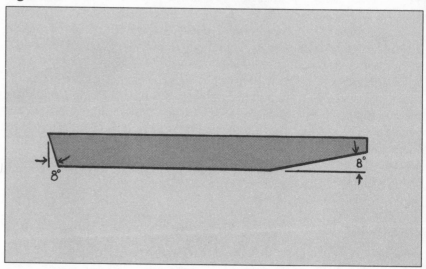

5. Cut 4 Hooves from walnut, each 2¼ x 3½ inches (57 x 89). The Eyes are cut from the remaining walnut, but they should be only half as thick. Slice the walnut in half (using the table saw) to create 2 thinner pieces. Trace the full-size drawing for the Eye given in **Figure C**, and cut 1 Eye from each of the thinner pieces of walnut.

6. Cut the ½-inch (13) diameter dowel rod into 8 pieces, each1½ inches (38) long. These will be used to peg the leg support joints. Cut the ¾-inch (19) diameter dowel rod into 3 pieces; 1 Handle 6½ inches (165) long, and 2 Footrests each 3¼ inches (83) long. Cut the 1-inch (25) diameter rod in half to form two 13-inch (330) long Tie Rods. The ¼-inch (6.35) diameter rod will be cut and used later for dowel pegs.

7. Several of the pieces need to be shaped before you assemble the horse. (It's always something!) Because each leg slants in two directions (sideways and either forward or backward), you have some mitering to do. On 1 Foreleg, miter the inner side (not the end) at an 8 degree angle, beginning 5½ inches (140) from the rounded upper end as shown in **Figure D**. On the same leg, cut an 8 degree compound miter (don't panic – read on) across the lower end as shown. To cut a compound miter, simply cut diagonally across the end from corner to corner, instead of straight across from side to side as you would for a simple miter. In this case, the miter should be widest at the inside back corner of the leg, and narrowest at the outside front corner. Cut the same miters on the other Foreleg, but be sure to cut them so that the legs are mirror images of each other.

Figure C

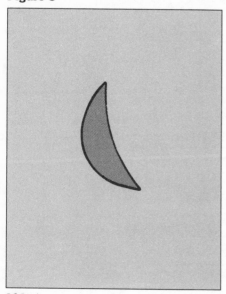

Figure F

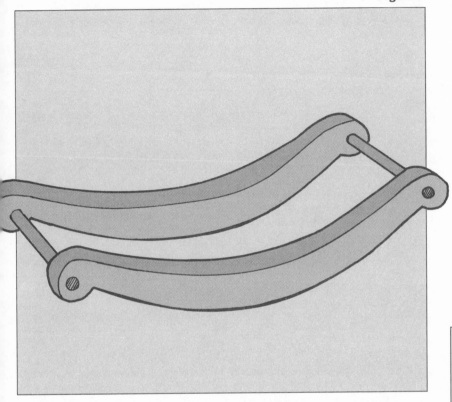

Figure E

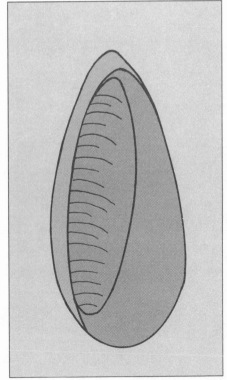

8. Cut similar miters on each Hind Leg. At the lower end, the compound miter should be widest at the inside front corner and narrowest at the outside back corner. Make the Hind Legs mirror images of each other.

9. Use the chisel to create a spoon-shaped indentation on the outside front edge of each Ear, where indicated by the shaded area on the scale drawing (**Figure B**). A correctly shaped ear is shown in **Figure E**. Be sure that the finished ears are mirror images of each other.

10. You just have a little drilling to do, and you'll be ready to start the assembly process. Drill a ¾-inch (19) diameter socket, about 1 inch (25) deep, into the outer side of each Foreleg where indicated on the pattern. Drill the holes through the Rockers and Body where indicated, using the drill bit sizes specified on the scale drawings.

Assembly   The horse and base are assembled separately and are then joined and finished. Begin by assembling the base section, which consists of Rockers, Leg Supports, and Tie Rods.

1. Align the Rockers side by side, about 10 inches (254) apart. Temporarily join them by inserting the ends of the Tie Rods into the aligned holes. The ends of the rods should be flush with the outer sides of the rockers (**Figure F**).

Figure G

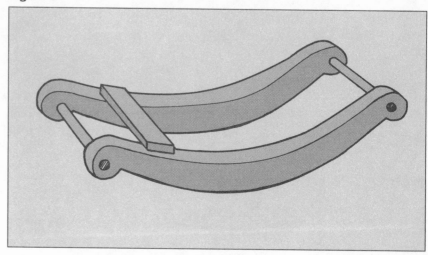

Figure H

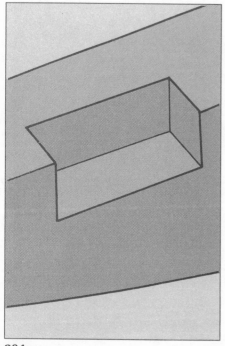

2. Rectangular grooves are cut into the tops of the rockers to accommodate the Leg Supports. Place 1 Leg Support on top of the rocker assembly, 5½ inches (140) from one end as shown in **Figure G**. The support should overlap each rocker by ¾ inch (19). If it doesn't, just scrap the entire project and go on to something else. No, sorry, don't do that – we just got carried away. If it doesn't, slide the rockers closer together or farther apart on the tie rods until the spacing is correct. Be sure that the support is at right angles to the rockers, and trace around each end of the support. Repeat this procedure at the opposite end of the rocker assembly.

3. Disassemble the rockers and tie rods. Cut a ¾-inch (19) deep groove inside each set of traced lines (**Figure H**), so that the end of the support will fit down into it. (You can chisel out the wood, or make initial cuts with a saber or table saw and then finish with the chisel.)

4. To permanently assemble the base section, glue the leg supports into the grooves, one at the front and one at the back. Replace the tie rods and glue the ends into the holes. Trim the ends if necessary.

5. The support/rocker joints are pegged for extra stability. To do this, you'll need to drill sockets to accommodate the dowel pegs. The sockets are drilled through the supports, into the rockers. Drill two ½-inch (13) diameter sockets through each joint, making each socket about 1⅝ inches (41) deep. Drill the sockets at an angle to avoid breaking through the inner side of the rocker. Glue a dowel peg into each socket, and trim the upper ends flush with the support. (You cut the pegs long ago in step 6 under "Cutting the pieces," remember?)

Figure I

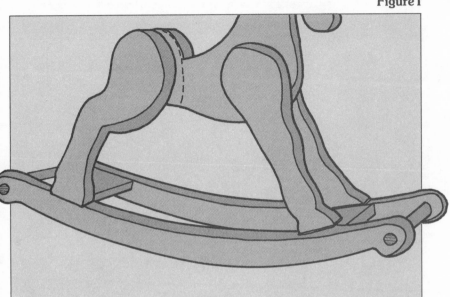

6. Now assemble the horse. Glue a Foreleg to each side of the Body inside the placement lines, placing the mitered side of each leg against the body. Place the partially assembled horse on the base, with the forelegs centered on one leg support. Place one Hind Leg against the horse, inside the placement lines, and check to be sure the hoof will sit on the leg support at the back of the rockers (**Figure I**). When you have adjusted the leg correctly, glue it in place. Attach the remaining Hind Leg in the same manner.

7. To accommodate dowel pegs, drill two ¼-inch (6.35) diameter sockets, approximately 2 inches (51) long, through each foreleg and into the body. Cut two ¼-inch (6.35) diameter dowel pegs, each 1⅞ inches (48) long, and glue them into the sockets. Peg the other foreleg joint and the two hind leg joints in the same manner.

8. Glue the Footrest dowels into the sockets in the forelegs, and glue a Hoof to the bottom of each leg. Insert the Handle dowel through the hole in the neck portion of the body, leaving equal extensions on each side. Glue it in place. Glue an Eye to each side of the head inside the placement lines.

9. Glue an Ear to each side of the head inside the placement lines as shown in **Figure J**. To peg the ear joints, drill a ¼-inch (6.35) diameter hole straight through both ears and the head. Cut a 3½-inch (89) length of ¼-inch (6.35) diameter dowel rod for the peg, and glue it into the hole. Trim the ends flush with the outer sides of the ears.

10. Glue a Saddle to each side of the body, just in front of the hind leg. The tops of the saddles should be flush with the upper edge of the body, and the front and back edges of the two saddles should be even. If you are desperately in love with pegged joints, by all means go ahead and peg these as you did the others.

Figure J

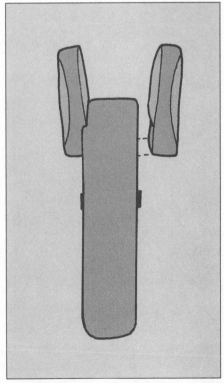

Figure K

Figure L

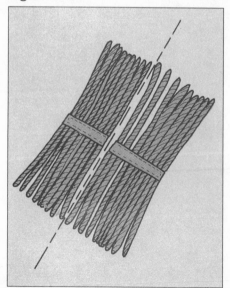

11. For the final assembly, first place the horse on the base so that the hooves are centered on the leg supports (**Figure K**). Glue the hooves to the supports. Insert 2 screws through the bottom of the support, through the hoof, and into the leg. Pre-drill the screw holes to avoid splitting the wood, and countersink the screws.

Finishing details   **1.** Use the wood rasp to round off the edge of the haunch on each leg. Carefully sand the entire horse, eliminating all sharp corners and edges. Stain and seal the horse.

2. Cut the mop head in half across the binding strip as shown in **Figure L**. On each half, glue together the cut ends of the binding strip, and fold the strings in half over the strip.

3. To create a tail, spread glue on the exposed side of the binding strip on one mop-head section. Attach it to the back of the horse at an appropriate spot. The remaining section will serve as the mane. Glue it to the upper edge of the head between the ears. To create the forelock, pull several strands of the mane forward and trim them to about 3 inches (76) long.

If you have trouble with the kick-starter on this model, try dangling a carrot in front of its nose.

Index

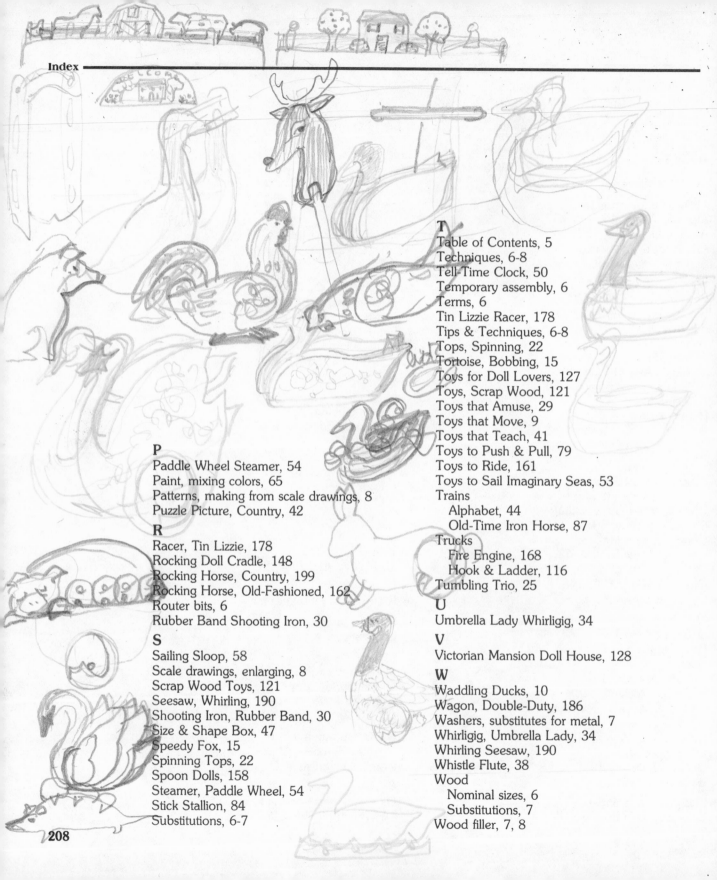